ISBN 978-1-330-99502-0
PIBN 10131188

English
Français
Deutsche
Italiano
Español
Português

www.forgottenbooks.com

Mythology Photography **Fiction**
Fishing Christianity **Art** Cooking
Essays Buddhism Freemasonry
Medicine **Biology** Music **Ancient
Egypt** Evolution Carpentry Physics
Dance Geology **Mathematics** Fitness
Shakespeare **Folklore** Yoga Marketing
Confidence Immortality Biographies
Poetry **Psychology** Witchcraft
Electronics Chemistry History **Law**
Accounting **Philosophy** Anthropology
Alchemy Drama Quantum Mechanics
Atheism Sexual Health **Ancient History**
Entrepreneurship Languages Sport
Paleontology Needlework Islam
Metaphysics Investment Archaeology
Parenting Statistics Criminology
Motivational

EMORIES

OF

A CENTURY

of Friendships

EDITED BY

C. LEHMANN, M.P.

FRONTISPIECE

DON

DER & C ., 15, WATERLOO PLACE

1908

MEMORIES

OF

ALF A CENTUR

A Record of Friendships

COMPILED AND EDITED BY

R. C. LEHMANN, M.P.

WITH A FRONTISPIECE

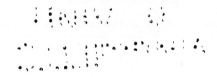

LONDON
SMITH, ELDER & CO., 15, WATERLOO PLACE
1908

BRADBURY, AGNEW, & CO. LD., PRINTERS,
LONDON AND TONBRIDGE.

PREFATORY NOTE.

I DESIRE to express my thanks to the Editors of *Chambers's Journal* and the *Cornhill Magazine* for allowing me to publish here those portions of the book which have already appeared in their periodicals.

No small part of this volume consists of letters from those who, at one time or another, corresponded with my parents.

My grateful acknowledgments are due to the following, whose kind permission, freely granted in every case, made it possible for me to put together this record of friendships:—

To Miss Hogarth, for the letters from Charles Dickens; to Mr. A. P. Watt, for the letters from Wilkie Collins; to Mr. Robert Barrett Browning, for the letters from his father; to Mr. J. W. Cross, for the letters from George Eliot; to the Earl of Crewe, for the letters from his father, Lord Houghton; to Mrs. Payn, for the letters from James Payn; to Lady Grove, for the letters from Sir George Grove; to Mr. Herbert Sullivan, for the letters from Sir Arthur Sullivan; to Mrs. C. B. Stuart-Wortley, for the letters from her father,

Sir John Millais; and to Mr. E. A. Lewes, for a letter from his father, George H. Lewes.

To Professor Charles Eliot Norton I am indebted for much valuable information and for the assurance that I was at liberty to publish a letter and poem, addressed by James Russell Lowell to Mrs. Procter, and kindly lent to me by their possessor, Mrs. George Murray Smith.

R. C. L.

October, 1908.

CONTENTS.

PART I.

CHAPTER I.

CHAPTER VII.

CHARLES DICKENS.

CHAPTER VIII.

ROBERT BROWNING.

CHAPTER IX.

CHAPTER X.

CHAPTER XI.

CHAPTER XII.

LETTERS FROM BIARRITZ AND ST. JEAN DE LUZ, 1867.

CONTENTS.

PART I.

B

PART I.

EMORIES OF HALF A CENTUR

CHAPTER I.

My Father and Mother—Robert Chambers—Alexander Ireland—Carlyle—A Festive Meeting in 1852.

I MUST premise that the memories of which I propose to write are not exclusively, or even mainly, my own. My certificate of birth forbids me (by a narrow and decreasing margin, it is true!) to think of looking back through the whole of the formidable period of fifty years.* No: it is from some MS. reminiscences left by my father and letters written to or by my father and mother, supplemented here and there by my own recollection, that I shall draw the materials of these memories. I can only hope that I may be able to communicate to those who read them here some part of the pleasure that I myself feel in calling to mind the beloved and honoured names of those who were for many years the friends of my parents, and who are endeared to me not only on that account, but also by the memory of great and unvarying kindness bestowed by them upon the son of their friends.

* This was written five years ago, and is no longer strictly accurate.

As I write I can summon a long procession of the departed. At its head marches Charles Dickens, and after him come Wilkie Collins, Lord Lytton, Lord Houghton, Barry Cornwall, Charles Reade, G. H. Lewes, George Eliot, John Forster, Sir Edwin Landseer, Sir John Millais, Sir Arthur Sullivan, Robert Browning, Sir Alexander Cockburn the Lord Chief-Justice, James Payn, Sir George Grove, and many another. Nor must I forget my grandfather, Robert Chambers, *clarum et venerabile nomen* not only to his descendants but to all who value great powers of intellect and a noble devotion to good causes. Of nearly all these I hope to have something to relate in the course of these chapters.

A few words by way of preface I must say about my father and mother. My mother was the eldest of the eight daughters of Robert Chambers. Born in Edinburgh in 1830, she was married there in 1852 to my father, he being her senior by four years. My grandfather on the paternal side was a distinguished portrait-painter living in Hamburg, and my father, the youngest of five sons, had left his home at a very early age, and had come to England to fit himself for a mercantile career. Later on he established himself in Leith, and it was while living there that he was introduced to the Chambers family.

My father was a man of great force of character, unbounded energy, and tireless industry. Immersed though he was in the daily struggle of his business, he never allowed it to dull his interest in art, music, and literature. He was the son and the brother of distinguished painters, and was himself an excellent performer on the violin. My mother, as the daughter of Robert Chambers, had lived from her earliest days in a literary atmosphere. She had known and conversed with great men, her own father not least among them. Moreover, like her mother and her sisters, she was musical to the finger-tips. Her playing of the piano was a revelation of the divine capacities of that difficult and much-abused instrument. She had a touch (alas that I should have to think of it as the touch of a vanished hand!) from which the notes seemed to flow in streams of liquid jewels. Her ear was faultless, and not less so was the instinctive sympathy with which she gave life and symmetry and charm to any piece that she played. Tenderness or rapture, yearning or passion—all the emotions that the musician strives to express were within the range of those frail but wonder-working fingers moving over the keyboard with a quickness, a precision, and an ease that would have been astonishing had the movements not seemed so perfectly natural and inevitable. The praise may seem high, but there are many still living who can testify to its simple truth.

Thus it came about that my father and mother after they were married were able to secure many friendships in the great world of art and music and literature.

It had been my father's intention to put together

for the pleasure of his family and his intimate friends his reminiscences. He began the task in 1884, but illness came upon him before he could carry it very far. Of Dickens, for instance, I find only a few rough notes of this character.

" With Dickens at Crystal Palace performance of Sullivan's 'Tempest.' Walked with Dickens from Crystal Palace to Chorley's, 13, Eaton Place.

"Dickens fond of Americans. But when I returned from America in the spring of '63, and expressed my firm belief in the ultimate triumph of the North, he treated my opinion as a harmless hallucination.

" Sunday walks with Dickens in 1862 (February to June) when he was at Hyde Park Gate. Walked back with him from Star and Garter, Richmond, April 2, after dinner to celebrate John Forster's birthday.

"With Dickens in Paris, Nov. 1862. Course of restaurants."

Wilkie Collins, too, was one of our closest friends, but in my father's MS. there is no mention of their long association. Fortunately I have many of Wilkie's letters, and of these I shall be able to give a selection. They will show better than any other record the kind and manly nature of our dear old friend : his humour, his power of work, and his courage in battling against pain and illness.

My first extract from my father's reminiscences relates to my grandfather, Robert Chambers :—

" I made the acquaintance of the Chambers family in 1851. My violin was the key which opened the house to me. All of them were passionately fond of music. Robert Chambers himself played the flute very fairly, and his wife and some of the daughters were not only excellent pianists, but were endowed with musical faculties to a very unusual degree. I remember a little dance for which Mrs. Chambers and one of the girls played the music on a piano and a harmonium. Musicians will understand my surprise when I heard the daughter interrupt her mother, saying, ' Not in G, mamma; let us play it in A ; ' whereupon they resumed in the altered key, as if such transposition, instead of being a difficult and intricate feat, was the simplest and most natural attribute of the performance.

" All strangers of distinction flocked to the house in Doune Terrace, Edinburgh, and eminent travellers made a point of bringing a letter to Robert Chambers, so as to have the advantage of being shown over the town by the author of ' The Traditions of Edinburgh.' I remember his coming home after a long day spent on some such errand, and saying, ' To-day I took a very pleasant party of Americans over Edinburgh, and I know they will think me one of the most charming and interesting of guides, for they talked incessantly, and never allowed me to get a word in edgewise.' I believe it was during one of the meetings of the British Association, when Robert Chambers had several eminent foreign men of science staying at his house, that the family narrowly escaped the catastrophe of an explosion, for a sweetly innocent professor from Pisa had, on retiring to rest, and being left alone with the, to him, novel incident of gas, blown it out instead of turning it off. Luckily not much had been turned on ; the professor, being presumably trained by the smells of Pisa, had had his slumbers only slightly disturbed, and the trouble was fortunately not discovered till daylight.

" What remained of Edinburgh literary society congregated at the house. Professor Aytoun and Sheriff Gordon, who, by the way, were Christopher North's sons-in-law, were constant visitors, and Mrs. Crowe, the authoress of ' The Night-Side of Nature,' ' Susan Hopley,' &c., often stayed there.

" Robert Chambers had three sons and eight daughters. Of the sons, two were at the time I am speaking of little boys, and the eldest, then a young man of about nineteen, was away from home. The eight daughters were of all ages, ranging from mere babyhood up to twenty-one, and the female element bore undisputed sway in the house. My mother-in-law, Mrs. Robert Chambers, was not only a most accomplished woman, but was the soul of kindness, and had a fund of the most delightful humour. Some of the daughters were strikingly handsome, and all were sprightly and attractive to an uncommon degree. As I write I still seem to hear the silvery peals of laughter which were continually ringing through the house. What innocent evenings of mirth and frolic we used to have, and when Robert Chambers, the most industrious of mortals, emerged late from his study, Jove-like, and with a little of the dampness of his Olympian clouds clinging to him, how the whole mad company would immediately be on its best behaviour, all the girls flocking to the feet of their father and trying to be fit company for him !

"The fact that Robert Chambers was the author of 'Vestiges of Creation' is at last established beyond all question since the last survivor of those who were in the secret, Mr. Alexander Ireland, of Manchester, has said his say. [Mr. Ireland, in an Introduction to the twelfth edition of the 'Vestiges of Creation,' published in 1884, gave a full account of the authorship of the book, and of the circumstances attending its original publication in 1844.] To the present generation, which has outlived Bishop Colenso and Darwin, and has been educated by Tyndall and Huxley, it will be almost impossible to convey an idea of the violent commotion to which 'Vestiges of Creation' gave rise on its appearance. The clerical press blew its loudest blast, and old-fashioned science, startled and uneasy, joined in the fray. The author, had he given his name, would not only have incurred the *odium theologicum*, but would have run great risk of being placed outside the pale of respectability. To a man with a large family and a flourishing business largely dependent on the goodwill of the general and easily led public, this was no slight matter, and I can easily understand now why Robert Chambers shrouded himself in impenetrable mystery. The veil was raised to me a few years after I married his daughter. I was staying at his house, No. 1, Doune Terrace. He and I had been out for a walk together, and as we were returning home I said to him, 'Tell me why you have never acknowledged your greatest work.' For all answer he pointed to his house, in which he had eleven children, and then slowly added, 'I have eleven reasons.' As Robert Chambers was the last man to let me infer he was the author if he could have truthfully denied it, the question was from that moment settled in my mind."

The publication of the "Vestiges" is referred to in the following interesting letter from the late Mr. Alexander Ireland to my mother:

"31, MAULDETH ROAD, FALLOWFIELD, MANCHESTER,
"Oct. 26th, 1892.

"MY DEAR MRS. LEHMANN,—It was a great pleasure to me to receive your kind letter. My wife was very much gratified by your good opinion of her 'Life of Mrs. Carlyle,' and has written to you to that effect. Have you seen her selections from Miss Jewsbury's 'Letters to Mrs. Carlyle'? It has only been published a week, and already more than thirty favourable reviews of it have appeared. I enclose one or two of them for your perusal. The *Times* gave a column to it. My wife has been in very precarious health for the last few years, and yet she has been able to do a great deal of literary work. . . . I was shocked by the news of Mrs. Wills's death.* It seems a very short time since we met her at Bowdon in Mr. Mills's house —so full of kindness and so cheerful. I always loved her very dearly from her youth upwards. Many a pleasant evening did I spend with her and her mother in Waterloo Place in the dear old Edinburgh days which I can never, never forget. Your dear father and mother and all their kindness to me will ever remain to me a sacred memory. For thirty-five years I enjoyed your father's friendship and confidence. He was, I may say, the dearest and best friend I ever had. His friendship was a constant blessing, and when he died I felt that something good and noble was for ever lost to me in this world; but the memory of him and of your mother will remain in me to the last hour of my life as a comfort and blessing. And now that Mrs. Wills is gone, the last earthly link of that generation is broken. One of the last letters I wrote her was about a year ago, when she wished me to put in writing a story I told her in her house in London about three years ago when I spent a delightful evening with her. The story I told her —a Scottish one—very much aroused her fine sense of humour, and she afterwards wished me to put it in writing for her.

* Mrs. Wills, sister of Robert Chambers and wife of W. H. Wills, the friend of Charles Dickens and his assistant in *House-hold Words, All the Year Round,* and the *Daily News.*

" Of course you know all about the history of
the ' Vestiges ' and my connection with the secret,
and the getting it published, so that no one could
know where it came from—all of which I related
in the edition of the book published in 1884, after
William Chambers's death.

" I intend, if life be spared me, to write a little
volume of cherished memories of some remarkable
men I have known : such as Campbell the poet,
Emerson (whom I knew and corresponded with for
fifty years), George Dawson, Leigh Hunt, Carlyle,
Lowell, Oliver Wendell Holmes, Charles and Mary
Cowden Clarke, Wordsworth, and an interview I
had with Sir Walter Scott in 1829, when I was a
lad of nineteen.   Your dear father will also be
included as one of the most interesting. . . . And
now, with all good wishes for you and yours, believe
me, with affectionate regards, your old friend from
the time you were a girl in the old house in Ann
Street,   ALEXANDER IRELAND."

Unfortunately Mr. Ireland was unable to carry
out the project of which he speaks in this letter.
He died two years afterwards, at the ripe age of
eighty-four.

With Carlyle my grandfather was well acquainted.
I have a letter written by Carlyle to him, and dated
" 5, Cheyne Row, Chelsea, 18th May, 1853," in
which he engages Mr. and Mrs. Chambers to visit
him on the following Sunday evening.   It contains
this characteristic sentence, which I venture to

quote : " Note, also, your coachman had better come by Cheyne Walk (*i.e.* the River Side) ; and you will probably have to get out at the bottom of our little street, and walk a few steps to us ; the *Commissioners of Sewers* [these words are under-lined] are hard on this poor population just now, and have rendered the houses here inaccessible to wheel-carriages for some time past : Bad luck to Block-headism everywhere ! " This, it must be admitted, is hard on the commissioners, who were probably only doing their duty in restoring defective drains.

Many years afterwards my mother met Carlyle at John Forster's house. I find the following pleasant account of the meeting in a letter written by her to my father, who was then on a journey round the world :

" On Tuesday, 8th [March, 1870], I dined with the Forsters to meet Carlyle quietly. Percy Fitz-gerald, his wife, and sister were the only other guests. Carlyle was so sweet. By the way, his young niece, a Scotch girl just home from school to keep his house, was there. Carlyle spoke to me so appreciatively and flatteringly of papa I could have kissed him. He said he had read iverything he had iver written since he was a vary young man, and had come out with his ' Reballion.' That he had been perteeclerly struck lately with a Life of Smollett by him. 'The vary best thing iver written about Smollett—vastly suparior to anything that has iver been written about him before,' &c.   He asked all about papa's life.   After dinner I played him one Scotch tune after another. He was pleased, even touched.   He said, ' Waal, I niver harrd a sweeter finger on the pianyforty in all my life.' "

Let me say here that my mother, like most of her sisters, was a letter-writer in the best sense of the word—not a mere chronicler of dull incidents or a retailer of chat about the weather or the price of provisions, but a writer with a style which was admirable because it was perfectly natural and unforced and simple—a style which was like good talk in its ease and its humour.   I hope to be able to make good my opinion by more than one extract from her letters to my father, every one of which I found he had religiously preserved from 1851 to 1891, the year of his death.   Here, to begin with, is an extract from a letter written to my father during their engagement.   My mother, then in her twenty-second year, was staying with friends near Newcastle, and was taken to what she calls "a presentation tea."   The date is 6th September, 1852 :

"I have now come home from that festive meeting.   Everybody is in bed, and I sit down to write to you.   Oh, what pleasure it was when we hailed the post-boy on the road as we went, and amongst other letters my eager eye recognised your precious handwriting !   It made me so happy, so strong in happiness !   It enabled me to stand all the speechifying with patience, and to see everything and everybody through rose-coloured eyes.

" You must know this was a meeting to present Mr. Clarke with silver plate, a purse of gold, and a watch, all for his invaluable services, &c.; and there was a tea given to about sixty people in a long room of an inn. Mr. Sopwith, as the great man of this district, presided in the chair, and *I* was requested by the people to be mistress of the festive board and to make tea. So behold me installed at the top of the table in *the* arm-chair, with every eye upon me, gracefully (of course) filling small cups with the brown beverage which enlivens but not, &c. Then I abdicated the chair to the rightful filler thereof, Mr. Sopwith, and took my place at his right hand, and then came the speeches. 'The Queen,' of course, and some very impertinent comparisons with the Continental management of affairs. Equally of course ' The Ladies ' were given with many cheers, and—what do you think ?—you will never believe it !—*I* got up to return thanks for that. I could not speak for about five minutes, they applauded so much; but I stood quite coldly eyeing them all round. My speech was brief, I am proud to say. It was merely this : ' In the name of all the ladies present, I take upon myself to thank the gentlemen for the last toast, which I think *decidedly the best of all.'*

" There was such a quantity of queer-looking

women there, so oddly dressed, too. The parson's wife was near me, a startled, haggard young woman with a large straggling mourning collar that flew away at corners and did not seem to belong to her dress at all, and a head of dried-up, desolate-looking hair which must have been slept upon and undisturbed by brush or comb since an early period of the owner's infancy. . . .

" But, oh ! that distressed woman Mrs. Clarke, so overwhelmed with the honour that was done to her husband, calling me ' Mum,' and trembling with delight and confusion at every fresh cup of tea with which I presented her. She had on a nervous pair of white silk gloves of a painful longitude at the finger-ends ; but pushing them on was a useful and blessed employment during the agitating moments when her husband's virtues were being descanted upon."

CHAPTER II.

Robert Chambers at Home—An Imaginary Lover—A Railway Accident in 1860—Mrs. Robert Chambers—A Benefit Concert—Wilkie Collins—Gratitude in Verse.

MY own memory of my grandfather, Robert Chambers, is, with the exception of one interview, somewhat vague and indistinct. He died when I was fifteen years old; and during the latter part of his life we, who were living in England, had not been able to see him frequently. That one interview, however, stands out in my mind with a startling distinctness. It must have taken place in 1864, when, as a boy of eight, I had just begun learning Latin with a tutor. This great intelligence had been communicated to my grandfather, and I can remember my feelings of mingled pride and apprehension when the towering and dignified figure took me by the hand and began to question me: "So, my little man, you're into Latin?" "Yes, grandpa." "That's good; that's good. Now then, can you go through *mensa*, a table?" "Please, grandpa, we call it *musa*, a muse, in our book. I can do that for you." And I did, without in the least understanding why my grandfather gave a Homeric shout of laughter. The consequent gift of a shilling was, however, thoroughly intelligible,

M.   C

and served to impress the little incident indelibly on my mind.

It is evident that Robert Chambers fully understood and practised *l'art d'être grandpère.* In July, 1858, my mother was on a visit to her parents in Edinburgh, and had taken me and my brother, aged respectively two years and a half and seven months, with her. She writes from 1, Doune Terrace:

" Papa is quite fidgety in the morning till I bring down the boys. Then he lights up, opens his arms, and clasps the laughing Frederico Jocoso, as he calls him, cuddles him, raves about him, foretells his future career of genius extraordinary and distinction generally; admires his nobly shaped head, his waggish eyes; calls him pearl of boys, the prince of babes, the dearest, funniest, wittiest child on earth; and allows him to pluck at his whiskers, disturb his shirt collar, and catch hold of his nose."

And again a day or two later:

" You should have seen us at breakfast this morning. Papa with Rudy on his knee getting bites of egg, sups of tea, and crumbs of roll. Freddy on Jan's knee, dadding on the table with his two chubby hands with all his might—a little giant, papa says, not knowing upon what to expend his strength; papa all the time keeping up a chorus of ' What a splendid babe! Oh, he is the prince of babes, the king of babes! Good heavens! I nev-v-v-v-er saw such a babe in my life.' Then, in a kind of rapture, he takes him in his arms, hugs him, kisses him, fondles him, says, ' Always smiling, always laughing—oh, the captain ! happy boy ! ' and enjoys him to the full. Then he gives Freddy jumps in the air, and makes him into a clock ; and Rudy is passionately fond of him ; and as for Freddy, his whole face is one grin when grandpapa appears."

My grandfather, no doubt, had a right to such little compensations as a visit from his grandchildren could give him, for the life of a philosopher in the midst of a family of cheerful daughters is not always an easy one. The following letter, written to my father in 1855 by my mother's sister Mary,* gives an account of some of the trials endured by the author of " Vestiges of Creation " at the hands of his girls :

" I must tell you such a good joke we keep up to frighten papa. Well, you must understand that we have an imaginary lover named ' Charles,' and sometimes on an evening when the curtains are drawn and papa comes abruptly into the room we all make a kind of underhand fuss, then make signs to each other, then look anxiously towards the

* Mary Chambers, known to her family as Mollie, was a beautiful and brilliantly gifted girl, who did not live to fulfil the high promise of her early years. She married Dr. Alexander Edwards, and died quite young.

curtains, and whisper loud enough for pa to hear, 'Keep in your feet, Charles; the tip of your boot is seen,' &c.   Then of course papa looks suspicious, and goes and examines behind the curtains, amidst our shouts of laughter.

" Well, to-night he came in as usual to read us some philosophical work or other ; and Tuckey, who cannot endure when he begins to read, and who generally acts as Charles on an emergency, went out of the room.   Presently there is the sound of a guitar heard outside in the garden, and we all look at each other and whisper, ' Oh ! there's Charles at last.   Good gracious ! I hope papa won't hear him.   Oh, heavens ! I wish he would be quiet until papa goes out of the room.   Annie ' (in a despairing tone), ' go to the window and sign to him to go away just now.'   Then papa, who has heard it all of course, looks up quite angry and says, ' Dear bless me, what's the use of my reading to you if you all go on making signs to each other in that way ? '   However, he goes on again.   Presently the door hastily opens and a head pops in, but the moment after disappears again on seeing papa, leaving nothing but a general impression of tremendous black moustache, a hat, and cane ; then, of course, we are all in fits of laughing.   Oh, we have such fun with the darling papa !   He is the best man in all the world.   I just adore him.   He takes us walks three times a week along the Dean Bridge, and entertains us with the most charm- ing, intellectual, and at the same time amusing conversation. These are the greatest treats we have, and we tell him that it is very bad policy on his part to make himself so fascinating to us, as we will never leave him to be married. . . .

"It was my birthday yesterday, and I was twenty, and none of them gave me a present (although I gave them all due warning some days before so that they might have sufficient time to prepare the presents) except mamma and Annie. Mamma gave me a pair of scissors, a thimble, a lovely coral stud for my neck, and a beautiful ring. Annie gave me a very pretty jug, Bob gave me his blessing (wretch!), and pa gave me a long lecture on the Dean Bridge, to the effect that although I had passed twenty years without seeing any misery and without experiencing any cares, yet I must often think that there *are* such things in the world of the extent of which l have no idea, &c."

The next letter is from my mother to my father, then in Sweden, and describes a railway journey (with a collision thrown in) to the Doune Terrace home in Edinburgh. With regard to the persons referred to in it I may say that Spaul, the funereal, was our butler; " Matilda " was Miss Volckhausen, our German governess, recently arrived. She was to stay with us for more than thirty years. "The Dodger " was W. H. Wills, the friend and assistant of Dickens ; " Auntie " was Mrs. Wills ; and " Prie " was our uncle, the late Sir William Priestley.

" 1, DOUNE TERRACE, EDINBURGH,
"*Monday*, 13*th February*, 1860.

"The first thing I do this glorious, sunshiny, dear frosty morning is to write to you as I promised in my hurried letter of last night. . . . I must tell you a little about our journey now. I was in a perfect ferment of anxiety as our journey approached and got up at five on Friday morning to be ready. At last all was ready, roped and down in the hall, Marian and I standing there waiting. The procession came down in this wise. First Matilda with Rudy in one hand and her bandbox in the other. Two steps above, Spaul with Freddy on his back. Two steps above that Baillie with Babe in one arm, and a bloated bag bursting with bottles and napkins in the other. The step above, Susan with a very stiff neck and a large basket of provisions followed by the mild Elizabeth, partially concealed by two railway rugs and one large fur. They all happened to be together on the one flight of steps and made me roar and forget all my anxiety. Marian bade us good-bye and off we set in a fly and a cab, Spaul looking like death with a fearful swollen jaw, &c., ready to bury us all in a respectable but *not* economical manner at the shortest notice and to retire subsequently into a separate but adjacent grave (being attached to the family, but too respectful to be *too* near).

"As our train was to start at 9.20, and I remembered your principles with regard to time of waiting at stations, you will not be surprised to hear I was not much more than an hour too soon.

"It was fortunate, as Matilda's box, of a baskety and German nature, and seemingly ballasted with stones, had been quietly left behind in the smoking room (where of course it had been put to be at hand and easily found). The misery of Spaul was touching :—back he had to go though, and back he came with it in time, the unconscious Matilda thinking— if she thought at all—it was safely tarpaulined on the top of the carriage all the time. This also put me into fits, her unconscious face and the idea of Spaul thinking that the bandbox had been her entire luggage. He handed in the *Times* with a funereal smile and eventually retired, leaving behind him an undertaker's blessing and a grave-digger's hope that we should all reach our long home safely in time. At the station were Auntie, [Mrs. Wills], inclined to pathos but disregarded, the Dodger [Mr. W. H. Wills], very spry, Jack, heavy, Prie, paternal and bearing outward signs of having sat up all night to be ready in time in the morning. Lastly came Hopie, bright and kind. We got packed into a centre carriage. The Dodger, I believe, tipped the guard, the bell rang, the door was shut, the window let down, more last words, and at last we were off.

"Well, I must cut the journey short. It went beautifully. I gave the party their dinner, consisting of roast fowls and orange jelly, between 12 and 1. York at 2.30—a danger signal—train slackening—proved to be Toozie as we neared the station. Large bottle of Pocklington milk and two cakes of toffy. Pause of twenty minutes, then off again, boys perfect bricks. Babe either sucking or sleeping or smiling, or doing all three at once.

"Very near Edinburgh, all the milk done,— there in half-an-hour say we. Baillie preparing all our things, stands emptying Babe's bottle—we run into a goods train—we all clash for a moment. Rudy's head is bumped, he howls—Freddy howls —baby howls. I call out for orange jelly—howls stop.

"I let the carriage window down. Guard *loquitur*, 'Anybody hurt here, mum?'

"'No, what's up?' 'Run into a goods train.' 'Oh, is that all—very well.'

"Sit down again and wait.

"Passenger from Berwick of a re-assuring nature walks up and down. 'It's a mehrrcy we werhnet all smashed — the goods train is all in rribands,' &c., &c. Suddenly think I should like to see a railway accident. Ask Berwick passenger to take me out and show me.

"Roofs of vans, splinters, smashes, intoxicated wheels and crazy engine strewed promiscuous. Invalid lady in carriage by herself. 'For God's sake let me out of here and take me where there is another lady.' I am that other lady. I say 'Don't be frightened. We're all right now. It's being telegraphed both ways. No danger. I'll take you in, if you don't mind the children.' 'Thank you,

thank you. How kind, how composed you are.'
' Ah, you see, I'm strong, and you're not.'

" Wait an hour ; engine hastens to our rescue,
back to Dunbar, very slow and stopping often.

" Then shunt on to the ' up line,' and go down
cautiously on that, past all the *débris*, lighted now
by the torches of fifty navvies or whatever they
are. Reach Edinburgh quite jolly at eleven. Find
Mollie bathed in tears at the station and papa cool
and kindly ; get into Mollie's carriage, baggage into
cab. Papa and Mollie walk behind. Reach Doune
Terrace ; they not a bit surprised that we didn't
arrive sooner. Mollie and papa arrive. Mollie tells
of her fright. Her coachman had come back from
the station saying there had been a collision and no
one knew when we might arrive, and nearly killed
Mollie. He ought to have added (but didn't know
himself), ' no passenger hurt.' Mollie had presence
of mind (being at Doune Terrace at the time) not
to say a word, but to fly upstairs, throw on her
bonnet, rush off to the station and wait in a state of
fearful distress till we came, when she fell sobbing
round my neck. The reaction was delightful, to
find all the dear ones safe and even merry. Poor
Rudy was the one that got a knock (of course),
being next the window, but it only ached one
night. Baillie's elbow was ill-used too, and her head,
I believe, as she was violently thrown I don't know
where, but she never so much as changed countenance. I never saw such a brave creature. Not
one of us but was cool and perfectly brave. Mind

you, it *was* a shock, and I am so glad you were not there, as your face would have turned white I know and frightened me. I felt I was the head there to whom all looked, and I was as unconcerned as possible, with my heart very nearly fainting within me once or twice. I had Babe in my arms in a centre seat luckily at the time, and Freddy sat opposite me by himself—also lucky. The passengers further in front were the worst used, but only the poor engine drivers were severely hurt. Mollie saw them in the train with their heads all bandaged. Our carriage and the forward ones were uncoupled from the rest of the train which bounded fifty yards back from us. But why should I bother you with what is over. The facts I suppose are that a goods train (as they usually do—particularly when they know an express to be behind—is it because they get paralyzed with fear?) had stopped. They had not hoisted a danger signal in time. Still we had time, barely, to slacken a little over forty mile speed, else I won't answer for consequences.

"Our engine leapt on the back of the goods van, and so and so and so—it was done; but it was well and neatly done, and really a most successful collision, and I'm not a grain the worse —indeed much the better. . . . So there's my description."

My grandmother, Mrs. Robert Chambers, has been already mentioned in the passages I have quoted from my father's note-book. She was a musician of no common skill, and played beautifully both on the harp and on the piano. Not only was she the very soul of kindness, but she had a charming gift of humour, sometimes conscious, sometimes (in appearance, at least) unconscious— humour always radiant and amiable, but often, too, of a detached and unworldly kind that made her society delightful to all who knew her. My mother, during the course of the Edinburgh visit, in 1860, to which the railway accident was the preface, writes to my father :

"About twelve o'clock I saw mamma hurrying up lunch, and asked why it was to be so early. 'Oh,' says mamma, 'I want to get lunch over, as Miss Y. said she would come in to-day, as she waited an hour and a half yesterday for me to come in, while I was sitting upstairs, and she had to go away ; but she left a message saying she would come back to-day, which I think is probable, as she has left her teeth behind.' 'Her *teeth ?*' I said. 'Yes ; they were found on the ground, just where she had been sitting, by cook when she did out the room this morning.' It gave poor mamma quite a turn, being the first thing she saw on coming down to breakfast this morning, and she has been on the sofa ever since. Well, we hurried our lunch, and got it over ; after which mamma prepared to vanish safely out of the ken of Miss Y. or any other visitor, first turning to Margaret the tablemaid, and saying gently, 'Margaret, if Miss Y. calls say we're all out, and that her teeth are on the dining-room mantel-piece.' The fits you are perhaps taking over this are nothing to what I am going into at this moment as it all comes back to me. There was the double set, eight-and-twenty of 'em, on the centre of the mantelpiece, covered decently by mamma with the *Scotsman* of yesterday, but exposed to view every now and then by everybody in turn taking up the *Scotsman* intending to read it. Papa can't get over it; he goes into tranquil fits over and over again, and says they were left as a ghastly reproach by Miss Y. because she had no lunch yesterday."

In 1862 Mrs. Chambers paid us a visit at Shanklin, in the Isle of Wight, and brought with her her youngest daughter Alice, a little girl who, though she was my aunt, was my senior by only a few years. In the following letter my mother describes a memorable incident of this visit:

"Mamma and Alice took a bedroom near, and lived with me till yesterday, when they took a parlour and bedroom next door; but of course we are always together, and Alice's cheerful voice rings about the house all day, pitched at such a height that one would think it *must* fall. Mamma enjoys the place in her own way immensely, and has already sniffed out all the drains and condemned them, particularly the Chine one by Sampson's. The Sampsons [the owners of the bathing-machines] are greatly impressed by her presence and dignity.

She goes about in her white dressing-gown, regard-
less of crinoline and all existing fashions, spends
small competencies on shrimps, never takes a meal
at the time we take it, and retires to her couch at
about 6.45, leaving Alice to spend her evenings and
sup with us.   Yesterday she announced with an air
of the deepest mystery and importance that she
was going to give a concert—Alice prima donna;
admission, by ticket, one halfpenny.   She intended
giving it in her own room, but came round and
asked if she might give it in mine, as the fact was
the upper notes of her piano were slightly defective,
and most of the lower ones wouldn't sound at all.
So I gave my consent.   Alice wrote the tickets,
and we were all obliged to purchase.   The boys
came clamouring for halfpence—the free list was
suspended—Liza [the parlour-maid], Julie [the
German nurse], and Matilda [our German gover-
ness], were commanded to disburse.   Julie plunged
a great brown paw in her pocket, and finally cleared
the required coin from a miscellaneous collection
of crumbs, local diamonds, nutmeg-grater, grimy
pocket-handkerchief, small hard apples, and safety-
pins.   Liza drew hers forth with more delicacy
from an old purse of yours where she keeps a small
fortune of halfpence and fourpenny-pieces.   Then
mamma said in a grand voice, ' Let Mrs. Colenutt*
know of this.   I desire she may come too.'   ' Free
list?' I whispered.   ' By no means. She must pay
for her ticket.'   So poor Mrs. C. had to buy her

* The landlady.

ticket; and finally, when we were all seated, she knocked at the door, held her ticket out timidly, and stood, without a smile, at the back of the door the whole time. Mamma had got Matilda to make a wreath for Alice, who looked like a midge in the sunshine with it on ! and all the boys had sprigs in their hats, and sat with the greatest solemnity the whole time. The concert consisted of mamma and Alice playing three duets, and before each mamma always turned to Mrs. Colenutt—who was ready to sink with awe—as being the principal feature in the audience, and said impressively, ' Scotch—Lowland ; ' ' English—very old ; ' ' Favourite air of Sir Walter Scott's—supposed to be Highland.' When it was over Mrs. Colenutt curtsied and said it was ' beautiful, and well worth the money.' Hopie and I retired after the whole thing, and actually danced with laughter. Mamma was, on the contrary, as serious as a judge ; and Alice subsequently confided to Hopie on the sands that she had made fourpence-halfpenny by the affair, having sold nine tickets. Mamma said afterwards to Hopie and me, ' Now, that is a thing Mrs. Walnut will never forget. She was deeply impressed.' "

I must now pass on, reluctantly enough, from these intimate family reminiscences, and next in order I call up from the past the figure of our dear old Wilkie Collins, the kindest and best friend that boy or man ever had. Wilkie—we never called him by any more formal name, even when we were little fellows—had known my mother before her marriage, and to us boys and to our sister he soon grew to be what he ever afterwards remained : not merely the grown-up and respected friend of our parents, but our own true companion and close associate.   He took our young imaginations captive with stories of Tom Sayers, with whom he had often conversed, whose face-destroying hand he had shaken, whose awful arm he had felt.   " He hadn't any muscle to speak of in his forearm," said Wilkie, " and there wasn't any show of biceps; but when I remarked on that, he asked me to observe his triceps and the muscle under his shoulder, and then I understood how he did it."   This story was told to us some time before Wilkie set out to denounce athletes and athleticism in " Man and Wife "—of which, by the way, he wrote a considerable part in our home near Highgate.   The book is dedicated to my father and mother ; and though, as budding cricketers and football-players and runners, we felt ourselves wounded in our tenderest places by its severity towards athletes, we were generous, and forgave the erring author for the sake of the un-varying friend.   Not very many years after, so great is the force of kindness and inconsistency, he congratulated me on having rowed in an eight-oar on the Cam and made some bumps !

I can see him now as I used to see him in those early, unforgotten days : a neat figure of a cheerful plumpness, very small feet and hands, a full brown beard, a high and rounded forehead, a small nose

not naturally intended to support a pair of large
spectacles behind which his eyes shone with humour
and friendship; not by any means the sort of man
imagination would have pictured as the creator of
Count Fosco and the inventor of the terrors of
" Armadale " and the absorbing mystery of "The
Moonstone." Yet he was, in fact, a very hard and
determined worker. In one of his letters to my
mother he describes how he finished the writing of
"The Guilty River": "You know well what a
fool I am—or shall I put it mildly and say how
'indiscreet'? For the last week, while I was
finishing the story, I worked for twelve hours a
day, and galloped along without feeling it, like the
old post-horses, while I was hot. Do you remember
how the forelegs of those post-horses quivered and
how their heads drooped when they came to the
journey's end?" It must be remembered that for
many years he had to struggle against attacks of
rheumatism, and later on of gout in the eyes; but
neither the acuteness of his pain nor the remedies
he was forced to take in order to abate it could
quench that indomitable spirit or freeze the genial
current of his soul. His conversation was easy and
delightful both in English and in French. "I
don't care a fig for the accent," he used to say, and
he certainly spoke truly. "The French are a
polite people, and they don't trouble to think about
accent if they understand you. They understand
me." Two peculiarities in his English I can
remember : he always pronounced the words

"really" and "real" as if they had been spelt "raily" and "rail," and he gave to the word "obliged" its old-fashioned sound of "obleeged."

I have said that Wilkie Collins knew my mother before she was married. The earliest specimen of his handwriting that I possess is a piece of verse addressed by him to her. It seems to have accompanied a gift of toffy sent in return for a similar gift from her. Here it is:

" Miss Chambers has sent me a very sharp letter,
　　With a gift of some Toffy (I never sucked better!).
　　'Tis plain, from her note, she would have me infer
　　That *I* should have first sent the Toffy to *her*.
　　I will only observe on the present occasion
　　(Thinking first gifts of sweets so much sugar'd temptation),
　　That, in tempting of all kinds, I still must believe
　　The men act like Adam, the women like Eve.
　　From mere mortal frailties I don't stand exempted,
　　So I waited, like Adam, by Eve to be tempted;
　　But, more fitted than he with 'The Woman' to grapple,
　　I return her (in Toffy) my bite of 'the Apple.'

　　　　　　　　　　　　　"W. W. C.

" *March* 27/52.

M.　　　　　　　　　　　　　　　　　D

Wilkie Collins's novels left him no time for sporting with the lighter muse; but it is plain from these playful and polished lines that he might, had he cared for the task, have set up as a frivolous rival to Mr. Locker or Mr. Austin Dobson in the writing of *vers de société*.

CHAPTER III.

It was through Mr. and Mrs. W. H. Wills that my mother came to know Wilkie Collins, the Dickens family, and others who were at that time distinguished in London literary circles. Mrs. Wills was, as I have said, the sister of Robert Chambers, and her husband thus became to us, as to our parents, "Uncle Harry"—the most popular uncle certainly that even a boyish imagination could have conceived. His close association with Charles Dickens, first in the *Daily News*, afterwards in *Household Words* from 1850 to 1859, and finally in *All the Year Round*, is a matter of literary history. The original agreement for the publication of *Household Words* is now in the possession of my aunt, Lady Priestley. It was made between Charles Dickens, William Bradbury, F. M. Evans, W. H. Wills, and John Forster; assigns to each of them a certain fractional share in the profits of the venture; and appoints Dickens to be editor and Wills to be "sub-editor" of the publication. In more modern parlance he would, I think, be styled assistant-editor. What is certain is that a very great part of the most laborious work of the editorial office was done by my uncle, for Charles Dickens was very busily occupied with his novel-writing and his public readings, and was necessarily compelled to leave a great deal to his assistant. It is equally true, however, that Dickens was no *roi fainéant*; indeed, it was not in his nature to be that. He kept all the literary threads of *Household Words* well in his hands. His correspondence with my uncle, which is now in Lady Priestley's hands, shows with what a high sense of responsibility and what anxious care he discharged his editorial duties. No promising manuscript escaped him; he took infinite trouble to arrange the chief features of each issue so that the public interest might be maintained. Article after article he wrote himself; others he collaborated in, and throughout the periodical his guiding mind made itself manifest. These letters form a profoundly interesting record of a long association in literature and friendship.

Amongst the contributors to *Household Words*, and afterwards to *All the Year Round* was Wilkie Collins. His first great novel, "The Woman in White," appeared in the pages of the latter publication, and the following note* written to my uncle, shows where and under what circumstances he hit upon the admirable title:

* This letter, as well as the two following ones, have been lent to me by Lady Priestley.

"CHURCH HILL COTTAGE, BROADSTAIRS,
                          "*Aug.* 15*th*, 1859.

"MY DEAR WILLS,—I send enclosed (and registered—for I should go distracted if it was lost) my first number. Please let me have duplicate proofs as soon as possible, for I want to see something in connection with the story which is not a mass of confusion. It is an awfully long number— between 8 and 9 pages; but I *must* stagger the public into attention, if possible, at the outset. They shan't drop a number when I begin, if *I* can help it.

"I have hit on a new title, in the course of a night-walk to the North Foreland, which seems to me weird and striking :

THE WOMAN IN WHITE.

"My love to Dickens. How does he do? When will he write? Have you a house to let? I am at mortal enmity with my London landlord, and am resolved to leave him. Where I am to go next 'God, He knows.' Ta-ta.

                                   "W. C."

It must be admitted that the North Foreland sent a happy inspiration.

The next letter gives an amusing insight into the methods of a story-writer, and the trials that come upon him in the course of his task. Wilkie Collins at the time was writing "No Name" for *All the Year Round:*

" The Fort House, Broadstairs,
" *September* 14*th*, 1862.

" My dear Wills,—Do you, or does Mrs. Wills, or does any kindly Scot to whom you can at once apply without trouble, know anything of the neighbourhood of Dumfries? My story will take me there next week. I am a total stranger to the locality, and I have no time to go and look for myself.

" I don't want any elaborate description. I only want answers to these questions:

" Is the neighbourhood of Dumfries—say for five miles round—hilly or flat? Barren and healthy, or cultivated and fairly stocked with trees? Is it pretty scenery or not? Is it like any neighbourhood of any English town? Is it sprinkled with villages? Or is it lonely? Are there any pretty cottages on the banks of the Nith in which I could put a married couple, anxious to escape observation, in their honeymoon? If so, what is the name of any village which could be near the said cottage? If the Nith won't do, the cottage can be put anywhere—north, south, east, or west—as long as it is a few miles from Dumfries. Am I right in supposing Dumfries to be a thriving manufacturing town? And if so, what does it manufacture? Lastly, is there any mortal book which you could send me by book-post, and from which I could crib the local knowledge which I want?

" Meditate, I beseech you, on these questions— and forgive ' No Name ' for worrying you as well as me.

"If the worst comes to the worst, I must write from pure imagination; and won't the letters come pouring in *then* to correct my mistakes! There is nothing the British reader enjoys so much as catching his author in the wrong.

"Where is Dickens? Will he be at Gadshill this week, and at the office on Wednesday? If this is so, I will send him up my second volume to read. I hear gladly from Beard, who has been staying here, that Georgina is better.

"I have been taking a holiday, and am hard at work again. If you see Reade, tell him to be of good cheer. I shan't have done before the end of the year—perhaps not before the end of January. They seem to like the story, and be d——d to them. The women write me letters begging for more each week. I wish they may get it!

"Will you come here and *tell* me about Dumfries? One of my servants was kicked out yesterday, and the other is going to-morrow; but if you don't mind waiting on yourself, *I'll* black your boots.— Ever yours, W. C."

The average novel-reader will learn from this letter one or two things that must surprise him. In the first place, the author, instead of being, as is commonly supposed, the planner and controller of the destinies of his story, is himself its unwilling but helpless slave. Wilkie Collins obviously did not desire to take his honeymoon couple to Dumfries. The place was a sealed book to him. He

knew nothing of its manufactures (tweeds and
hosiery, by the way), its scenery or its surroundings; nothing except that it stood on the river Nith.
In spite of this complete ignorance of the locality,
he was forced by characters and circumstances over
which he had manifestly no control to take his
masters to Dumfries, and not only to take them
there, but to pretend that he had known the place
from his cradle.   In this pathetic extremity he
applied to Mr. Wills, who, it may be believed,
managed to give him a good deliverance.   A reference to the novel, however, shows that even if Mr.
Wills supplied the various details asked for, Wilkie
Collins made but little use of them.   In the first
chapter of the fifth " scene " of " No Name," Noel
and Magdalen Vanstone are found spending their
honeymoon at " Baliol Cottage, Dumfries."   To be
strictly accurate, I should say that Noel is living
there, for Magdalen has just left him.   The only
description given of the neighbourhood is contained
in the following passage : " The prospect from the
window overlooked the course of the Nith at a bend
of the river a few miles above Dumfries.   Here
and there through wintry gaps in the wooded bank
broad tracts of the level cultivated valley met the
eye.   Boats passed on the river, and carts plodded
along the high-road on their way to Dumfries.   The
view, noted in Scotland for its bright and peaceful
charm, was presented at the best which its wintry
aspect could assume."

Finally, it may be noted in Wilkie's letter that

he seemed to look upon the public who devoured his book and called for more rather with anger than with affection. They were his hard taskmasters, with their confounded liking for his story, and it was they who were driving him along this thorny and untrodden road to Dumfries. It was a humorous inversion of sentiment, and I am sure it did not last long, for no writer had at the bottom of his heart a more genuine regard for those who read his books, and whose servant, in a sense, he was proud to be, than Wilkie Collins.

In any case, whatever may have been Wilkie's troubles while his story was still on the stocks, he must have felt many a thrill of pleasure when "No Name" appeared in book-form. Here is his account of its reception :

"12, HARLEY STREET, W.,
Decr. 31*st*, 1862.

"MY DEAR WILLS,—I have this day sent you (to Regent's Park Terrace) a copy of 'No Name.' We published to-day—an edition of four *thousand* copies. At five this afternoon only four *hundred* were left. This is a good rattling sale to begin with.

"I heard at the office to-day that you had kindly put everything in proper train with Mr. Bernard, and that nothing was wanted but the last act. Perhaps the end of the story staggers my worthy collaborator ? Or perhaps the festivities of the season are a little in his way ? I have promised Emden at the Olympic a first look at the Drama as

soon as it is done.   The sage Low recommends our
sending a copy to the British Museum, as a solemn
act of publication.   What do you think?

"My liver still torments me, and the fiend
rheumatism gnaws at my right knee.—Ever yours,

"WILKIE COLLINS.

"*P.S.*—I had just hobbled out, unluckily, when
you called."

The next letter is to my father (my mother and
the family being then *en pension* in Shanklin), and
shows Wilkie in a new light as an intending
yachtsman :

"12, HARLEY STREET, W.,
"*August 6th,* 1860.

"MY DEAR LEHMANN,—Delighted to hear you
are coming!   The only hitch in the programme is
that I can't go to Shanklin this week—as I am
already engaged to Gadshill.   But you will give
me another chance?—and we will discuss the question of time on Thursday.   The autumn is 'all
before us when to choose, and Providence our
guide' (Milton).   I suppose you don't feel inclined
to take a cruise off the west coast of Ireland on the
15th of September?   I and two other British tars
propose to plough the main for a fortnight or so,
on that occasion, in a Welsh boat of our own
hiring.—Ever yours,

"W. C."·

In the summer of 1862 my father had to go to America on business. The civil war was then raging, and the cause of the North seemed to many Englishmen to be a hopeless one. My father never wavered in his strong sympathy for the Northern side, and his conviction that it must ultimately prove triumphant. Most of his friends, however, held a contrary opinion, Wilkie Collins and Charles Dickens amongst them. Both these distinguished men at a later period came to know Americans well, and to like the people, as all who know them well must like them. In the early sixties, however, they shared the beliefs then prevalent amongst a large section of Englishmen with regard to Americans and their destinies. When my father was about to start on his voyage Wilkie Collins wrote to him the following letter :

"THE FORT HOUSE, BROADSTAIRS,
"*July 28th*, 1862.

"MY DEAR LEHMANN,—Here is a line to wish you most heartily a safe voyage out and a prosperous return. I need not tell you, I am sure, how sorry I am to miss the chance of having you here —and how glad I should be to hear, even at the eleventh hour, that the American voyage was put off—for Mrs. Lehmann's sake as well as for yours and for mine. But I suppose there is no hope of this.

"The one chance for that miserable country on the other side of the Atlantic is, that those two blatant impostors, Lincoln and McClellan, will fail to get the 300,000 new men they ask for. If I thought it would be the least use, I would go down on both my knees, and pray with all my might for the total failure of the new enlistment scheme. But the devil being the ruling power in American affairs, and I not being (as I venture to hope) on particularly good terms with him, it seems hopeless on this occasion to put any trust in the efficacy of fervent aspirations and cramped knees.

"All I do most seriously and earnestly hope is that you will come back with all personal anxieties in the American direction set at rest. We will then drink confusion together to your customers for light steel and my customers for light reading. I have hundreds of American correspondents, but no friends there. If you want anything special in the literary way, tell Harper of New York you are a friend of mine, and he will be gladly of service to you. So would Fields (of the firm of Ticknor and Fields), Boston.

"Good-bye, my dear fellow, and once more may you have the best of voyages out and the speediest of voyages back again.—Ever yours most truly,

"WILKIE COLLINS.

"Pray thank Mrs. Lehmann for two additions to your letter. I am not a good correspondent generally; but if she will write to me in those long evenings, I promise to write back. We are in nearly the same situations—she is shut up with her boys, and I am shut up with my books."

Amongst my father's memoranda in the note-book is one which I have already cited, relating to Charles Dickens : "Dickens fond of Americans. But when I returned from America in the spring of 1863, and expressed my firm belief in the ultimate victory of the North, he treated my opinion as a harmless hallucination." Here is a letter my father received from Dickens at that time :

"GAD'S HILL PLACE,
"HIGHAM, BY ROCHESTER, KENT,
"*Thursday, Twenty-eighth June*, 1863.

"MY DEAR LEHMANN,—On Thursday the 4th of June [July], at 7, I shall have much pleasure in dining at Westbourne Terrace. (My Ascot horse being sure to win; I have no need even to go down to see him run for the cup.)

"Although you have so lately been in America, and although I know what a raging mad topsy-turvy state of things obtains there, I can *not* believe that the conscription will do otherwise than fail, and wreck the War. I feel convinced, indeed, that the War will be shattered by want of Northern soldiers.—Ever faithfully,

"C. D.

" Of course, the more they brag the more I don't believe them."

To leave these old, unhappy, far-off things and battles long ago, and to end in a simpler strain, I

quote a letter to my mother from Wilkie Collins on
the subject of sulphur baths :

"NUELLEN'S HOTEL, AIX-LA-CHAPELLE,
                    "*April 29th*, 1863.

"MY DEAR MRS. LEHMANN,—Under any circumstances I should have written to tell you all my
news, and to ask for all your news in return.   But
a letter from my brother telling me that you too
have been ill, puts the pen at once into my hands.
I gather from what Charlie says that you are now
better; but I want to hear about you and yours
from yourself, and I am selfishly anxious for as long
an answer as you can send, as soon as you can write
it.   There is the state of my mind expressed with
the most unflinching candour !

"As for me, I am all over sulphur, inside and
out; and if ever a man felt fit for the infernal
regions already, I (in respect to the sulphurous part
of the Satanic climate) am that man.   The invalid
custom here is to rise at seven in the morning, to
go out and drink the water hot from the spring,
and to be entertained between the gulps with a
band of music on an empty stomach.   You who
know me will acquit me of sanctioning by my
presence any such uncomfortable proceeding as
this.   I have an excellent carrier.   I send him
to the spring with a stoppered bottle, and I drink
my water horizontally in bed.   It was nasty
enough at first; but I have got used to it
already.   The next curative proceeding discloses

me, towards the afternoon, in a private stone-pit, up to my middle in the hot sulphur spring; more of the hot water is pouring down on me from a pipe in the ceiling; a worthy German stands by my side, directing the water in a continuous shower on all my weak points with one hand and shampooing me with the other. We exchange cheerful remarks in French (English being all Greek to him and German all Hebrew to me); and, oh, don't we massacre the language of our lively neighbours! In mistakes of *gender*, I am well ahead of the German—it being an old habit of mine, out of my love and respect for the fair sex, to make all French words about the gender of which I feel uncertain, feminine words. But in other respects my German friend is far beyond me. This great creature has made an entirely new discovery in the science of language—he does without verbs. '*Trop fort? Bon pour vous fort. Trop chaud? Bon pour vous chaud. Promenade aujourd'hui? Aha! aha! bon pour vous promenade. Encore la jambe—encore le dos—frottement, ah, oui, oui, frottement excellent pour vous. Repos bon pour vous—à votre service, monsieur—bon jour!*" What an excellent method! Do think of it for your boys—I would practise it myself if I had my time to begin over again. The results of all these sulphurous proceedings—to return to them for the last time, before I get to the end of my letter—are decidedly encouraging in my case. So far I can't wear my boots yet, but I can hobble about with my stick much more freely than I could when I left London; and my general health is benefiting greatly by the change. As for the rest of my life here, it is passed idly enough. The hotel provides me with a delightful open carriage to drive out in, contains a cellar of the best hock and Moselle wines I ever tasted, and possesses a Parisian cook who encourages my natural gluttony by a continuous succession of *entrées* which are to be eaten but not described. My books have made me many friends here, who supply me with reading and make me presents of excellent cigars. So, upon the whole, I get on well enough ; and as long as the Baths do me good, so long I shall remain at Aix-la-Chapelle.

" There is a nice egotistical letter ! But what else can you expect from a sick man ? Write me another egotistical letter in return, telling me about yourself and Lehmann, and Lehmann's time for coming home, and the boys—and believe me, ever most truly yours,

" WILKIE COLLINS."

CHAPTER IV.

BETWEEN 1863 and 1866 increasing cordiality had abolished the last trace of ceremoniousness between Wilkie and my parents. My father had become "Fred" and my mother was "the Padrona."

[WILKIE COLLINS *to* MRS. F. LEHMANN.]

"MILAN,
"*October* 26, 1866.

"MY DEAR PADRONA,—Are you angry with me for leaving your charming letter so long unanswered? You well might be—and yet it is not my fault. I have been living in a whirlwind, and have only dropped out of the vortex in this place. In plain English the first quarter of an hour which I have had at my own disposal since you wrote to me, is a quarter of an hour to-night, in this very damp and very dreary town. Last night my travelling companion (Pigott) and I went to a public ball here. We entered by a long dark passage, passed through a hall ornamented with a large stock of fenders, grates, and other ironmongery for sale on

M.   E

either side, found ourselves in a spacious room lit
by three oil lamps, with *two* disreputable females
smoking cigars, ten or a dozen depressed men,
about four hundred empty chairs in a circle, one
couple polking in that circle, and nothing else, on
my sacred word of honour, nothing else going on!
To-night I am wiser. I stay at the hotel and write
to you.

"Let us go back to England.

"How came I to be so dreadfully occupied when
your letter reached me? Surely I need not tell
you, who know me so well, the particular circumstance in which my troubles took their rise. *Of
course I caught a cold.* Very good. I had four
different visits to pay in the country, and they had
to be put off till I was better. I also had a play,
('The Frozen Deep') accepted at the Olympic
Theatre and to be produced at Christmas. I also
had my engagement with Pigott to go to Rome on
a certain day. Very good again. It turned out as
soon as I was better that all my four visits must be
paid together in ten days—in consequence of the
infernal cold seizing on me by the nose, teeth, face,
throat, and chest in succession, and keeping me at
home till the time for going to Italy was perilously
near at hand. To make matters worse, the play
with which the Olympic season opened proved a
failure, and 'The Frozen Deep' was wanted in
October instead of at Christmas. I paid a visit in
the country, and came back to London and read
the play to the actors. I paid another visit, and

came back and heard the actors read their parts to
me. I paid another visit and came back to a first
rehearsal! I paid a last visit and came back to see
the stage 'effects' tried—and went away again to
say good-bye to Mama Collins at Tunbridge Wells
—and came back again to sketch the play bill and
hear the manager's last words—and went away
again to Folkestone and Boulogne, and stopped in
Paris a day to discuss the production of my other
play, 'Armadale,' on the French stage, with my
good friend Regnier, of the Théâtre Français, and
went away again through Switzerland and over the
Splügen with Pigott, whose time is limited, and
whose travelling must not be of the dawdling and
desultory kind—and so it happened that to-morrow
night, if all goes well, I shall be at Bologna while
'The Frozen Deep' is being performed for the
first time in London, and the respectable British
Public is hissing or applauding me, as the case may
be. In the midst of all this, where is the time for me
to write to the best of women? There is no time
but between ten and eleven to-night at the Albergo
Reale in Milan. Have I justified myself? Hem?

"We shall go all the sooner to Rome, I think,
and when we leave Rome towards the end of next
month and take the steamer for Marseilles I will
write again and say my last word about a visit to
Pau.* If I *can* come, though it may be only for a
few days, depend upon it I will. It will all depend

* My mother was passing the winter at Pau for the sake of
her health.

on my letters from London and Paris next month,
and as soon as those letters are received you shall
hear from me once more.

"In the meantime need I say how glad I am to
hear such good news of you. You know how glad
I am, but are you learning to take care of yourself
for the future? Don't say 'Stuff!' Don't go to
the piano (especially as *I* am not within hearing)
and forget the words of wisdom. Cultivate your
appetite, and your appetite will reward you. Purchase becoming (and warm) things for the neck
and chest. Rise superior to the devilish delusion
which makes women think that their feet cannot
possibly look pretty in thick boots. I have studied
the subject, and I say they *can*. Men understand
these things; Mr. Worth, of Paris, dresses the fine
French ladies who wear the 'Falballa,' and regulates
the fashions of Europe. He is about to start
'comforters' and hobnail boots for the approaching winter. In two months' time it will be inde-
cent for a woman to show her neck at night, and if
you don't make a frightful noise at every step you
take on the pavement you abrogate your position as
woman, wife, and mother in the eyes of all Europe.
Is this exaggerated? No! A thousand times no!
It is horrible—but it is the truth.

"Has Fred returned to you? If he has, give
him my love, and ask him to bring you to Rome
in the middle of next month. Oh dear, dear! how
pleasant it would be if we could all meet in the
Forum! But we shan't. Kiss Miss L. for me,

and give my love to the boys.   The lamp is going out, and I must start early to-morrow morning, and there is nothing for it but to repeat that everlasting business of unbuttoning and going to bed.   Good-bye for the present.   Yours affectionately,

"W. C."

[WILKIE COLLINS *to* MRS. F. LEHMANN.]

" 9, MELCOMBE PLACE, DORSET SQUARE, LONDON,
" *Dec.* 9, 1866.

" Injured and admirable Padrona ! Observe the date and address ! !

" What does it mean ?   Am I a wretch unworthy of your kindness, unworthy of your interest ?

" I affirm with the whole force of my conviction that I am only the unluckiest of men.

" Hear me !

" I had made all my arrangements for returning by way of Pau, and was on the point of writing to you to say so, when letters arrived for me from Paris and London.

" The letter from Paris only informed me of a difficulty.   The letter from London announced a disaster.

" My collaborator in the new French dramatic version of ' Armadale ' was at a standstill in Paris for want of personal explanations with the author of the book.   He had urgent reasons for wishing to see me as soon as possible.   Having laid this letter down I took up next the letter from London.

It was from the manager of the Olympic Theatre, and it announced the total failure (in respect of attracting audiences) of 'The Frozen Deep!' Not a sixpence made for me by the play (after all the success of the first night!)—the account books of the theatre waiting to be examined by me—and the manager waiting to know what was to be done next! There was nothing for it but to resign myself to the disappointment of missing my visit, and to get back to Paris and London as fast as I could. I caught the steamer at Civita Vecchia, went to Leghorn, from Leghorn to Marseilles, Marseilles to Macon (to rest after ten hours' shaking on the railway), Macon to Paris. At Paris a long day's work with my collaborator which put things right again. Next day from Paris to London. Next day investigation of the accounts of the theatre—plain evidence that the play has not even paid its expenses—no alternative that I can see or the manager either, but to put 'The Frozen Deep' on the shelf by or before Christmas. Such is my brief narrative of disaster. Now you know the facts, will you be a dear good soul and forgive your faithful Wilkie? When a man's affairs are all going wrong in his absence abroad what is the man to do? He can do nothing but go back.

"The play is (I am *told*, for I have not yet had the courage to go and see it) beautifully got up, and very well acted. But the enlightened British Public declares it to be '*slow*.' There isn't an atom of slang or vulgarity in the whole piece from beginning to end; no female legs are shown in it; Richard Wardom doesn't get up after dying and sing a comic song; sailors are represented in the Arctic regions, and there is no hornpipe danced, and no sudden arrival of 'the pets of the ballet' to join the dance in the costume of Esquimaux maidens; finally, all the men on the stage *don't* marry all the women on the stage at the end, and nobody addresses the audience and says, 'If our kind friends here to-night will only encourage us by their applause, there are brave hearts among us which will dare the perils for many a night yet of —'The Frozen Deep.'

"For these reasons, best of women, I have failed. Is my tail put down?   No—a thousand times, no! I am at work on the dramatic 'Armadale,' and I will take John Bull by the scruff of the neck, and force him into the theatre to see it—before or after it has been played in French, I don't know which— but into the theatre John Bull shall go.   I have some ideas of advertising next time that will make the public hair stand on end.   And so enough, and more than enough, of theatrical matters.

"Oh, I wanted you so at Rome—in the Protestant cemetery—don't start! No ghosts—only a cat. I went to show my friend Pigott the grave of the illustrious Shelley.   Approaching the resting-place of the divine poet in a bright sunlight, the finest black Tom you ever saw discovered at an incredible distance that a catanthropist had entered the cemetery—rushed up at a gallop, with his tail at right angles to his spine—turned over on his back with his four paws in the air, and said in the language of cats: 'Shelley be hanged! Come and tickle me!' I stooped and tickled him. We were both profoundly affected.

"Is this all I have to tell you about Rome? By no means. Then why don't I go on and tell it? Because it is five o'clock—the British muffin-bell is ringing—the dismal British Sunday is closing in. I have promised to dine with the Benzons (where I shall meet Fred), and to take Charley and Katie * (who is in the doctor's hands again) on my way. I must walk to keep my horrid corpulence down, and the time is slipping away; and though I want to go on talking to you, I must submit to another disappointment, and give it up.

"Will you write and say you have forgiven me? The most becoming ornament of your enchanting sex is—Mercy. It is the ornament, dear lady, that *you* especially wear! (Mercy on me, I am drifting into the phraseology of Count Fosco!) Let me revert to W. C. again. Will you ask me to come and see you when you are back in the fine weather at Woodlands? Do please—for it isn't my fault that I am in London instead of in Pau. I must work and get some money, now my play has declined to put a halfpenny in my pocket. Yours ever affectionately,

"W. C."

In 1867 Wilkie Collins, busily occupied then, as

---

* Charles A. Collins (Wilkie's brother) and his wife, the younger daughter of Charles Dickens.

always, with his literary work, was devoting his intervals of leisure to house-hunting. He pitched at last upon the comfortable house, 90, Gloucester Place, Portman Square, where he remained till his death, more than twenty years later. We were then (1867) living near London, at Woodlands, Southwood Lane, Highgate, and there Wilkie was always a welcome guest. Here is a letter written by him to my father in that year:

"SOUTHBOROUGH,
"*Tuesday, September* 10*th*, 1867.

"MY DEAR FRED,—Have you made up your mind that I am a Humbug? Naturally, you have.

"Weeks since, you wrote me a kind letter from Rothesay, giving me delightful accounts of the Padrona, and asking me to join you; and that letter remains unanswered to the present date!

"Disgraceful! What is the cause of this ungrateful silence? The cause is: 90, Gloucester Place, Portman Square, W.

"When your letter reached me, I had an old house to leave—a new house to find—that new house to bargain for, and take—lawyers and surveyors to consult—British workmen to employ—and, through it all, to keep my own literary business going without so much as a day's stoppage. Is there no excuse in this? *Ach, Gott! Ja wohl! Si! gewiss!*

"Here, then, is a letter of apology which—if Mamie Dickens's information is correct, ought to meet you on your return to Woodlands. My best love and congratulation to the Padrona. The same from Mama Collins—with whom I am staying to get a little quiet for working in. I return on Thursday next. Come and see me on my new perch. My dining-room is habitable—and the drawing-rooms are getting on.—Ever yours,

"WILKIE COLLINS."

The next letter refers to a theatre-party arranged by Wilkie for my brother and me. I remember the occasion well enough, and the delightful sense we had of dining out in state ; but the details of the pantomime have vanished from my mind.

"Lock Fred up—or he will be taking places !

"90, GLOUCESTER PLACE, PORTMAN SQUARE,
"4th Jan., 1868.

"Stop ! Stop ! Stop ! Don't, for God's sake, go to the Pantomime at the Royal Alfred Theatre before Saturday. _I_ want to take you _there_. I hear it is a good Pantomime—it is also close by.

"Dinner on Saturday punctually at FIVE, instead of half-past four.

"The Surrey business has broken down—as I guess. A note from the inimitable Reade* informs me that he encloses a letter from the manager, which 'is without a parallel in his (Reade's) experience.' _Of course_ there is no letter enclosed ! ! ! But I infer that we are treated by this atrocious manager with the utmost contempt. Oh, Heavens !

* Charles Reade, the novelist.

have we lived to be rejected by a transpontine theatre? But no matter, we gain half-an-hour for dinner-time on Saturday—and we have only a little distance to go to the theatre—and we shall do as well in Marylebone as in Surrey—if I am only in time to stop you and Fred from seeing *that* Pantomime also—without *me!* Yours affly.,

"W. C.

"*P.S.*—The Royal Alfred Theatre is in Church Street, Portman Market. A gorgeous building, opened by His Royal Highness Prince Alfred in person. There!"

[WILKIE COLLINS *to* MRS. F. LEHMANN.]
"90, GLOUCESTER PLACE, PORTMAN SQUARE,
"*January* 10*th*, 1868.

"IN VINO VERITAS.

"While drinking healths on New Year's Eve
    I promised all you ask'd me.
Next day excuses you receive
    Which say you overtask'd me.
'Ungrateful man!' my lady cries,
    'With falsehood's mark I brand him!'
To which your humble slave replies,
    'Pray, madam, understand him!'
The wine once in, the truth comes out,
    (This proverb may assist you)
When sober, I can pause and doubt;
    When *not*—I can't resist you!

"W. C."

" 90, Gloucester Place, Portman Square,
" *Monday, January 4th*, 1869.

" Dearest Padrona,—I have just seen Fechter *
—he has called here. The great culinary artist is
dismissed in disgrace. You must not think of
engaging her. She has done all sorts of dreadful
things. Alas! such but too frequently is the fatal
gift of genius! I wish I knew of another cook to
recommend—but unless you will take *me*, I know
of nobody. And I am conscious of one serious
objection to myself. My style is expensive. I
look on meat simply as a material for sauces. Yours
affectionately,
                                        " W. C."

[Wilkie Collins *to* F. Lehmann.]
" 90, Gloucester Place, Portman Square,
" *October 25th*, 1869.

" My dear Fred,—The Stoughton bitters arrived
this morning from Liverpool. At the same time
appeared a parcel of country sausages from Beard.
I sent him back a bottle of the bitters with instructions to drink your health in brandy and bitters,
and to meditate on the innumerable virtues of
intoxicating liquors for the rest of the day. On
my part I suspended an immortal work of fiction,
by going downstairs and tasting a second bottle
properly combined with gin. Result delicious!
Thank you a thousand times! The first thing
you must do on your return to England is to

* The French Actor.

come here and taste gin and bitters.   May it be soon!*

"Have I any news? Very little. I sit here all day attacking English institutions—battering down the marriage laws of Scotland and Ireland and reviling athletic sports—in short, writing an *un*-popular book ["Man and Wife"] which may possibly make a hit, from the mere oddity of a modern writer running full tilt against the popular sentiment instead of cringing to it. The publishers are delighted with what I have done—especially my American publishers, who sent me an instalment of 500*l*. the other day, on receipt of only the first weekly part. I call *that* something like enthusiasm. Produce me the English publisher who treats his author in this way.

"I am to meet the Padrona at Procter's† on Thursday. And I *did* meet her at Payn's‡ last week, looking very well and beautifully dressed. But two events occurred worth mentioning. The Padrona, assisting the force of a few sensible remarks by appropriate gesticulation, knocked over her tumbler of champagne, and flooded the table. Shortly afterwards *I* assisted a few sensible re-marks, on my part, by appropriate gesticulation, and knocked over *my* tumbler, and flooded the table. *And* Mrs. Payn, seeing her cloth ruined, kept her temper like an angel, and smiled upon me

* My father was in the United States, on his way round the world.
† Barry Cornwall.
‡ James Payn, the novelist.

while rivulets of champagne were flowing over *my* dress-trousers and *her* morocco leather chair. Excellent woman!

"Reade has been here, and has carried off my book about the French police ('mémoires tirées des archives'). He begged me to go and see him at Oxford. I said, 'Very well! write and say when.' Need I add that he has *not* written?

"I had a friend to dinner at the Junior Athenæum the other day. Our remonstrance has produced its effect. I declined to order *any*thing after our experience. 'A dinner at so much a head. If it isn't good I shall personally submit myself for examination before the committee, and shall produce specimens of the dishes received by myself.' The result was a very good dinner. When you come back let us try the same plan. Nothing like throwing the whole responsibility on the cook.

"I had a day at Gadshill a little while since. Only the family. Very harmonious and pleasant—except Dickens's bath, which dripped behind the head of my bed all night. Apropos of Gadshill, your cutting from the *New York Times* has been followed by a copy of the paper, and a letter from Bigelow. I don't think Dickens has heard of it, and I shan't say anything about it, for it might vex him, and can do no good. Why they should rake up that old letter *now*, is more than I can understand.* But then a people who can spell Forster's name without the 'r,' are evidently capable of anything.

* I have been unable to trace this allusion.

"Fechter has refused, what appears to everybody but himself, to be an excellent offer from America. He seems determined to go 'on his own hook' in December next, and will find the managers whom he has refused his enemies when he gets there. I am afraid he has made a mistake.

"Charley and Kitty are back in town. Charley dined here yesterday—no, Saturday. He is fairly well.

"Mrs. John Wood has made the St. James's Theatre a perfect fairy palace, and is playing old English comedy with American actors. Scenery and dresses marvellously good. A great success. The other great success I am going to see on Wednesday—monkeys who are real circus riders, jump through hoops, dance on the horse's back, *and* bow to the audience when they are applauded. We shall see them in Shakespeare next—and why not? They can't be worse than the human actors, and they *might* be better.

"Where will you be when this reaches you? I am told you have got to San Francisco. That will do. Come back. Leave well alone, and come back. I will describe Japan to you, and take you to see the manufactures afterwards at the Baker Street Bazaar.

"Good-bye for the present. Yours, my dear F., ever W. C.

"As for my health, I am getting along pretty slick, sir! A third of my book just done. Have seen nothing of Forster. *Shall* see him if we all last till November 21, at dear old Procter's birthday celebration. Reade and Charley send loves."

CHAPTER V.

WILKIE COLLINS always expressed the greatest possible contempt for the ordinary methods of English education and, in particular, for the grand old fortifying classical curriculum. On one occasion, however, he was good enough to help me in my school-work, and the result of his intervention was that I secured very good marks on the following morning. Our form had been ordered to translate into English verse Horace's Ode (Book I. 12), beginning,

" Quem virum aut heroa lyra vel acri
Tibia sumis celebrare, Clio ? "

Wilkie, who was staying at our house near Highgate, saw me cudgelling my brains, and asked if he could help me. I told him the nature of the task, whereupon he said, " Give me the crib. I'm no good at the Latin, I'm afraid; but I'll see what I can do with the English." Our old friend Bohn was produced, and Wilkie, taking it in his hand, dictated a set of couplets quite as fast as I was able to write them down. This was the result of his intervention :—

"*August 23rd*, 1872.

"HORACE (*Book I., Ode* 12).

"What man or hero, Clio, dost thou name,
On harp or lute, to swell the roll of fame?
What god whose name doth sportive Echo sound
On Hæmus cold or lofty Pindus' mound?
Or Helicon, whence followed Orpheus' strain
The winds and rivers, flowing to the main?
Taught by his mother's art—unwonted sight—
He led the woods themselves in headlong flight.
What more beyond the Father's wonted praise
Can touch my heart or echo in my lays?
He rules the sea—divine and human powers—
And sways the earth with ever-changing hours.
From him nought greater than himself can rise,
Nor aught be like him in th' Olympian skies.
Yet Pallas, next th' immortal gods among,
Holds foremost rank and claims a worthy song.
Thou too, O Liber, dost my Muse inspire,
Tried in the conflict and the martial fire!
And thou, Diana, here shalt bear a part
With Phœbus, champion of th' unerring dart.
Alcides too, and Leda's god-born twain,
Must find a place in this my sounding strain.
This one delights to show his skill on horse,
The other joys in brave and manly force.
Their guiding stars on storm-tossed sailors shine
And point the track across the heaving brine.

M.   F

At their command the wind, the wave, subsides,
The tempests flee, not e'en a cloud abides.
Next Romulus, the haughty Tarquin's pride,
Pompilius' peace, how noble Cato died,
Divide my mind.   I know not which to choose,
Which first, where all deserve an equal Muse.
But Regulus, the Scauri, Paullus' death,
Who loved his country with his dying breath,
Though Carthage conquered—such and such as
  these
In glorious numbers do Camœna please.
The stroke of poverty, the homely farm,
The ancient hearthstone nerved Fabricius' arm.
Rough Curins, too, and brave Camillus' name
Through these have gained an everlasting fame.
The might of Claudius grows as forest trees,
Which grow, we know not how, by slow degrees
For ever; yet above this mighty throng
Doth Julius shine as moon the stars among.
Father and guardian of the human race,
From Saturn sprung, thou hast a worthy place,
The care of Cæsar, Cæsar second reigns,
Thou art supreme, thy glory first remains.
Whether he shall have checked the Parthian's bow
Which oft has laid the Latian warrior low,
Or bound with fetters fast the Indians' pride;
Let him be second, thou the first abide.
Olympus trembles, though the gods be round,
It needs must tremble when thy chariots sound.
Upon polluted groves thou hurl'st thy fire,
And teachest man to reverence thine ire."

Wilkie spent the winter of 1873—4 in America on a reading tour. The following letter to my father describes some of his experiences and impressions :—

"BUFFALO, NEW YORK,
"*January* 2, 1874.

"Strange to say, my dear Fred, I have actually got some leisure time at this place. A disengaged half-hour is before me, and I occupy it in writing a sort of duplicate letter for the Padrona and for you.

"I hear you have called like a good fellow at Gloucester Place, and have heard something of me there from time to time. No matter where I go, my reception in America is always the same. The prominent people in each place visit me, drive me out, dine me, and do all that they can to make me feel myself among friends. The enthusiasm and the kindness are really and truly beyond description. I should be the most ungrateful man living if I had any other than the highest opinion of the American people. I find them to be the most enthusiastic, the most cordial, and the most sincere people I have ever met with in my life. When an American says, ' Come and see me,' he *means* it. This is wonderful to an Englishman.

"Before I had been a week in this country I noted three national peculiarities which had never been mentioned to me by visitors to the States. I. No American hums or whistles a tune either at home or in the street. II. Not one American in

500 has a dog.   III. Not one American in 1,000
carries a walking stick.   I who hum perpetually,
who love dogs, who cannot live without a walking
stick, am greatly distressed at finding my dear
Americans deficient in the three social virtues just
enumerated.

"My readings have succeeded by surprising the
audiences.   The story surprises them in the first
place, being something the like of which they have
not heard before.   And my way of reading surprises them in the second place, because I don't
flourish a paper knife and stamp about the platform,
and thump the reading desk.   I persist in keeping
myself in the background and the story in front.
The audience begins at each reading with silent
astonishment, and ends with a great burst of
applause.

"As to the money, if I could read often enough
I should bring back a little fortune in spite of the
panic.   The hard times have been against me of
course, but while others have suffered badly I
have always drawn audiences.   Here, for example,
they give me a fee for a reading on Tuesday
evening next—it amounts to between £70 and £80
(English).   If I could read five times a week at
this rate (which is my customary rate), here is £350
a week, which is not bad pay for an hour and
three-quarters reading each night.   But I cannot
read five times a week without knocking myself
up, and this I won't do.   And then I have been
mismanaged and cheated by my agents—have had

to change them and start afresh with a new man. The result has been loss of time and loss of money. But I am *investing* in spite of it, and (barring accidents) I am in a fair way to make far more than I have made yet before the last fortnight in March, when I propose to sail for home. I am going ' Out West ' from this, and I *may* get as far as the Mormons. My new agent, a first-rate man, is ahead making engagements, and I am here (thanks to the kindness of Sebastian Schlesinger) with my godson Frank as secretary and companion. I find him a perfect treasure; I don't know what I should do without him. As for the said S. S., he is the brightest, nicest, kindest, little fellow I have met with for many a long day. He wouldn't hear of my dining at the hotel while I was in Boston this last time. Whenever I had no engagement (and I kept out of engagements, having work to do) I dined at his house, and dined superbly. It is not one of the least of S.'s virtues that he speaks with the greatest affection of *you*. He also makes the best cocktail in America. Vive Sebastian !

" The nigger waiters (I like them better than the American waiters) are ringing the dinner bell. I must go and feed off a variety of badly cooked meats and vegetables ranged round me in (say) forty soap dishes. Otherwise I am comfortable here; I have got the Russian Grand Duke's bed-room, and a parlour in which I can shake hands with my visitors, and a box at the theatre, and the freedom of the club.

"Write soon, my dear boy, and tell me about yourself and the Padrona, to whom I send my best love and sincerest good wishes. She is happily settled I hope in the new house. I want to hear all about the new house and about the boys. God forgive me! I am writing of Rudy as if he was a boy. Don't tell him! The fact is I am getting to be an old man. I shall be fifty if I live till the eighth of this month, and I shall celebrate my birthday by giving a reading at Cleveland. I wish I could transport myself to London.

"Yours, my dear Fred, always affectionately,

"WILKIE COLLINS.

"Providence (the city, not the Deity) paid me 400 dollars in spite of the panic."

[WILKIE COLLINS *to* MRS. F. LEHMANN.]

"90, GLOUCESTER PLACE, LONDON, W.,
"*December* 28*th*, 1877.

"DEAREST PADRONA,—I guess I shall be just in time to wish you and Fred, and the sons, and the daughter, all possible health and happiness in the year that is to come. If I could have offered you my good wishes at your villa [in Cannes], need I say how much better I should have been pleased? But there are all sorts of impediments—literary and personal—which keep me in England at the most hateful of all English seasons (to me), the season of Cant and Christmas.

" Good-natured friends tell me that I look twenty
years younger after my travels. I am certainly
much stronger than I was, and I hope to fight
through the winter. The fog and rain met me
at Paris, and prepared me for the horrors of
London.

"I am charmed to hear that the Cannes climate
has done you so much good. Thirty years ago, I
remember it as a delightfully snug, small, cheap
place, with two English people only established in
it—Lord Brougham and another Britisher whose
name I forget. It is plain that I should not know
Cannes again if I saw it now. Brougham—beginning
with a B—reminds me of 'Samuel Brohl et Cie.' I
am going to begin the book to-night in bed ; thank
you for remembering to send it. But for Christmas-
time, I should have read it long ago. I have
returned to heaps of unanswered letters, bills, pay-
ments of pensioners, stupid and hideous Christmas
cards, visits to pay, and every other social nuisance
that gets in the way of a rational enjoyment of life.
As to modern French novels in general, I have read
them by dozens on my travels, and my report of
them all is briefly this : Dull and Dirty. 'The
Nabab,' by Daudet (of whom I once hoped better
things), proved to be such realistic rubbish that I
rushed out (it was at Dijon) to get something 'to
take the taste out of my mouth,' as the children
say. Prosper Mérimée's delicious 'Colomba' appeared
providentially in a shop window ; I instantly secured
it, read it for the second time, and recovered my

opinion of French literature. You know the book of course? If not, I must send it to you instantly.

"There is no news; everybody is eating and drinking and exchanging conventional compliments of the season. You are well out of it all. Give my love to Fred, and thank him for his kind letter; and write again and tell me that you are getting immense reserves of health, and announce when *you* too are likely to be recaptured by the great London net.—Good-bye, dear Padrona.—Yours affly.,

"W. C."

"90, GLOUCESTER PLACE,
"PORTMAN SQUARE, LONDON, W.,
"20th Dec., 1878.

"I have but one excuse, dearest Padrona, for not having long since thanked you for your kind letter —the old excuse of hard work and poor health. But I hold up my head still, and lead the life of a hermit, and (may I confess it?) enjoy the life. Your Wilkie is getting old—there is no mistake about that!

"And how do you like Paris? And how does my dear '*blonde* mees' Nina finish her education? She must remain like herself, mind— she must not be made into a French *ingénue*. With this important message, take my love, and give a lot of it to N.

"Do you sometimes lie awake, and want a little something to read you to sleep again? I send you by book-post two little stories which they have bribed me to write in America, and which have been, of course, republished here. Don't trouble to send them back. Tear them up when you have done with them.

"Later I shall have more proofs (of the long story which is coming out in *The World*) to send you—perhaps to bring, if I can make a holiday six weeks or so hence.

"We have had lights *all day long* in London, and the fog has got into my head, and I must go and walk it out again, and get an appetite for the glorious *pâté* which the good Fred has sent to me.

"Will you write again, I *wonder*, to your affectionate

"W. C. ?"

"90, GLOUCESTER PLACE, PORTMAN SQUARE, W.,
"*Saturday*, 28*th Feb.*, 1880.

"DEAREST PADRONA,—Need I say that I engage myself with the greatest pleasure?—but also with a certain feeling of awe. You know in your boudoir in Berkeley Square what I say and do *here*. Yesterday morning you heard me use "ungentlemanlike language," and saw me throw into the fire an unoffending morsel of muffin polluted by ——'s cart-grease. I declare it is true. Your delicious butter came on the very day when I was thinking of keeping a private cow in the back-yard, and presiding myself over the pastoral churn. Judge of my gratitude, if you can—words fail to express my feelings.

"Ever yours,

"W. C.

"Oh! I was foolish enough to eat slices of plain joints two days following. The bilious miseries that followed proved obstinate until I most fortunately ate some *pâté de foie gras.* The cure was instantaneous—and lasting."

"90, GLOUCESTER PLACE,

"25*th Feb.*, 1883.

"DEAREST PADRONA,—The sight of your handwriting was delightful, and the sight of you will be better still. Anybody who says there is no such thing as luck, lies. Last year I was too ill to get to you at all. This year I am only not well enough to get out to dinner at night, but I might come to lunch—when you have no company—if you will choose your own day and hour, and make several allowances for Wilkie's infirmities. For six months, while I was writing furiously—without exception, one part sane and three parts mad—I had no gout. I finished my story, discovered one day that I was half dead with fatigue, and the next day that the gout was in my right eye.

"No more of that! I am nearly well, and I pull off my black patch indoors. But I am forbidden night air, and I am so weak that I slip down in my chair towards night, like old Rogers. But *he* was only eighty—I am a hundred.

"With love to you particularly, and everybody else generally, yours always affly.,

"W. C.

"*N.B.*—Weak brandy-and-water, and no wholesome joints."

"*Thursday, October* 25 [1883 ?].

"My Dearest Padrona,—Whatever you ask me to do is done as a matter of course. I will lunch with you all to-morrow at 1.30 with the greatest pleasure. N.B.—Please order up a handy stick out of the hall for your own use at lunch—(in this way)—namely, to rap me over the knuckles if you find me raising to my guilty and gouty lips any other liquor than weak brandy and water.

"Always yours affectionately,

"W. C."

[Wilkie Collins *to* F. Lehmann.]

"90, Gloucester Place, Portman Square, W.,
"*December* 14, 1886.

"My dear Fred,—Thank you for your letter. Saturday next at 1.30—with the greatest pleasure.

"When my Fred mentions oysters, he never was more happily inspired in his life. And when I add that I am allowed to drink two glasses of dry champagne—'now and then'—I offer a statement which does equal honour to my doctor and myself.

"Ever yours,

"W. C."

[WILKIE COLLINS *to* MRS. F. LEHMANN.]

"90, GLOUCESTER PLACE,
"*February* 2, 1887.

" Oh ! what a wretch I am, dearest Padrona, to be only thanking you now for your delightful letter, and for that adorable photograph of the boy. I may tell you what I told his father when I had the pleasure of meeting him at Berkeley Square, that I must be introduced to your grandson at the earliest possible moment after his arrival in England. I brought away with me after our luncheon such an agreeable impression of Sir Guy Campbell that I must repeat my congratulations to Nina on her marriage. There was but one drawback to my enjoyment when I found myself in those familiar rooms again—the dreadful word ' Dead ' when I asked after dear little ' Buffles.'*

"If you were only at the North of Scotland—say Thurso—I would rush to you by steamer and become young again in the fine cold air. But when I think of that fearful French railway journey, and of the southern climate of Cannes, I see madness on my way to the Mediterranean and death in lingering torments on the shores of that celebrated sea. We have had here—after a brief paradise of frost — the British sirocco. Figets, aching legs, gloom, vile tempers, neuralgic troubles in the chest—such are the conditions under which I am living, and such the obstacles

* A favourite Skye terrier.

which have prevented my writing to you long since. 'The Guilty River' (I am so glad you like it) has, I am afraid, had something to do with the sort of constitutional collapse which I have endeavoured to describe. You know well what a fool I am—or shall I put it mildly, and say how 'indiscreet'? For the last week, while I was finishing the story, I worked for twelve hours a day, and galloped along without feeling it, like the old post-horses, while I was hot. Do you remember how the forelegs of those post-horses quivered, and how their heads drooped when they came to the journey's end? That's me, my dear, that's me.

"Good God! is 'me' grammar? Ought it to be 'I'? My poor father paid £90 a year for my education, and I give you my sacred word of honour, I am not sure whether it is 'me' or 'I.'

"After this the commonest sense of propriety warns me to remove myself from your observation. I have just assurance enough left to send my love to you, and Nina and her boy, and to remind you that I am always affectionately yours,

"WILKIE COLLINS."

[WILKIE COLLINS *to* F. LEHMANN.]

"82, WIMPOLE STREET, W.,
"*September* 3, 1889.

"MY DEAR FRED,—A word to report myself to you with my own hand. I am unable to receive

Martin to-day, for the reason that I have fallen asleep and the doctor forbids the waking of me. Sleep is my cure, he says, and he is really hopeful of me. Don't notice the blots, my dressing-gown sleeve is too large, but my hand is still steady. Good-bye for the present, dear old friend; we may really hope for healthier days.

"My grateful love to the best and dearest of Padronas. Yours ever affectionately,

"WILKIE COLLINS."

On the 23rd of September Wilkie Collins died.

CHAPTER VI.

CHARLES DICKENS.

Long Walks—A Dinner *Chez Voisin* in 1862—W. H. Wills at
Compiègne—Dickens as Editor—A Reading in Edinburgh,
1861—A Bet about *Masaniello*.

It was, as I have said, through the introduction
of our uncle, Mr. W. H. Wills, that my parents
became acquainted with Charles Dickens. They
were then living near Sheffield, and the great
novelist was on a visit to the town with his
dramatic company. I have no record of this first
meeting; but a family legend has it that Charles
Dickens and I became very intimate friends—I was
then about two years old—and that he adopted me
as his nephew. Indeed, he so refers to me in the
following letter to my mother:

> "Gad's Hill Place,
> "Higham, by Rochester, Kent,
> "*Thursday, Twenty-first June*, 1860.

"My dear Mrs. Lehmann,—As to Tuesday
evening, the 26th, your slave is a mere helpless
Beast. I shall have Mr. —— here, and shall
abstain from Wellington Street in consequence,
and shall (I fear) indubitably "put on a bored
aspect" long before then, and keep it on for a

week.   I should have been delighted to come to you otherwise, but Destiny is too heavy for me. I beg to send my regards to Lehmann, and my love to my Nephew, and the most inflammable article to yourself that it is lawful to transmit by post.—Ever faithfully yours,

"CHARLES DICKENS."

Between my father and Dickens there was a special bond of intimacy : they were both great walkers. During the first half of the year 1862, as I find from my father's notes, while Dickens was living in Hyde Park Gate South, he and my father used regularly to take long Sunday walks together. On April 2 of that year a dinner was given at the "Star and Garter," Richmond, to celebrate John Forster's birthday, and when it was over my father and Dickens walked back to town together. For two pedestrians so determined and so well trained this was, of course, a mere trifle. In November of the same year Dickens was in Paris with his sister-in-law, Miss Hogarth, and his elder daughter, and my father and mother ran over and joined them there for a short time. My father notes that he and Dickens did a course of restaurants together. Of this course I possess one very pleasant memento. It is a *carte* of the Café Voisin, not a mere *menu* of the day, but a substantial catalogue, extending to many pages, of all the dishes and wines provided by that establishment, printed in French and English, with all the prices added. On the title-page are written in pencil these words : " 19th Nov. 1862. —In grateful memory of a wonderful dinner at the Café Voisin, from [here follow the signatures] Nina Lehmann, Charles Dickens, Georgina Hogarth, Frederick Lehmann, W. H. Wills, Mamie Dickens, to Mrs. Wills." The whole, encased in one of the red leather covers of the restaurant, was sent as a peace-offering to Mrs. Wills, who had remained in London while Mr. Wills was away. As a matter of fact, he had gone over to arrange the Christmas Number of *All the Year Round* with Dickens, and had taken with him a gift of a boxful of flowers from Miss Burdett Coutts to the Empress Eugénie. This is his account, written to Mrs. Wills, of how he executed his mission :

" 27, RUE DU FAUBOURG ST. HONORÉ, PARIS,
" *Sunday, 16th November*, 1862.

" I had a queer passage across. A rough sea, though there was no wind; but arrived comfortably at Creil at six o'clock in the morning. Of course I was anxious about the contents of the big box, and set to work unscrewing it with my pocket-knife. It got an awful *clite* at Dover. It being low tide, it was shot down into the vessel as if it had been a pig of lead, and turned quite over. Well, in the gray, mysterious dawn of morning, half-asleep, I could not help feeling, as I undid the screws, as if I were exhuming a dead body out of a coffin. However, though there had been a little crushing and one or two heads had tumbled out, the corpses were in very good preservation. By this time the buffet-women and porters crowded round me, and, as I watched them looking inside the box—some admiring, some pitying the accident, others awed by the fact that the bouquets were so gigantic and for so great a person as the Empress— I felt more like a body-snatcher than ever. They screwed down the half-alive flowers, however, and I went off at eight to Compiègne. At this station I found that the entire hireable locomotive power of the town was one omnibus, and that continually plying between the inn and the station. However, I hired that on the spot, went off to titivate, dressed in a delightful little bedroom out of a courtyard gallery prettily trellised and covered with creepers, and finally departed triumphantly in the omnibus for the Palace. The driver, before I started, asked me with a kind of humour whether I wished to be driven into the *cour d'honneur*. I answered with dignity, 'Decidedly.' I can't say that my reception was encouraging at the *conciergerie*. However, a frown and some bad French sent off a valet with my letter and card to the Duke of Atholl, and I was shown into the apartments he occupied. They are gorgeous, but self-contained, exactly as in an hotel or *étage* in a private house. His Grace was not up. Would I wait? And I was shown into a bright, comfortably furnished room where tea and coffee were set for two. By-and-by out came his Grace, attired in a dressing-gown. Would I have

tea or coffee ?   He poured me out a cup of tea,
took a little for form's sake himself, and talked
away about whatever he could muster as a topic.
Then he sent for his servant, who sent for the box,
which was brought into his private passage.   The
bouquets were exhumed, and pronounced to be
in wonderful preservation considering.   He would
undertake everything : deliver Miss Coutts's letter
to the Duchesse de Bassano, get the Imperial
gardener to touch up the bouquets, and save me
all bother.   Then the Duchess was sent for to
see the flowers.   She came in simply but most
elegantly dressed, in a dove-coloured silk.   A
handsome woman whose gestures, if she were
sweeping the stairs or opening oysters, you would
call lady-like, about Miss Coutts's height, and a
good deal of her sweetness of address.   A little
chat about the flowers, and I took a graceful leave
of both.   At my hotel (de la Cloche) I found a
capital fillet-steak and fried potatoes, and was off
again for Paris at one, having written meanwhile
to Miss Coutts describing my mission as having
been a perfect success ; which I think it was.

" The omnibus brought me to the room Dickens
had ordered for me ; a capital one with a good fire,
and I went over the way.   I found Mary and
Georgina, Dick being out (it was half-past four).
Very glad to see me ; inquired after you very
cordially ; didn't know that Nina and Fred were on
their way.   Dick, when he came in, very cheery
We had a capital dinner at 6 P.M., from the house

at the corner of the Place Madeleine, where you remember we dined twice; they have all their dinners from there.

"Didn't I sleep last night! and here I am in the middle of the Xmas Number, writing this between whiles as Dick goes over his proofs."

One memory of Dickens is indelibly impressed on my mind. I can recall the whole scene as if it had happened yesterday. I cannot have been more than six or seven years old when my father and mother took me to one of his readings at, I think, St. James's Hall. First he read the death of Paul Dombey, which left me in floods of tears, and next came the trial-scene from " Pickwick." I shall never forget my amazement when he assumed the character of Mr. Justice Stareleigh. The face and figure that I knew, that I had seen on the stage a moment before, seemed to vanish as if by magic, and there appeared instead a fat, pompous, pursy little man, with a plump imbecile face, from which every vestige of good temper and cheerfulness—everything, in fact, except an expression of self-sufficient stupidity—had been removed. The upper lip had become long, the corners of the mouth drooped, the nose was short and podgy, all the angles of the chin had gone, the chin itself had receded into the throat, and the eyes, lately so humorous and human, had become as malicious and obstinate as those of a pig. It was a marvellous effort in transformation. When the reading was over my father and mother took me round with them to the room behind. As soon as Dickens caught sight of me he seized me up in his arms and gave me a sounding kiss.   And so it comes that,

> While Memory watches o'er the sad review
> Of joys that faded like the morning dew,

this particular recollection comes up bright and delightful and unfading out of the chambers of my mind. "*Principibus placuisse viris non ultima laus est*," even for a little fellow of six or seven.

I must now hark back a little in order to give a selection from Dickens's correspondence with his assistant-editor, my uncle, W. H. Wills.   The first two letters are concerned with *Household Words*. They show not only how carefully and sympathetically Dickens discharged the task of reading manuscripts submitted to him, but how fertile he was in suggestions even when he was busy with his work of novel-writing :

" FOLKESTONE,
" *Sunday, Twenty-second July*, 1855.

"DEAR WILLS,—I have been so very much affected by the long story without a title—which I have read this morning—that I am scarcely fit for a business letter.   It is more painfully pathetic than anything I have read for I know not how long.   I am not at all of your opinion about the details.   It seems to me to be so thoroughly considered that they are all essential and in perfect keeping.   I could not in my conscience recommend the writer to cut the story down in any material degree. I think it would be decidedly wrong to do so; and I see next to nothing in the MS. which is otherwise than an essential part of the sad picture.

"Two difficulties there remain, which I fear are insurmountable as to *Household Words*. The first is, the length of the story. The next is, the nature of the idea on which it turns. So many unhappy people are, by no fault of their own, linked to a similar terrible possibility—or even probability— that I am afraid it might cause prodigious unhappiness if we should address it to our large audience. I shrink from the responsibility of awakening so much slumbering fear and despair. Most unwillingly, therefore, I come to the apprehension that there is no course but to return it to the authoress. I wish, however, that you would in the strongest language convey to her my opinion of its great merits, while you explain the difficulties I now set forth. I honestly think it a work of extraordinary power, and will gladly address a letter to her, if she should desire it, describing the impression it has made upon me. I might, perhaps, help to soften a publisher.

"Miss L——'s story shows to considerable disadvantage after such writing. But it is what she represented it in her draft, and it is very clever. Now, as it presents (to cursory readers) almost the reverse of the medal whereof Miss J—— presents the other side, I think it will be best *to pay for it at once*, and, for the present (say even for a few months) to hold it back ; not telling her the exact reason, but merely saying that we are pledged first to the insertion of other stories in four parts, already accepted. Miss J——'s is more wholesome and more powerful, because it hits the target (which Miss L—— goes a little about) with a rifle-shot in the centre of the bull's-eye, and knocks it clean over. Therefore it should have precedence—both on its own account and ours.

" But observe—I do not conceive it possible that Miss J—— can alter her story within the time you mention. What I want done to it is much too delicate for such swift jobbing-work. I question, on the other hand, whether it may not be politic just now, to have *one monthly part without a long story*—merely for the sake of variety.

" My thoughts have been upon my books since I came down, and I do not know that I can hit upon a subject for the opening of the new volume. I will let you know, however, by to-morrow night's post.

" I have written to Mr. B——, whose paper *will do*. I expect my brother down to-day, and, if he comes, will send it and the pathetic story up to you by him.

" Miss L——'s notions of a criminal trial are of the nightmarest description. The prisoner makes statements on oath, and is examined besides !

" Ever faithfully,

" C. D."

"49, CHAMPS ELYSÉES,
"*Thursday, January tenth*, 1856.

"MY DEAR WILLS,—

"*H*[*ousehold*] *W*[*ords.*]

Forster does not think those two little poems
are otherwise than original. That is to say, he
cannot find them anywhere, though he has my
general impression about them. Therefore, get
them back from him, and insert them.

"My head is necessarily so full of my own subjects that I have not thought of that point to any
advantage, though I have thought of it at various
times. The police inquiry was never done, though
I spoke to you about it when you were here.
Accounts of the constitution of foreign armies,
especially as to their officering, and as to the
officer's professional business being his professional
pride and study, and not a bore, are highly desirable. An article on the prices of fares on foreign
railways, on the cost of making them, on the
public accommodation, and the nature of the
carriages, &c., contrasting their law with our law,
and their management with our management, would
be highly desirable. I suppose D—— could do it
directly. Would it be possible to strike out a
new man to write popularly about the monstrous
absurdity of our laws, and to compare them with
the Code Napoléon? Or has Morley knowledge
enough in that direction, or could he get it? It is
curious to observe here that Lord Campbell's Acts

for making compensation to bodily-injured people are mere shreds of the Code Napoléon. That business of the Duke of Northumberland and his tenantry : couldn't Sydney do something about it ? It would be worth sending anybody to that recusant farmer who leads the opposition. Similarly, the Duke of Argyle, whom the papers drove out of his mind by agreeing to consider him a phenomenon, simply because he wasn't a born ass. Is there no Scotch source from whence we can get some information about that island where he had the notice stuck upon the church door that ' no tenant under £30 a year was to be allowed to use spirits at any marriage, christening, funeral, or other gathering ' ? It would be a capital illustration of the monstrous nonsense of a Maine Law. Life assurance : are proposals ever refused ? if so, often because of their suspicious character as engendering notions that the assured life may possibly be taken ? I know of policies being refused to be paid on the ground that the person was murdered—and could insert an anecdote or so. Poisoning : can't Morley do something about the sale of poisons ? I suppose Miss Martineau's doctrine of never, never, never interfering with Trade, is not a Gospel from Heaven in this case.

" For a light article, suppose Thomas went round for a walk to a number of the old coaching-houses and were to tell us what they are about now, and how they look. Those great stables down in Lad Lane whence the horses belonging to the ' Swan with Two Necks' used to come up an inclined plane—what are they doing? The 'Golden Cross,' the 'Belle Sauvage,' the Houses in Goswell Street, the 'Peacock' at Islington—what are they all about? How do they bear the little rickety omnibuses, and so forth? What on earth were the coaches made into? What comes into the yard of the General Post Office now at five o'clock in the morning? What's up the yard of the 'Angel,' St. Clement's? *I* don't know. What's in the two 'Saracens' Heads'? Any of the old brains at all?

"Mr. Payn might do this, if Thomas couldn't.— Ever faithfully,   C. D."

The next letter gives an inimitably graphic description of a scene that took place at one of Dickens's readings in Edinburgh:

"CARRICK'S ROYAL HOTEL, GLASGOW,
"*Tuesday, Third December*, 1861.

"MY DEAR WILLS,—From a paragraph, a letter, and an advertisement in a *Scotsman* I send you with this, you may form some dim guess at the scene we had in Edinburgh last night. I think I may say that I never saw a crowd before.

"As I was quietly dressing, I heard the people (when the doors were opened) come in with a most unusual crash, and I was very much struck by the place's obvious filling to the throat within five minutes. But I thought no more of it, dressed placidly, and went in at the usual time. I then found that there was a tearing mad crowd in all the passages and in the street, and that they were pressing a great turbid stream of people into the already crammed hall. The moment I appeared fifty frantic men addressed me at once, and fifty other frantic men got upon ledges and cornices, and tried to find private audiences of their own. Meanwhile the crowd outside still forced the turbid stream in, and I began to have some general idea that the platform would be driven through the wall behind it, and the wall into the street. You know that your respected chief has a spice of cool-ness in him, and is not altogether unaccustomed to public speaking. Without the exercise of the two qualities, I think we should all have been there now. But when the uproarious spirits (who, as we strongly suspect, didn't pay at all) saw that it was quite impossible to disturb me, they gave in, and there was a dead silence. Then I told them, of course in the best way I could think of, that I was heartily sorry, but this was the fault of their own townsman (it was decidedly the fault of Wood's people, with maybe a trifle of preliminary assist-ance from Headland); that I would do anything to set it right; that I would at once adjourn to the Music Hall, if they thought it best; or that I would alter my arrangements, and come back, and read to all Edinburgh if they wished (meantime Gordon, if you please, is softening the crowd out-side, and dim reverberations of his stentorian roars are audible). At this there is great cheering, and they cry, 'Go on, Mr. Dickens; everybody will be quiet now.' Uproarious spirit exclaims, ' We *won't* be quiet. We won't let the reading be heard. We're illtreated.' Respected chief says, ' There's plenty of time, and you may rely upon it that the reading is in no danger of being heard until we are agreed.' Therefore good-humouredly shuts up book. Laugh turned against uproarious spirit, and uproarious spirit shouldered out. Respected chief prepares, amidst calm, to begin, when gentleman (with full-dressed lady, torn to ribbons, on his arm) cries out, ' Mr. Dickens!' ' Sir.' ' Couldn't some people, at all events ladies, be accommodated on your platform?' 'Most certainly.' Loud cheering. ' Which way can they come to the platform, Mr. Dickens?' 'Round here to my left.' In a minute the platform was crowded. Everybody who came up laughed and said it was nothing when I told them in a low voice how sorry I was; but the moment they were there the sides began to roar because they couldn't see! At least half of the people were ladies, and I then proposed to them to sit down or lie down. Instantly they all dropped into recumbent groups, with the respected chief standing up in the centre. I don't know what it looked like most---a battlefield---an impossible tableau---a gigantic picnic. There was a very pretty girl in full dress lying down on her side all night, and holding on to one leg of my table. So I read 'Nickleby' and the Trial. From the beginning to the end they didn't lose one point, and they ended with a great burst of cheering.

"Very glad to hear that Morley's American article is done. Rather fagged to-day, but not very. So no more at present.—Ever faithfully,

"C. D.

"Will you reply to enclosed letter? 200 stalls let here for to-night!"

Finally, here is the record of a hospitable bet:

"Office of *All the Year Round*,
"No. 11, Wellington Street North, Strand,
"London, W.C.,
"*Wednesday, Twenty-second January*, 1862.

"Dick bets Stanny* that 'Masaniello' was produced, *as an opera*, at Drury Lane Theatre thirty years ago; reference is supposed to be had to the date of the year, without reference to months. The bet is, a Dinner for four at Greenwich, Richmond, or elsewhere, for the party present—that is to say, Stanfield, Dickens, Wilkie Collins, Wills."

Here follow the signatures. On the document somebody (I think Mr. Wills) has added in pencil:

"I think C. D. lost, for 'Masaniello' was produced as a *ballet*."

* Clarkson Stanfield, the artist.

CHAPTER VII.

CHARLES DICKENS.

A Wedding at Gad's Hill, 1860—The Far, Far West—A Child Story—A Visit to Gad's Hill—Dickens's Dogs—A Sunday in Edinburgh—H. F. Chorley—The Last Letter—My Father and the Fire-escape.

The Dickens family and ours eventually became great friends. My father and mother were Dickens's guests at Gad's Hill on more than one occasion; my father was present at the marriage of his second daughter to Charles A. Collins (the brother of Wilkie), and both he and my mother were amongst those who had the melancholy privilege of being summoned to Gad's Hill to pay a last tribute of friendship and regard to his lifeless body.

The letters I possess from Dickens to my parents extend from 1860 to April 14th, 1870, the year of his death. Four of these have been already printed in the collection of Dickens's letters published by Miss Dickens and Miss Hogarth. I reprint them here by Miss Hogarth's special permission. Two I have printed in former chapters. I will preface a selection from those that remain by a letter from my father to my mother, who was recruiting her health and that of her small family at Vernon Cottage, Shanklin, during July of 1860. The letter describes the festivities that took place at Gad's Hill on the occasion of the marriage of Dickens's younger daughter, Katie, to Charles Collins. In a letter of May 3rd, 1860, to M. de Cerjat ("Letters," vol. ii., p. 113), Dickens says : "My second daughter is going to be married in the course of the summer to Charles Collins, the brother of Wilkie Collins, the novelist. The father was one of the most famous painters of English green lanes and coast pieces. He was bred an artist, too, and does 'The Eye-Witness' in *All the Year Round*. He is a gentleman, accomplished and amiable."

My father writes from London on July 18th : "On Monday evening I went to the French play after a lonely dinner at the club. The piece, 'Pattes de Mouches,' is excellently played and very French, a mere airy nothing. I enjoyed it as much as one can enjoy anything alone. When I got home the butler was in bed, and there was nobody whom I could order to call me at 7 A.M. I regret to inform you that your great and infallible husband overslept himself, and awoke cheerfully at a quarter to nine. Hurrah! To be at London Bridge at 9.40 was impossible. Still, I rushed into my clothes, into a cup of coffee, and into a hansom, and arrived at the station at 10.15, just in time, not for the special, but for another train about to leave for those parts. When I arrived at Higham Station at 11.45 the stationmaster said the wedding would be nearly over, and I had better go at once to the house. So I did, and was overtaken on the road by the whole party coming in ever so many carriages from church. First Charlie and Katie, and didn't I give them a cheer! Then Wilkie, Holman Hunt, Tuck,* and Miss Crawford, who insisted on picking me up. When the others joined us at the house the astonishment at my presence was general, as I had been given up, but Mamie rushed towards me and greeted me most affectionately—so I had lost the ceremony, but came in for all the essentials. Katie looked sweet in her bridal dress. There was a little exhibition of presents, the description of which I will leave to Tuck; and, in order to despatch the bride and bridegroom from the scene, I will say at once that they just sat down at the breakfast, to reappear again in travelling dress: Katie crying bitterly on her father's breast, Mamie dissolved in tears, Charlie as white as snow. No end of God bless yous; King John Forster adding in his most stentorian voice, 'Take care of her, Charlie. You have got a most precious treasure.' Shaking of hands, a vision of a postillion in red, a shower of old shoes, and exeunt Mr. and Mrs. Charles Collins.

"The party consisted of Mr. and Mrs. Forster, Tuck, Chorley [the musical critic of the *Athenæum*], Miss Crawford, Holman Hunt, Mr. and Mrs. Malleson, and Mr. and Mrs. Hulkes (neighbours), Uncle and Auntie [Mr. and Mrs. W. H. Wills], old Mrs. Collins, and Mr. Townshend. The house is a perfect

* Miss Chambers, my mother's sister, who was one of the bride's-maids. She afterwards married my father's brother, Rudolf Lehmann, the artist.

gem—not a Vernon Cottage for poetry, but a down-right pretty, honest, English country house, red brick, and no end of smooth lawn. No great view, but everything that's pleasant and kind to the eye. The breakfast was a gorgeous affair. Everything on the table in the way of decoration was white, flowers and all. After breakfast (without a single speech, and only one toast) we had games on the lawn, and Aunt Sally was the great attraction. About three o'clock we all drove to Rochester, and had a good time in that delicious old ruin, Rochester Castle. . . . Thence to Chatham, where we listened to a military band performing in a park. The programmes handed round being signed ' W. Collins, Bandmaster,' exposed Wilkie to innumerable bad jokes. About 6.30 we were back at Gad's Hill, had time for a game of croquet, saw the children of the neighbouring people get tea and cake, and went in to dinner at seven. I sat next old Forster, a most unmanageable, wild man, whom, however, I tamed successfully, at least for the evening. Dinner over at nine ; a cigar in the garden ; Tuck sings, to everybody's enthusiastic delight ; a country dance ; and we all fly at eleven to our special waiting our return at Higham."

I now begin the Dickens letters :

"OFFICE OF *All the Year Round,*
"*Tuesday, Sixth November,* 1860.

"MY DEAR MRS. LEHMANN,—I have been in Cornwall and have missed your note. Came back only last night.

"It unfortunately happens that I am engaged to-morrow. Don't give me up because of my misfortunes. Have faith in me. Try me again, and your Petitioner will ever pray!

"I hear rumours that Mary is at the present moment advancing towards the Metropolis on crutches!—Ever faithfully yours,

"CHARLES DICKENS."

Mary Dickens had had a riding accident, which is thus described in a letter from Dickens to Wilkie Collins ("Letters of Charles Dickens," vol. ii. p. 129): "I also found a letter from Georgina describing that Mary's horse went down suddenly on a stone, and how Mary was thrown, and had her riding-habit torn to pieces, and has a deep cut just above the knee—fortunately, not in the knee itself—which is doing exceedingly well, but which will probably incapacitate her from walking for days and days to come."

When my father was proposing to go to America in 1862 on business he had the following letter from Dickens:—

"GAD'S HILL PLACE,
"HIGHAM, BY ROCHESTER, KENT,
"*Tuesday, Twenty Second July*, 1862.

"MY DEAR LEHMANN,—I write in the greatest haste, being pressed by all manner of business and botheration.

"Here is a note to Fields, who is a capital fellow and of strong English sympathy. So many years have passed since I was at Boston, and so many of the people whom I knew there have gone to that Far Far West which is behind the sun and moon, that I cannot hurriedly recall any other likely names.

"Heaven speed you in that distracted land of troublesome vagabonds!—Faithfully always,

"C. D."

There follows a series of letters written in 1863, and relating to a family matter about which Dickens had consulted my father. He writes to him about it from Paris, where he had gone to give readings at the Embassy, and adds (3rd February, 1863) : "If I had carried out my original intention and had Readings of my own in Paris, I don't know where they would have stopped. The Parisian audiences run away with them in a most astonishing and most rapturous manner."

[CHARLES DICKENS *to* MRS. F. LEHMANN.]

"OFFICE OF *All the Year Round*,
"NO. 26, WELLINGTON STREET,
"STRAND, LONDON, W.C.,
"*Tuesday, March* 10*th*, 1863.

"DEAR MRS. LEHMANN,—Two stalls for to-morrow's reading were sent to you by post before I heard from you this morning. Two will always come to you while you remain a Gummidge, and I hope I need not say that if you want more, none could be better bestowed in my sight.

H 2

"Pray tell Lehmann, when you next write to him, that I find I owe him a mint of money for the delightful Swedish sleigh-bells. They are the wonder, awe, and admiration of the whole country side, and I never go out without them.

"Let us make an exchange of child stories. I heard of a little fellow the other day whose mamma had been telling him that a French governess was coming over to him from Paris, and had been expatiating on the blessings and advantages of knowing foreign tongues. After leaning his plump little cheek against the window glass in a dreary little way for some minutes, he looked round and enquired in a general way, and not as if it had any special application, whether she didn't think 'that the Tower of Babel was a great mistake altogether?' —Ever faithfully yours,

"CHARLES DICKENS."

In 1865 my father and mother were to have been Dickens's guests at Gad's Hill. I find the prospect of this visit referred to in the following letters :

"16, SOMERS PLACE,
"*Twenty Seventh April*, 1865.

"MR DEAR LEHMANN,—If I had not settled to go out of town between my two Nos. your kind note would have made sure of me at once. But I had, and settled it these ten days. It is really necessary to the pains I am taking with my book—always was indispensable to my working at my best—and has

not become the less so as my botherations have
grown taller. I can throw anything off by going
off myself. Not otherwise.

"To-day I am going out to dinner for the first
time. But whether I can keep a boot on, and get
it on again for the Academy Dinner on Saturday,
remains to be seen. If I can't, I shall go off on
Saturday for a week. If I can, I shall go off on
Sunday.

"Mary is going to propound to Mrs. Lehmann a
certain distinct time early in June for a visit to
Gad's Hill, where I shall be heartily glad to see you
and walk with you.—Faithfully yours always,

"C. D."

"Gad's Hill Place,
"Higham, by Rochester, Kent,
"Tuesday, June 29th, 1865.

"Dear Mrs. Lehmann,—Come (with self and
partner) on either of the days you name, and you
will be heartily welcomed by the humble youth
who now addresses you, and will then cast himself
at your feet.

"I am quite right again, I thank God, and have
even got my voice back; I most unaccountably
brought somebody else's out of that terrible scene.*
The directors have sent me a resolution of thanks
for assistance to the unhappy passengers.

"With kind regards to Lehmann, ever yours,

"Charles Dickens."

* The railway accident at Staplehurst.

It seems, however, that this visit did not take place, for on the 13th July of the same year Dickens writes to my father:

"MY DEAR LEHMANN,—I was vexed that you were put off from coming here by the inscrutability of Mary's arrangements. But we will try the Fates again when you come back from Heligoland, and I hope they may be propitious. I have no present idea of being away from here for longer than a day or two together, until the autumn is out.

"So I still hope to see you, and you must undertake to report your return. Meantime all good go with [you] and return likewise.—Faithfully yours always,

"C. D."

Dickens's fondness for dogs is well known. Forster ("Life," vol. iii. pp. 191—193) gives an account of his favourites, Turk, a mastiff, "a noble animal, full of affection and intelligence, whose death by a railway accident, shortly after the Staplehurst catastrophe, caused him great grief. Turk's sole companion up to that date (1865) was Linda, puppy of a great St. Bernard brought over by Mr. Albert Smith, and grown into a superbly beautiful creature." After Turk came Sultan, whom Forster describes as "an Irish dog, given by Mr. Percy Fitzgerald, a cross between a St. Bernard and a bloodhound." It is not easy to understand how, with such an ancestry, he came to be Irish at all. Dickens, however, according to Forster, "always protested that Sultan was a Fenian, for that no dog, not a secretly sworn member of that body, would ever have made such a point, muzzled as he was, of rushing at and bearing down with fury anything in scarlet with the remotest resemblance to a British uniform." In a letter to Mr. Fitzgerald ("Letters," vol. ii. p. 264) Dickens thus refers to him : " Your mention of the late Sultan touches me nearly. He was the finest dog I ever saw, and between him and me there was a perfect understanding. But, to adopt the popular phrase, it was so very confidential that ' it went no further.' He would fly at anybody else with the greatest enthusiasm for destruction. I saw him, muzzled, pound into the heart of a regiment of the line, and I have frequently seen him, muzzled, hold a great dog down with his chest and feet. He has broken loose (muzzled) and come home covered with blood, again and again. And yet he never disobeyed me, unless he had first laid hold of a dog." Sultan's untamable ferocity brought him to a tragic end. Having seized a little girl, sister to one of the servants, he was sentenced by Dickens to be shot on the following morning at seven o'clock. "He went out very cheerfully," says Dickens in a letter to M. de Cerjat, "with the half-dozen men told off for the purpose, evidently thinking that they were going to the death of some-body unknown. But observing in the procession an empty wheelbarrow and a double-barrelled gun, he became meditative, and fixed the bearer of the gun with his eyes. A stone deftly thrown across him by the village blackguard (chief mourner) caused him to look round for an instant, and he then fell dead, shot through the heart."

The unfortunate Sultan was succeeded by Don, a Newfoundland, brought over to this country in early doghood by my father, and by him presented to Dickens. He and the St. Bernard, Linda, another great favourite, became the parents of Bumble and another who survived their master. Here, in a letter to my father, is Dickens's recipe for a big dog's dinner:

"OFFICE OF *All the Year Round*,
"*Tuesday, Seventh November*, 1865.

" MY DEAR LEHMANN,—The recipe for one dog's allowance is this : 2 pints oatmeal, 1 pint barley meal, 1 pound mangel wurzel, boiled together, and then mixed with pot-liquor, which is poured over it. If there be no pot-liquor in the house, a sheep's head will make it very well. Any bones that happen to be about may be put into the mixture for the exercise of the dog's teeth. Its effect upon the body and spirits of the creature is quite surprising. I have my dogs fed once a day, always at the same hour.

" I am very sorry to say I cannot take my pleasure to-morrow, having to 'make-up' the Xmas No. with the printer. Always a tough job.—Ever yours,

"CHARLES DICKENS."

[CHARLES DICKENS *to* MRS. F.LEHMA N N.]

"KENNEDY'S HOTEL, EDINBURGH,
"*Sunday, Dec. 6th*, 1868.

"MY DEAR MRS. LEHMANN,—I hope you will see Nancy with the light of a great audience upon her some time between this and May; always supposing that she should not prove too weird and woeful for the general public.

"You know the aspect of this city on a Sunday, and how gay and bright it is. The merry music of the blithe bells, the waving flags, the prettily-decorated houses with their draperies of various colours, and the radiant countenances at the windows and in the streets; how charming they are! The usual preparations are making for the band in the open air in the afternoon; and the usual pretty children (selected for that purpose) are at this moment hanging garlands round the Scott monument preparatory to the innocent Sunday dance round that edifice with which the diversions invariably close. It is pleasant to think that these customs were the customs of the early Christians, those early birds who didn't catch the worm—and nothing else—and choke their young with it.

"Faithfully yours always,

"CHARLES DICKENS."

"OFFICE,
"*Wednesday, Feb. 3rd*, 1869.

"DEAR MRS. LEHMANN,—Before getting your kind note, I had written to Lehmann, explaining why I cannot allow myself any social pleasure while my farewell task is yet unfinished. The work is so very hard that every little scrap of rest and silence I can pick up is precious. And even those morsels are so flavoured with *All the Year Round* that they are not quite the genuine article.

"Joachim* came round to see me at the hall last night, and I told him how sorry I was to forego the pleasure of meeting him (he is a noble fellow!) at your pleasant table.

"I am glad you are coming to the 'Murder' on the 2nd of March. (The house will be prodigious.) Such little changes as I have made shall be carefully presented to your critical notice, and I hope will be crowned with your approval. But you are always such a fine audience that I have no fear on that head. I saw Chorley yesterday in his own room. A sad and solitary sight. The widowed Drake, with a certain gincoherence of manner, presented a blooming countenance and buxom form in the passage; so buxom indeed that she was obliged to retire before me like a modest stopper before I could get into the dining decanter where poor Chorley reposed, like the dregs of last season's last wine.   "Faithfully yours always,

"CHARLES DICKENS.

"P.S.—My love to Rudie."

The last letter I possess is written to my mother, and relates to a German translation of "Edwin

* Dr. Joseph Joachim, the renowned violinist.

Drood," which was being written by an uncle of mine :

"OFFICE OF *All the Year Round,*
" *Thursday, Fourteenth April,* 1870.

" MY DEAR MRS. LEHMANN,—I think the enclosed must have crossed a letter to Dr. Lehmann from my publishers, whom I instructed to send—and who, I know, sent—the 1st No. to Hamburg for translation. All other Nos. will duly follow, and there will be twelve in all.

" If you pay to my account at Coutts's, at any time, £50, you will have done your duty in that station of life in which, &c. (see 'Church Catechism').

" Faithfully yours always,

" CHARLES DICKENS."

In Mr. C. L. Graves's "Life of Sir George Grove " there is a letter from Grove (p. 97) referring to a dinner at our house in Westbourne Terrace some time in June, 1865. " On Thursday," he says, " we went to a great dinner-party there, followed by a musical ' at home.' At dinner were Dickens and his sister-in-law, R. Browning, R. Chambers, Miss Gabriel, and ourselves. It was very pleasant. Dickens was very amusing, but not the least forced, and Browning was also interesting. Dickens was full of a ship of Mormon emigrants which he had been seeing : 1,200 of the cleanest, best conducted, most excellent people he ever saw." I wish I myself could recall Dickens at dinner under the

influence of cheerful company and pleasant enter-
tainment. All I can remember, however, is our
family tradition which has handed him down as
the prince of companions, always brilliant, humorous, and delightful. I like to remember that my
own father in such feasts of a later date as I can
call to mind was *haud impar congressus Achilli*, even
when Achilles was for the moment represented by
Robert Browning or James Payn or J. E. Millais
or Arthur Sullivan; for he was a man of commanding
mind, well read, a fine musician, and of keen artis-
tic sympathy. Above all he had, before illness
came upon him and depressed his later years, a
special gift of humour which rendered his society
attractive to his friends. I may perhaps be pardoned
on the score of filial piety if I give one example of
that quality which was supplied to me, while the
earlier chapters of these "Memories" were appearing
in serial form, by Mr. Thomas Widdows, of West-
combe Park, S.E. Mr. Widdows (whose permission
I have to make use of his letter) wrote to me as
follows :

"I have wondered what relation you were to a
Mr. Lehmann whom I met a great many years
ago, when an incident occurred which amused me
extremely at the time, and which I have never
forgotten.

"It must be thirty years ago or more [as a
matter of fact it must have been in 1868 or 1869]
when I was staying at Enfield from Saturday to

Monday with an uncle of mine, an architect, Mr. F. G. Widdows. He proposed on the Sunday morning that we should drive over and look at a house where he was carrying out extensive alterations for a Mr. Lehmann, and we accordingly did so. The house was between Highgate and Hampstead [strictly speaking, it was a mile or so beyond Highgate, on the way to Muswell Hill]. I do not know whether my uncle wished to see Mr. Lehmann on business, or whether, as he always took a great pride and interest in his work, he only wished to have the pleasure of looking at it, as the peasants in, I think, one of George Eliot's novels used on Sunday mornings to go and look admiringly at the ricks which they had thatched during the week.

"Mr. Lehmann, however, very kindly showed me the house, and regretted that he could not take me into one particular room, as Wilkie Collins was at work there. We eventually got to the top floor, where we were joined by the builder, a Mr. Colls. I suppose the staircases up to the last flight but one were of stone, but from the top of this last flight there was an arrangement for dropping a folded iron ladder which, opening by its own weight, would in case of fire give access to the floor below. Mr. Colls, in a quiet, mechanical way, just to show the perfection and simplicity of the arrangement, opened the trap-door, and had taken hold of the ladder, when Mr. Lehmann from a little distance off said in a commanding and serious tone, 'Stop!

It is above all things necessary that I should understand the working of the arrangement.' He then placed himself carefully where he could have a perfeet view of the procedure, and, Mr. Colls having the ladder ready in his hand, Mr. Lehmann gave the word 'Now!' Mr. Colls thereupon let go, but the machinery did not work. The ladder was to fall easily when he let go, but it did not move; nor did a slight shake or two even effect the desired result. Mr. Lehmann looked on solemn and expectant, and after a little time said, 'Remember, the flames are roaring and raging around us.' Thus urged, Mr. Colls shook and shook again, all without result, till at last, when it was evident that it would not work at all, Mr. Lehmann cried out, still looking on, 'Great Heaven, this is death!' Mr. Colls remained perfectly serious, and the whole incident, though I have imperfectly described it, was irresistibly funny."

Many such scenes I feel that I myself ought to be able to remember. Gleams of them come to my memory, but when I try to grasp them they are gone. It gives me all the greater pleasure, therefore, to be able to set down Mr. Widdows's story, which I recognise as highly characteristic of the man to whom it relates.

CHAPTER VIII.

ROBERT BROWNING.

"Waring"—A scene with John Forster—Browning's eyesight—His Greek—Gift of a pony—Light correspondence—Friendly hyperbole—An anecdote from Wanley, 1677—A picture by "Pen"—An impromptu translation.

My parents became acquainted with Robert Browning soon after Mrs. Browning's death, when the poet settled in London at 19, Warwick Crescent, and from that time forward until his death his friendship with us never varied. My own memory of him, even in the early days, is very vivid. I can remember something of the awe with which at first I looked upon the man of whom I had been told that he was a great poet, but his extraordinary cordiality soon banished that feeling. He had the happy knack of making even a small boy feel that it gave him real pleasure to shake that small boy by the hand or to pat him on the back and talk to him about the little interests of his life. No man was ever more free from bardic pose, and, indeed, from affectation of any kind, than Browning. His dress was simple, his manner was genial, and his appearance, though he was by no means a tall man, was in the highest degree manly and impressive. His massive, noble head was splendidly set on a strong neck; his shoulders were solid, and his chest was deep, a fit generator for the resonant voice with which he held you in conversation. A vision of him standing four-square and firmly poised rises before me as I write, and I can still feel the grip of his hand and see the kind light in his eyes as he looked into mine. Then my mind's eye follows him to the dining-room table, where his special decanter of port had been set by his place, and I can hear him, " while the great poet rolled us out his mind," throughout the dinner. Of such dinners I have only one note written by me in a fit of (unfortunately) brief enthusiasm for the task of keeping a diary :

" 17th Nov. 1887.—Dinner at home [15, Berkeley Square] : F. L. [my father], Browning, Pym, Bancroft [Sir Squire], A. Shand, Sir James Hannen [President of the Probate, Divorce and Admiralty Division of the High Court], Comyns Carr, R. C. L. Much good talk, though at first Hannen and Browning seemed at issue over a question as to whether Browning had dined and spoken at the Inner or the Middle Temple on a certain occasion. Browning told us that the Waring of his poem was Alfred Domett, who was afterwards first Prime Minister of New Zealand, ' a man who always impressed me,' said Browning, ' as capable of greater things than he achieved.' Speaking with reference to the present disturbances and the calling out of special constables, Sir James Hannen told me that, at the time of the Hyde Park Riots,

he, as Attorney-General's devil, attended a confer-
ence at the Home Office, at which Spencer Walpole
(Home Secretary), Holt (Attorney-General), Karslake (Solicitor-General), and Disraeli himself were
present, and that it was then and there decided to
close the Park and prevent the meeting. He (Sir
James) ventured to say that it was not by any
means clear that the public had not a right to meet
peaceably in the Park; but his objections were
overruled, Disraeli assenting, and he was unable to
make any impression on Karslake, though he argued
with him up to the very doors of the House of
Commons. The result everybody knows. Comyns
Carr was brilliant as usual. In a reminiscent
humour he afterwards mentioned a certain festive
occasion, years ago, on which, in making a chaffing
speech, he had spoken of M. (who was then present)
as 'a clown without the colour, a pantaloon without
the experience, hovering midway between the
cradle and the grave, not yet having lost the folly
which is associated with the one, and having already
anticipated the dullness which is inseparable from
the other'—a remark to which M. replied in perfect good humour. Speaking of X., Carr said he
had recently met him, and that X., after imbibing
freely, had passed into the didactic stage, 'the
stage in which,' Carr added, 'he first lays down the
law, and then falls upon it.' Altogether a most
cheery gathering."

I can remember how heartily Browning enjoyed

M.   I

these sallies.   It must not be supposed, however, · that Browning was always in a state of
indiscriminating good temper.   I have myself seen
him flash into anger at some incident that displeased
him, and I may add an account of one of his rare
explosions as related in my father's uncompleted
reminiscences, from which I have previously quoted :

"The third and last quarrel " [my father had
already related two others, one between Sir Edwin
Landseer and Sir A. Cockburn, and the other between
Lord Houghton and the fiery Lord Chief Justice*]
" was between Robert Browning, the poet, and John
Forster, the well-known editor of *The Examiner* and
biographer of Dickens.   These two men had lived
for years in the closest intimacy.   Forster's great
literary judgment, his willingness to take trouble,
and his passionate desire to be consulted about all
the ventures of his literary friends made him for
many years a kind of Court of Appeal on all literary
matters.   I believe he had, during many years, prepared all Browning's and Mrs. Browning's works for
the press.   However valuable such aid and interference may have been to Browning while he was
living in Florence, it may have become irksome
when Browning took up his domicile in London.
Forster exercised a kind of patent-right or owner-
ship over Browning.   It was an understood thing
that on Sundays Browning had to dine with Forster,
and that any one wanting Browning to dinner on

* See pp. 199 and 256.

Sundays could only secure him after some diplomatic negotiations, of which one of the fundamental conditions was that Mr. and Mrs. Forster were to be invited together with Browning. Forster was kind but ponderous ; Browning was nervous and sensitive, and had, no doubt, grown restive under this kind of literary bear-leading. There may have been other combustibles, but at any rate a mere nothing brought about a sudden and violent conflagration. At a dinner at 10, Kensington Palace Gardens, the house of my brother-in-law, Mr. Benzon, Browning and Forster began to nag at each other, and so continued for some time, till Browning spoke of the incredible neglect which had lately occurred at Marlborough House, where, when the Princess of Wales had suddenly been taken very ill, no carriage could be got for the purpose of fetching a doctor. Forster at once ridiculed the story as a foolish invention. Browning gave chapter and verse, adding that he had it from Lady ——. Forster retorted that he did not believe it a whit more on account of that authority. Suddenly Browning became very fierce, and said, ' Dare to say one word in disparagement of that lady '— seizing a decanter while he spoke —' and I will pitch this bottle of claret at your head ! ' Forster seemed as much taken aback as the other guests. Our host, who had left the room with Sir Edwin Landseer, on his return at this moment found Browning standing up in great anger, with a decanter in his hand ready for action. He had the greatest difficulty in realising the situation. I soon made him hurry every one from the room, but all attempts to bring about an immediate apology or reconciliation were in vain. A kind of peace was, however, patched up before Forster's death."

One little incident in which Browning took a chief part I particularly remember. It occurred on New Year's Day, 1886, when Browning dined with us at 15, Berkeley Square. After we had joined the ladies the conversation turned upon eyesight, my father, I think, remarking that he found writing more and more difficult every day owing to his failing sight. Browning, however, declared that he himself found no difficulty whatever, his eyesight being as good then as it had ever been. He offered to prove his statement, and called for paper, pen, and ink, which were at once produced. He then wrote, in an extraordinarily minute but perfectly legible hand, the following :—

> Shall we all die ?
> We shall die all :
> Die all shall we,
> Die all we shall.
>
> ROBERT BROWNING, Jan. 1, '86·

> Afflictions sore
> Long time I bore,
> Physicians were in vain :
> Till God did please
> To give me ease,
> Release me from my pain.

Having done this he paused, and then suddenly

said, "I'll give you some Greek too," and, in the same tiny hand, added these three lines, the first three of the Seven Against Thebes—

Καδμου παλαιου χρη λεγειν τα καιρια
οστις φυλασσει πραγος εν πρυμνῃ πολιος
οιακα νωμων βλεφαρα μη κοιμων υπνῳ.

His son, who was standing by, suggested that the lines would be the better for accents and breathings, but Browning refused to add them.   There is, by the way, a misquotation of παλαίου for πολῖται, which makes nonsense of the first line, but nothing was said about that at the time.   Moreover πολιος ought to be πόλεως.   I ought to add that I can remember nothing that could account for the gloomy character of the English part of this curious MS.

My budget of Browning letters begins with the following three to my father about a pony which was to have been given to me, then aged seven. This kind intention was frustrated, as it appears, by the size and ferocity of the animal, which was afterwards, I believe, given to Elwin, the editor of the *Quarterly*:

"19, WARWICK CRESCENT,
     "UPPER WESTBOURNE TERRACE, W.,
               "*June* 19, '63·

* "DEAR LEHMANN,—Pen and I think we cannot do better for the pony than give him to you.   He will be happier as you will treat him than if we

* I have to thank my old friend "Pen," Mr. R. Barrett Browning, for permission to publish here these letters from his father.

parked him up prematurely—for he is not above six years old—during four of which Pen has ridden him. Being an entire horse, he is abundantly spirited; but your boy rides well, I am told. Of vice, or fear, or anything unpleasant to a good rider, he has not a particle.

"I know you will never put him to any other work than that to which he has been accustomed, and that if from any cause he should not suit, or become invalid, you will return him to me. Consequently, at the end of next month he is yours with all the heart of—Yours faithfully,

"ROBERT BROWNING.

"All kind regards to Mrs. Lehmann."

"19, WARWICK CRESCENT,
"UPPER WESTBOURNE TERRACE, W.,
"*June* 23, '63·

"MY DEAR LEHMANN,—It will be best for you to have the pony at once. Robert is far too heavy for him, and you may just as well take him at his best and while fine weather lasts. You can therefore send for him on the earliest day convenient to you—the sooner the better, since a parting must be!

"The more I see of you, the greater delight to me, be certain. Next two Saturdays, however, we are engaged. I shall remember, however, where I may go so pleasantly, and meantime we'll talk about it ere long.—Ever yours most truly,

"R. BROWNING."

"19, WARWICK CRESCENT,
          " UPPER WESTBOURNE TERRACE, W.,
                              "*June* 25, '63.

"MY DEAR LEHMANN,—You are quite right. To tell you the truth, I don't know by what stupid misconception I had got into my head that your boy was some four years older. The pony has always been abundantly spirited even with Robert's weight, and required his strength, unless more steadily worked than was the case of late. I would not have had an accident spoil Rudie's pleasure for the world.—Ever yours faithfully,

                              "ROBERT BROWNING."

The three letters that follow are pleasant examples of Browning's pretty deftness in light correspondence :

                              "*October* 21, 1867.

"MY DEAR MRS. LEHMANN,—' Renew our interrupted acquaintance,' is a sadly inadequate expression for *my* share in the matter : say rather that by seeing you again I shall complete the delight with which I heard of your return and restoration to health. I do hope we are past ' acquaintanceship ' long ago, or your kindness and your husband's kindness have been inconsiderately bestowed. Of course I shall be most happy to go to you on Wednesday.—Ever truly yours,

                              "ROBERT BROWNING."

" 19, Warwick Crescent,
" Upper Westbourne Terrace,
" *July* 17, 1869.

" Dear Mrs. Lehmann,—You should not bid me be 'like my old self'—because my last self is always the most affectionately disposed to you of all the selves ; and I can do myself (honestly to speak) no greater pleasure than to go to you on Monday week. I always think my heart is on my sleeve, and that who likes may see it, and know whether it means kindly or otherwise to them— for all one's excuses, refusings, and misleading stupidity ; and unless it play me false indeed, it must beat very gratefully whenever your name is mentioned ; with such recollections of long kind-ness unvaried by a minutest touch of anything like the contrary ! So let me have the enjoyment you promise me—if by help of your brother, well—if by my own means and act, still well enough. But, understand that I don't care a straw about seeing anybody but yourself and your husband—for my eyes rather ache just now with such sights as you promise. With all love to your husband,

" Ever affectionately yours,

" R. Br."

" 19, Warwick Crescent, W.,
" *Tuesday Evening, July* 27, 1869.

" Dear Friend,—I hardly know whether you are quite in earnest, but *I* am, in—more than grieving—being frightened a little at all this ill-luck.

"I ought to have started in a cab the moment things grew doubtful: why did I not? Because I was unwell—having been so for some time—and felt the grasshopper a burden all day long in the house from which I never stirred.

"Besides, I am of a dull, unadventurous turn in these matters. Of course, to-day I fancy how easily and happily I might have reached you, even if a little late. Don't cast me off next time, if there be a next time, and be sure I will try hard to break the ugly spell. I had no expectation that you would think of arranging for me at all, as I was so long in hearing from you. I supposed you left me to my own resources, as I bade you—and should certainly have reached Woodlands at the punctual quarter past, but for your superfluity of goodness.

"Thank you for your beautiful flowers—I can give nothing in return—unless you bear with a photograph? Yes, you will, and here it shall be. Good-bye over again, dear friend. I am ever—so believe it—in all affection, yours,

"ROBERT BROWNING."

The next letter to my father, a delightful specimen of Browning's friendly gift of hyperbole, has already appeared in Mr. C. L. Graves's "Life of Sir George Grove." My father was not himself at that time a member of the Athenæum, but became one a good many years later:

"19, WARWICK CRESCENT, W.,
"*Feb.* 24, '71·

"MY DEAR LEHMANN,—I wish I could fairly promise to oblige you by voting for Mr. Grove, as your friend; but it happens that I simply oblige myself in so doing, and that I have already signed his certificate in the rooms as earnest of my purpose to do all in my power on Monday next. You must, in justice to the extreme desire I cannot help feeling to make you some slight attempt at return for the manifold kindness you have shown myself— you must tax your ingenuity to pick out, among your acquaintances, some really unpleasant and ineligible person; you will have difficulty enough, I know—but find him, and, for your sake, be assured he shall have the vote of—

"Yours ever truly,
"ROBERT BROWNING."

"19, WARWICK CRESCENT, W.,
"*December* 4, 1873.

"MY DEAR LEHMANN,—See how prettily the story is told in the good old style of Wanley, 1677. 'A certain young man came to Rome, in the shape of his body so like Augustus that he set all the people at gaze upon that sight. Augustus hearing of it, sent for the young man, who, being come into his presence—"Young man," says he, "was your mother ever in Rome?" He, discerning whither the question tended, "No, sir," said he, "but my father hath often;" wittily eluding the intended suspicion of his own mother, and begetting a new concerning that of Augustus.' Ever yours,

"ROBERT BROWNING."

The next letter is to my mother:

"19, WARWICK CRESCENT, W.,
"*Dec.* 16, '73·

"DEAR MRS. LEHMANN,—Nothing would give me so much pleasure as forgetting sad old Christmas Days in your house, where sadness never yet came to me; but we have an engagement to receive that day, our very selves, a 'lone woman' friend, now abroad, with whom it is impossible to make another arrangement. My sister feels your kindness deeply, and bids me return you the truest thanks that ever were. Pen also, who would be so happy to join your party, is only able to be abundantly grateful along with—Ever affectionately yours,

"ROBERT BROWNING."

Browning's son, "Pen," had in the meantime devoted himself to painting and had been studying in Antwerp. One of his first pictures was a very striking piece of work on a large scale. It represented an old French *curé* sitting comfortably beside an assortment of liqueurs and coffee and reading a French novel. It was entitled "Half Hours with the Best Authors." My father, having seen the picture at Browning's house, bought it, and received the following letter from Browning:

"19, WARWICK CRESCENT, W.,
"*January* 24, 1876.

"MY DEAR LEHMANN,—With this note you will receive the picture. What can I say in sending it that you do not perfectly understand? Really, I doubt if anything ever made me more happy than such a prodigious incitement to Pen's industry, and, what he has always wanted, a confidence in his own power of doing good and original work. We can't but believe (all of us here) that your personal kindness had more to do with the purchase than you would desire us to think. Still it is not hard to fancy that you find sufficient pleasure in being the first to bring forward a young fellow who may— and ought—to justify such a distinction by future success. It is simply the truth to say that your approval of the picture would have been preferable immeasurably to its purchase by almost anybody else; you must know *why*, well enough. There, I shall say no more, but remember this circumstance so long as ' this machine is to him.'—Yours truly,
                                     "R. BROWNING."

"19, WARWICK CRESCENT, W.,
"*Feb.* 22, '83·

"DEAR MRS. LEHMANN,—When I say that I am already engaged for the 28th I might leave off, so

unnecessary is it to add another word about the
vexation.   I feel that it should be so.   Do give me
a second chance—have you an afternoon as of old?
I am now a hunger and thirst to see you again, and
your husband, who was so dear and kind to go and
see Pen at Dinant, and all of you—such friends as
you always have been and will be to yours affectionately ever,

"ROBERT BROWNING."

"19, WARWICK CRESCENT, W.,
"*November* 10, 1884.

"DEAR MRS. LEHMANN,—It will indeed be a
delight for me to see you again, and dine with you
and your husband on the 23rd.   Tell him so,
please, with my best regards.

"As for Pen, 'how he is and where'—he has
just entered into a good and adequate studio at
Paris, unlike the poor holes he has hitherto
occupied.   His Dryope is obtaining great success
in Brussels, where they allowed it to arrive a fortnight after the last day for receiving works at the
Exhibition, and gave it the best place there.   He
told me, months ago, that he had painted a little
picture as his proper tribute to your Nina.   Oh,
you dear Scotch! while writing the above bit, I
got a telegram asking me to be the Rector at
Glasgow (as I have more than once refused to let
my friends attempt to make me), 'by unanimous
election' this time!   NO, once more, but I am
grateful enough all the same.   So am I grateful

for such scraps as this, by one of their best critics,
I hear :

"'Un bronze empoignant et qui se fait aisément pardonner
certaines lourdeurs, c'est *Dryopée* fascinée par Apollon sous la
forme d'un serpent.   Voilà qui est grandement vu et éminem-
ment sculptural !   Qui donc osera contester encore aux Anglais
le sentiment de la plastique ? M. Browning renverse victorieuse-
ment ce préjugé.'

Bear with me, and believe me ever, though 'a
parent,' affectionately yours,

"ROBERT BROWNING."

"19, WARWICK CRESCENT, W.,
"*December* 29, 1884.

"MY DEAR LEHMANN,—Here you have, as
well as I can remember, the translation [Horace,
Sat. I. 3] I made impromptu for Felix Moscheles,
and which hangs in his music room :

"'In the whole tribe of singers is this vice,
    Ask them to sing, you'll have to ask them twice ;
    If you don't ask them—that's another thing,
    Until the Judgment-day, be sure they'll sing.'

"Ever yours truly,
"ROBERT BROWNING."

"29, DE VERE GARDENS, W.,
"*Nov.* 8, '87·

"MY DEAR LEHMANN,—I have been troubled of
late with a cough which made it as necessary for
my friends' sake as my own that I should stay at
home of an evening ; but the sight of you again—

and, it may be, of Mrs. Lehmann—is an altogether irresistible temptation, and I joyfully yield to it, accepting your kind invitation for the 17th with all my heart.   Yes, Pen was immediately informed of the exceeding goodness in the matter of the present.   He acknowledged it in a letter from Venice, which I hope reached Mrs. Lehmann, and on arriving here last Saturday week, he was able himself to appreciate the very beautiful clock. . . .

"With true love to Mrs. Lehmann, keep me ever in mind as you have hitherto done, and believe me most affectionately yours,

"ROBERT BROWNING."

"29, DE VERE GARDENS,
"*April* 2, '89·

"MY DEAR LEHMANN,—I am bound to inform you—Pen's very earliest patron—that in case you pass this way any day in the course of the week, Pen's portrait of myself will be on view.   Don't be at any trouble, as you may see it at the Grosvenor, but I could not leave you unapprised that the picture may be seen.   With all regards to Mrs. Lehmann.—Ever yours truly,

"ROBERT BROWNING."

On the 31st December of this same year my father and I were present when the great poet who had been our friend was borne to his place in Westminster Abbey.

CHAPTER IX.

John Forster—George Eliot and G. H. Lewes—A reading by Tennyson—George Eliot as musician—George Eliot in Pau, 1867—Her letter from Barcelona—Ben Jonson's perfect woman.

In the last chapter I have given an account from my father's reminiscences of the unfortunate fracas between John Forster and Robert Browning. I have myself a very distinct memory of the biographer of Goldsmith and Dickens. I recall him as a very big, square, beetle-browed, black-haired piece of solid humanity, with a voice that made the glasses jingle on the table. Yet he could roar you (on paper) as gently as any sucking dove, for with all his arbitrariness and resolute roughness he had one of the kindest hearts that ever beat in the breast of a literary dictator. As a proof of that I may cite three letters written by him to my mother when she was recovering from a dangerous attack of inflammation of the lungs :

"Palace Gate House, Kensington, W.,
"19th March, 1866.

"My dear Mrs. Lehmann,—It was a great grief to me last night to hear of your illness.

"I returned to town only a few days since; and, remembering our engagement before I left, was looking forward to the pleasure of an early meeting when this sad disappointment came.

"You are forbidden to see friends at all, I hear; but when the prohibition is removed you will, I hope, give me the privilege of coming to you. I feel that I deserve this by the pain the news has given me which I heard last night.

"Earnestly do I trust that better news will reach me soon. The weather lately has been such as to try us all; but we have no winter before us now; and you, with your youth on your side, and spring and summer coming on so fast, will soon again be merriest of us all.

"Of course this note is not to give any one the trouble of answering; for my wife (herself a prisoner to-day) will bring me word to-morrow how you are, after inquiring; and when *I may see you*, I know that Mr. Lehmann will kindly send me a line to tell me so.

"With all kindest wishes, my dear Mrs. Lehmann, very affectionately yours,

"JOHN FORSTER."

My mother must have answered this kindly letter very promptly, for on the following day Forster writes again:

"MY DEAR MRS. LEHMANN,—I will not believe that any note from me gives you any pleasure if you trouble yourself again to send an answer to what I write. So now, you see, I shall test you.

If I don't hear from you I'll write, and if I do —— Well, I cannot bring myself to say I won't write ; but I certainly shall not write with half so much pleasure.

"My wife sends her best love to you. She has not been out of doors since we dined on Sunday at Southwick Place, or she would have gone to inquire after you. She has been saving herself up to be able to dine with the Dilkes to-night, and I fear won't be able to go after all.

"The fact is, everybody's ill with this weather, and whatever secret little ailment one has it fastens upon and exaggerates. It has discovered a little weakness in you, and the lesson it teaches is that you should guard that place with greater care when you are well. The secret of long life is to know where the enemy is always lying in wait to assail us, and to provide and fortify against him. You will do this more carefully in future—will you not? For your husband's and children's sake first and for all our sakes afterwards.

"You have the best of doctors—a doctor to disarm a sick-room of not a little of its weariness and pain ; and I am sure you will soon be well. Not only that, I am sure you will in future be more prudent, not defying, but temporising with east winds and savage airs, especially at night.

"Always, my dear Mrs. Lehmann, very affectionately yours,

"JOHN FORSTER."

And then comes the third and last of this set of pretty messages of friendship :

"Palace Gate House, Kensington,
"29th March, 1866.

"With no common pleasure, my dear Mrs. Lehmann, I have heard of your ability to take a drive the other day; and now I hope this fine weather which is really come will help the good De Mussy*, and another doctor more potent even than De Mussy (we call him Youth) triumphantly to set you up again.   And then with a little—no, I will say a great deal—of prudence, you will be able for the future to defy your enemy, and to save from infinite anxiety all your friends.

"As soon as I hear that I may call and see you I mean to inflict myself upon you for a few minutes, just to be satisfied upon my own seeing that what I hear is true.

"And so, good-bye for the present, and ever believe me, my dear Mrs. Lehmann, very affection- ately yours,

"John Forster.

"I shall bear this myself, and learn how you really are."

In the winter of 1869—70 my father, who was then in America, had sent John Forster some canvas-back ducks, of which he received the follow- ing pleasant acknowledgment:

* Dr. Guéneau De Mussy, the eminent French doctor, at that time practising in London.

"PALACE GATE HOUSE, KENSINGTON,
"18th January, 1870.

"MY DEAR LEHMANN,—My thanks for your kind remembrance has been too long delayed, but you must not on that account think them less grateful and sincere.

"Both of us here were indeed much touched by your having thought of us at all that distance, and in such seasonable Christmas fashion. Nor was there a wish belonging to the season which your splendid present seemed to bring with it that we did not desire to return fifty-fold for all future happiness to you and yours.

"I call the present splendid, for how magnificent the birds were! I never saw such plumage. It seemed a horrible sacrifice to the spit; but the result justified it, and the two brace we had here were a wonderful success. One brace only I could find in my heart to part with: and Coleridge (the Sol.-Gen.), to whom I sent it, told me his son, who is a bit of an ornithologist, would far rather have stuffed the birds than have let them stuff anybody else.

"We went to Torquay immediately after Xmas Day, and only returned on Friday last. We had horrible weather, and much of the pleasure of the visit was lost to me by a miserable cold.

"I shall rejoice to hear that health attends you everywhere in your wanderings, and that these will have, in every possible way that you can wish, a prosperous issue.

" With my wife's kindest regards, I am ever, my dear L., very sincerely yours,

"JOHN FORSTER."

It was well said by the *Times* after Forster's death that those who at first sight found him obstinate and overbearing were ready to confess that they had in reality found him to be one of the tenderest and most generous of men.

GEORGE ELIOT AND G. H. LEWES.

I find in my father's "Reminiscences" the following passage relating to George Eliot and G. H. Lewes:

" G. H. Lewes was on intimate terms with my father-in-law, Robert Chambers, and I met him first in 1853 at Chalcotts, a house Robert Chambers had taken for the summer of that year at Haverstock Hill. Lewes was then chiefly engaged upon the *Westminster Review*. His more solid works belong to a later period. Through him I became acquainted with George Eliot, and at one time saw a great deal of her. What first struck one about her was the strange contrast between the large head, the masculine, Dantesque features, and the soft melodious voice, which always cast a spell over me. One might almost have forgotten that she was a woman, so profound was her insight; but I, at least, could never forget while in her company that I was with an exceptional being.

" In the winter of 1866 my wife and family were at Pau, while I was alone in London. George Eliot was a very fair pianist, not gifted, but enthusiastic, and extremely painstaking. During a great part of that winter I used to go to her every Monday evening at her house in North Bank, Regent's Park, always taking my violin with me. We played together every piano and violin sonata of Mozart and Beethoven. I knew the traditions of the best players, and was able to give her some hints, which she always received eagerly and thankfully. Our audience consisted of George Lewes only, and he used to groan with delight whenever we were rather successful in playing some beautiful passage. Now that both he and George Eliot are no more, the scene is to me a strange, sad, and quite unique memory.

" Some years afterwards they were kind enough to ask me and my wife to join a very small audience, invited to hear Tennyson read his poetry, at their house. I had at first some little difficulty in accustoming myself to his very marked Northern dialect, but that done I thoroughly enjoyed the reading. He would interrupt himself every now and then to say quite naïvely, ' We now come to one of my best things. This has been tried before me, but not successfully,' and so on, acting through-out as his own not quite impartial Greek chorus. He read ' The Northern Farmer,' and almost the whole of ' Maud.' We were spell-bound, and he seemed to enjoy it so much that his son had at last to make him stop by reminding him of the lateness of the hour."

The following undated letter from George Eliot evidently refers to one of the visits mentioned by my father :

"THE PRIORY,
"NORTH BANK, REGENT'S PARK.

"DEAR MR. LEHMANN,—Friday the 16th will suit us perfectly.

"I will forgive you for disappointing me as to Wednesday, since I got the compensation of knowing that there still exist personages so romantic as Wandering Minstrels.*

"George continues so far better as to be able to write a sheaf of philosophy every morning, and we feel that it will be very agreeable to listen to your violin in the evening.—Very truly yours,

"M. E. LEWES."

Here is another of an earlier date to my mother :

"THE PRIORY,
"*April* 30, '64·

"MY DEAR MRS. LEHMANN,—In Mr. Lewes's absence I opened Mr. Lehmann's letter, which is altogether a conjugal one, and can be answered by me to you.

"Yes, I do hope to be able to see you to-morrow; but in my uncertainty as to my state of headache

* My father was a member of the well-known musical society of that name.

(that is the name sometimes for my head) I should be much easier if you would *not* send the carriage, but would simply leave us to find the way to you [to Southwood Lane, Highgate] for ourselves ; and, if I am able to come to you, to allow the carriage to bring us home.

"Mr. Lewes is sure—so far as one can be sure—of presenting himself to you between five and six.

"I wish I had been fortunate enough to see you yesterday. You are not one of those dreadfully healthy women who stare in utter scepticism at one's alleged miseries and inabilities. But I *do* mean to be at Highgate to-morrow if I can.

"Ever yours truly,
"M. E. LEWES."

The following undated letter from that sprightly correspondent, G. H. Lewes, to my mother also, in all probability, belongs to 1864. There is another enclosed in an envelope addressed to "The Mother of the Gracchi (in smalls as yet)," which was conveyed by my brother and myself on ponies, the same juvenile postmen having carried the note to which it was an answer :

"THE PRIORY,
"*Wednesday.*

"ADMIRABLE WOMAN,—The extremely youthful George will certainly break through his rule (for what are rules good for but to be broken?) and present himself arrayed in great splendour (*i.e.* a tail-coat and waxed whiskers) on Tuesday next.

But oh! how little impression his pothooks and signature must have made on your insensible soul that you should have mistaken them for his better two-thirds'! I wrote to you—alone I did it!— Polly* having installed me in the office of general secretary, with directions to give her hearty love, and wish to see you, which of course I forgot. Come up on Sunday if you can; if not, any other afternoon after two.

"Ever yours faithfully,
"G. H. Lewes."

My mother spent the winter of 1866—67 in Pau, in order to restore her health after her attack of inflammation of the lungs. While she was there G. H. Lewes and George Eliot paid her a visit, of which she gives an account in two letters to my father. The first is undated, but must have been written, I think, on January 21st, 1867:

"When I came home," she says, "I found the *Lewes's card!* They had turned up at last, and both had called, and were at the Hôtel de France, so I wrote a note instantly and asked them to tea, which come they did, and a very sweet evening we had. There is such a gentle graciousness about Mrs. Lewes one must love her, and she seems to adore him. He is worn out and thin and languid, has lost his old spirits, but they'll come back with change and rest. I made myself pretty in my gray

* "Polly" is, of course, George Eliot herself.

silk and lace *kragen*, and they admired my dress so
much.   When I got up to play, Mrs. Lewes said,
'I am inclined to quarrel, do you know, with Mr.
Rudolf Lehmann about a portrait of you I saw at
his house.   It does not do you justice.'   I told her
she was the first person who said so, as it was
usually thought, and *I thought* it, flattered.   (Do
you remember Aunt J——'s, 'It's much too pretty
—why it's quite a handsome woman,' before me,
the unhappy original?)   I played to them, and
wound up with 'Adelaida' by particular request,
Mr. Lewes having told her that I played such a
beautiful arrangement!   Arrangement!   Why, I
never knew it was arranged, and if it is, it's certainly my own.   They are coming to-day to breakfast at twelve.   Then I have persuaded him to go
and call on the Savages, poor things, whilst she
will remain with me.   Then they do what they
like till six, when they dine with me.   I felt I
must make an effort, because they told me it was
solely on *my account* they came to Pau.   'We look
upon you as a sort of heroine, dear Mrs. Lehmann,
parted so long from your husband and your home,
and take a deep interest in you,' for which I thanked
her, and felt inexpressibly soothed in the idea that
somebody at last had found out I was a heroine,
which I had been suspecting all along myself.   If
people would only say such things and smooth my
fur the right way, instead of lecturing me as they
do, I would take a much more cheerful view of my
position.   I begin to think it's abominable the way

my friends roar out when I meekly say I would like
to come home, and write me severe philosophical,
physiological treatises, and put me down, and when
they've got me down keep me down.   Mrs. Lewes
knows better, so please understand for the future
I am a sort of heroine. . . . The Lewes's were
enchanted with our dog Chang.   They say he is a
real Maltese ; they like Deutsch.*   He is the *brightest*
German (always excepting you, I trust and believe)
they ever saw.   That is a nice little word for his
hop-sparrowishness, I daresay, but they like him.
He likes De Mussy too, and she said she was so
anxious to see him (I can't tell why) that she did a
rude thing at the theatre and turned round and
stared at him when he was with us once.   I am
sure he did not remark it, and if he had, would
have been flattered. . . . Fancy, Lewes intended
Goethe for *Nina*, having heard of her passion for
Goethe from you, and in a vague way fancied she
was a great big girl !—Heard afterwards she was
five.   However, he'll see her to-day at déjeuner."

                                    " PAU,
                                        " 23rd [*Jan.*].

   " The Lewes's are gone after two delightful cosy
days.   I have got to know her as I never should
have done in years in London, and I think she loves
me—we are sworn friends.   What a sweet, mild,
womanly presence hers is—so soothing, too, and
elevating above all.   It is impossible to be with that

   * Emanuel Deutsch, the distinguished Orientalist.

noble creature without feeling *better*. I have never
known any one like her—and then her modesty, her
humility. A modesty, too, that never makes her
or you awkward, as many modesties do. I am full
of her. She makes a great impression on me, and I
long to see more of her and be with her. She said,
without my asking it, she would write me from
Barcelona to tell me how it went with 'George,'
and if they were going on as they now intend.
They don't go to Madrid, but Seville, Cordova,
Granada, &c. When she went away last night I
said something of hoping she would like me, and
we should be friends. She said, 'I do; I love you
better every hour.' She said it so sweetly, with
her soft penetrating voice, it did not sound as such
a compliment would from any other lips. How
they like you! This was such a tie between us—
and she thinks you so handsome. I can't remember
the word she used for your head. I had to give
her the 'head-medallion' photo of yours, so send
me another; she didn't like the one she had, and
admired this so much. . . . I walked down to the
station with them this lovely summer morning.
The weather has been glorious these two days, and
the old white mountains so grand; in fact, the little
visit has been a *complete success*. She made me tell
her the whole story of our courtship and marriage,
which seemed to interest her intensely. In fact,
she was like a dear, loving elder sister to me the
whole time. I gave them a nice little dinner; first,
a light lunch at twelve—then he went and rejoiced

poor Mr. Savage's heart by a visit, whilst I walked
in the garden and told her my love-story.   I wanted
to take them a drive, the day was so perfect—not
a *voiture* to be had of any kind, a *chasse* going on!
Provoking, wasn't it? . . . Nina said her little
poem of Goethe to them to-day, sweetly.   My dear,
she, Mrs. L., was so sweet, so attentive to Matilda
[our German governess]!   She often brought her
gently into our conversation by talking of Germany,
and appealing in her charming, gentle way to the
delighted Tilla.   It was such a contrast to the way
that upstart Miss P. treats her—hardly deigning to
take notice of her, and that very day, in the *Place*,
having in an insolent way held out a finger of her
left hand as she passed to Tilla to shake, which
Tilla did not take—bravo!   She says this insolent
baggage always gives her her left hand when she
condescends to do it at all.   So she was determined
not to take it next time. . . .

"What cold you have suffered!   Here it is
sirocco again to-day—like going into a hothouse
when you go out.   The valley was full of a seeth-
ing mist over which the mountains towered clear
and serene.   George Eliot in looking at this mist
said, 'I love to see that mist—it is beautiful—it
looks as if creation were going on underneath.'
. . . She asked me if there was anything characteristic here to take home.   I said, ' Hardly!' then
went to my drawer and pulled out a beautiful large
beaded rosary of the box-root, which perfectly
enchanted her.   She said it was strange: she had

longed for a rosary, and had never seen anything more charming than those beads made of a root. I also gave her a knitted wool shawl, in which she much rejoiced. They are looking forward to having you again when they come home."

The letter promised by George Eliot duly arrived:

"BARCELONA,
"*February* 3, 1867.

"MY DEAR MRS. LEHMANN,—When one's time is almost all spent out of doors in churches or in theatres, it is not easy to find time for letter writing. But I should have wanted to say a few words to you before we go further South, even if I had not promised to do so. Of course you have been knit into my thoughts ever since we parted from you, and the memory of you would have been a pure addition to my pleasures if it had not been mixed with repentance at my want of consideration in not insisting on saying a final good-bye to you at night, instead of disturbing you in the morning, when you ought to have been resting from extra excitement. I am sure you felt ill that last morning, and I wish there were any chance of my knowing soon that you are as well as ever again. I have only good news to tell you about ourselves. George is much stronger and looks quite well, but he is not yet fat or robust enough to support a slight sore throat without depression. However, he is in excellent circumstances for getting better, enjoying our travel, and

breathing every day delicious air, for since we left
Biarritz for San Sebastian, on the 26th, we have
had perfect weather, weather such as makes even
me feel as if life were a good even for my own
sake.   We stayed three days at San Sebastian, and
were only troubled with two smells out of the
registered twenty-five.   We walked for hours on
the fine sands of the bay, and each evening the
sunset was memorable among our sunsets.   I hope
you saw Passages, and were rowed out there in the
sunshine, listening to the soft splash of the oar.
From San Sebastian we went to Saragossa, and I
think we never enjoyed landscape so much by railway as on this journey : the reason probably is
that the rate of swiftness is much lower, and objects
remain before the eyes long enough for delight in
them.   Until we got into Aragon I thought I had
never seen so many pretty women or people with
such charming manners as in the few days after
we left France.   But at Saragossa the people are
brusque and the beauty had disappeared.   Still
they were not rude ; the Spaniards seem to me to
stare less, to be quicker in understanding what
foreigners say to them, and to show more good will
without servility in their manners than any other
nation I have seen anything of.   I longed to be
able to sketch one or two of the men with their
great striped blankets thrown grandly round them,
and a kerchief tied about their heads, who make
the chorus to everything that goes on in the open
air at Saragossa.   They and the far-stretching

brown plains with brown sheep-folds, brown towns and villages, and far off walls of brown hills, seemed to me more unlike what we think of as European than anything I had seen before. Looking at the brown windowless villages, with a few flocks of sheep scattered far apart on the barren plain, I could have fancied myself in Arabia. We stayed a night at Lerida, and here we saw a bit of genuine Spanish life, such a scene on the brown slope of the high hill which is surmounted by the fort—groups of women sitting in the afternoon sunshine, at various kinds of small woman's work, men gambling, men in striped blankets looking on, handsome gypsies making jokes probably at our expense, jokes which we had the advantage of not understanding, and which gave us the advantage of seeing their (the gypsies') white teeth. Then the view from the fort was worth a journey to see, no longer a barren plain, but an olive garden; and the next day, in proportion as we got far into Catalonia, the beauty and variety increased. Catalonia deserves to be called a second Provence, or rather, I should say, it is more beautiful than Provence.

"Barcelona is of the class of mongrel towns that one can never care for much, except for the sake of climate, and this we are having in perfection. For the rest we are at a good hotel, the cathedral is fine, the people strikingly handsome, and we have popular theatres, a Spanish opera, and an Italian opera, where we can always get good seats. Yesterday we saw a mystery play, 'The Shepherds of

Bethlehem,' at a people's theatre in the little Prado. Except that the notion of decorations was modern, the play itself, in its jokes and its seriousness, differed little from what people delighted in five centuries ago. There was a young actor who played one of the shepherds, with a head of ideal beauty. In the evening we heard a charming Spanish opera, the music really inspiriting, and this evening we are going to hear the Faust at the great Opera House, to say nothing of our being now in a hurry to be ready for a popular drama at 3 o'clock. Pray admire our energy. You can imagine that everything of this sort is interesting to us. We watch the audience as well as the actors, and we try to accustom our ears to the Spanish pronunciation. All this morning we have been bathing in the clear soft air, and looking at the placid sea. If it continues placid till Wednesday, think of us as starting for Alicante in the steamboat, ultimately for Malaga and Granada.

"But I am scribbling unconscionably without much excuse—my only excuse is that I like to fancy myself talking to you. George sends his best love, and we both should like the children to be reminded of us. Please ask the rosebud Nina to accept a kiss on each cheek, and think one is from Mr. Lewes and the other from Mrs. Lewes. Our joint good wishes and regards to Miss Volekhausen. Get strong, and like to think of us kindly.

"Ever yours, most sincerely,
"M. E. Lewes.

"We have found no hardships hitherto. Even at unsophisticated Lerida, the odours and insects are hybernating."

Later, in 1867, after they had both returned to England, George Eliot wrote to my mother. There is no date, except "Tuesday morning," on the letter:

"My dear Friend,—I shall say yes very gladly, for just now I want to see you of all dear people that I know, if there were not this insurmountable obstacle, that to-morrow morning we go to Niton, where we have taken a house for a fortnight.

"Poor George, after being so blooming that you would hardly have known him, has got all wrong again, has had headache for ten days, and begins to ask, "What good shall my life do me?" But he revives so quickly under favourable circumstances that I hope you will see him looking bright when we come back.

"Thus unkind Fate has willed it, else I should have felt as happy as a schoolgirl invited out to have gone to see you on Saturday in your pretty home, and I should have chosen to meet just the friends you mention—including Mr. Deutsch. If I had not heard you cough too much! And you do not tell me that you have lost that old enemy who overtook you again in Paris.

"I wonder if I like you better because you are not well. I have a trick of caring more for any one who has a trouble than for those who seem quite scathless.

"We shall take care to advertise our return to friends whom we want to see, and therefore to you, without any delay. George tells me to send his love with mine to you and your husband. You know already that he would have been delighted to see you all again.—Always yours affectionately,

"M. E. LEWES."

George Eliot's friendship for my mother continued to the last, and was extended to the younger members of the family. Once a little essay written by my sister was shown to her. She took it away, and afterwards wrote to my mother:

"THE PRIORY,
"*April* 2, 1877.

"DEAR FRIEND,—Nina's little paper is full of the best promise. It has the double strength of simple, direct expression, and of observant lovingness.

"You remember what old Ben Jonson wished for his perfect woman. Besides 'each softest virtue' she was to have 'a manly soul.' And I hope we shall see that grander feminine type— at once sweet, strong, large-thoughted—in your Nina.

"But don't let us tell her all the good we think of her.

"I suppose the word ' abrupt ' is meant as an admonition by the teacher. But to me, the beginning to say at once what she has to say without the artificiality of an introduction is one of the good signs.—Yours affectionately,

"M. E. LEWES."

CHAPTER X.

I REMEMBER on a certain afternoon many years
ago—it must have been somewhere about the year
1864—my mother took me out with her in the
carriage, and impressed upon my mind the fact that
I was about to see and to shake hands with a poet.
I did see him, and I did shake hands with him, a
very old and a very amiable and pathetic-looking
gentleman. Did he wear a silk skull-cap? No, I
think not; but he was reclining in an easy-chair or
on a sofa, and he spoke in a high and rather quaver-
ing voice. This was Barry Cornwall, otherwise
Bryan Waller Procter, who was born in 1787, had
been at Harrow with Byron and Peel, had enjoyed
the intimate friendship of Charles Lamb—Procter's
name was one of the last that Lamb murmured
before he died—and was to become (in 1866) his
biographer. Dyer, too, he had known—George
Dyer, the friendly, short-sighted, would-be poet of
whom Lamb relates that he saw him, " upon taking
leave, instead of turning down the right-hand path
by which he had entered—with staff in hand and
at noonday—deliberately march right forwards into
the midst of the stream that runs by us, and totally

disappear." Mr. E. V. Lucas, in his delightful "Life of Charles Lamb" (i. 377), says: "In that year [1817, when Procter first met Lamb at Leigh Hunt's] the author of 'Charles Lamb: a Memoir,' to which all who write of Lamb are so much indebted, was thirty. He was in business as a solicitor, was living a very gay life as a man about town, keeping his hunter and taking lessons in boxing from Tom Cribb, and contributing to the *Literary Gazette*. There is no doubt but that intercourse with Lamb, who seems to have liked him extremely, led to his thinking more seriously of poetry, and we may attribute the composition of his 'Dramatic Scenes' largely to Lamb's influence. Lamb admired them a little, perhaps, beyond their deserts, possibly from this paternal association; he said that they were worthy of a place in his 'Specimens.' It was not, however, until 'Marcian Colonna' (1820) and 'A Sicilian Story' (1821) were published that Procter took his place as one of the poets of the day."

Certainly, when I saw Barry Cornwall nearly fifty years later, there was nothing in his appearance to suggest a former association with Tom Cribb. No man could have looked, as I remember him, less pugnacious. Still, in his devotion to the noble art he did not stand alone among the writers of that earlier day. Byron boxed for purposes of slimness; Hazlitt has left us a description of a prize-fight which is one of the finest pieces of prose in the language; and the friend of Keats (himself a fighter), John Hamilton Reynolds, has celebrated the Fancy in stirring lines.

As for the sea (*cf.* "The sea, the sea, the open sea," &c.), of which Barry Cornwall wrote with an enthusiasm so infectious and seemingly so sincere, it is well known that he was himself one of the worst sailors in existence—I speak in relation to colour and health, not to nautical skill.   A Channel crossing was a dread to him.   I do not say that all marine singers have this vice ; but I seem to remember that Dibdin, the laureate of poor Jack, never managed to get beyond Gravesend in his actual investigations of the ocean.

If Barry Cornwall was happy in his friends, he was even happier in his wife.   In 1823, at the age of thirty-six, he married Anne Benson Skepper, the charming and beautiful daughter of Basil Montagu's third wife.   Born in the last year of the eighteenth century, this delightful lady lived until 1888, an example to later generations of the sprightly humour, the vivacious and indefatigable intelligence, and the genuine friendship that ruled amongst the heroes of the past.   I am thankful to say that I knew her well.   She loved my mother, and was one of her best correspondents.   For her benefit she employed the untiring activity of her pen, and for us, the representatives of a later race, she brought forth from the store of her experience treasures of memory and conversation.   She could hold her own, and more than her own, with the youngest and liveliest, for she herself was the very embodiment of perennial life and youth. These characteristics of hers are celebrated by James Russell Lowell in his own inimitable way in a letter which the kindness of its possessor, Mrs. George Murray Smith, enables me to print here. At the time when he wrote it Lowell was the American Minister in this country :—

"10, LOWNDES SQUARE, S.W.,
"15*th Jany.*, 1882.

"DEAR MRS. PROCTER,—I have been out of town ; I have been arrested for sympathy with suffering Ireland !   I have been in a lunatic asylum, shut up there by relatives who thought I had property ! But wherever I have been I have thought incessantly of you ! Ungrateful being, is this the return I might fairly have looked for ? But a truce to mutual recriminations. I send you the copy of an ode which I picked up on my floor and which I believe you to have written yourself. I keep the original for purposes of identi- fication. Two experts have already pronounced the handwriting to be yours.   I send you the copy in case somebody has been counterfeiting your hand.

' I know a girl (they say she's eighty)
  Who finds not years, as we do, weighty,
  But moults them softly one and all
  As roses let their petals fall,
  Certain that Nature has in store,
  For eighty shed, as many more:

Youth loved her at first sight, and locked her
In lifelong arms—'tis Mistress P——r !
When I feel old and bare of wit
And nothing with my mood will fit
Nor Wine nor Woman, no, nor Song
(Life's three best things, or Luther's wrong)
Nothing, if I must tell the truth,
But an heroic dose of youth,—
I hasten to the only Doctor
That keeps the drug : the name is P——r !
And she pretends (but I've the sense
To know that all is mere pretense)
She makes believe that I forget
The creditors if not the debt,
That I, who'm neither fool nor mad,
Cannot distinguish good from bad
And cleave thereto ! What fiend has mocked her
(So clever too) ?   *Can* this be P——r ?
Ah, well, it is the thing, I see,
Called nowadays *espièglerie*,
A girlish wile to counterfeit
Anger, and draw me to her feet—
As if she fancied (Holy Virgin !)
That flies to sugar needed urgiu—
But I shall come, unless life's docked or
Worse fate befall—for who's like P——r ! '

" I am writing in great haste and with a summons
to which that to Tower Hill was a trifle—an artist
is waiting upstairs to take my head off ! So good-
bye for the present. Mrs. Lowell and I have a

plan of getting you here for dinner and a game of whist. What say you? With kindest regards to your daughter,

> "Faithfully yours,
>> "J. R. LOWELL."

On one occasion, nearly eighty years ago, Mrs. Procter had seen Charles Lamb in a state of exaltation. Mr. E. V. Lucas tells the story ("Life of Charles Lamb," ii. 223): "A glimpse of Lamb in his cups," he says, "is given by Mrs. Procter in a letter to Mrs. Jameson in 1830 or thereabouts. 'Charles Lamb,' she writes (from 25, Bedford Square), 'dined here on Monday at five, and by seven he was so tipsy he could not stand. Martin Burney carried him from one room to the other like a sack of coals. He insisted on saying, "Diddle, diddle, dumpty, my son John." He slept until ten, and then woke more tipsy than before; and between his fits of bantering Martin Burney kept saying, "Please God, I'll never enter this cursed house again." He wrote a note next day begging pardon, and asking when he might come again.'

"The late Mr. Dykes Campbell," continues Mr. Lucas, "sent Mrs. Procter, fifty-six years later, a copy of this letter, when it was sold at Christie's, and drew from that wise and witty lady a pleasant reply, in which she remarked, 'I could not help laughing when I read your extract. I have entirely forgotten the dinner. If people will dine at five what can be expected ? We have no time to get tipsy now, and that is our excuse.'"

Let those read on who are attracted by the prospect of some minutes of intimate conversation with Barry Cornwall and his wife, and let them, if they like, imagine they are listening in a room peopled with the great shades of Wordsworth, Coleridge, Keats, Landor, Tennyson, Walter Scott, Browning, Hazlitt, Carlyle, Dickens, and Thackeray; for to all these, as to Lamb and many others, Mr. and Mrs. Procter were friends.

The first letter is from Barry Cornwall to my mother, who had just established herself at Pau for the autumn and winter :—

" ESSINGTON'S HOTEL, MALVERN WELLS, ENGLAND,
" *Sunday, September*, 1866.

" MY DEAR MRS. LEHMANN,—My wife says, ' I am writing to Mrs. Lehmann. Won't *you* write a few lines ?'

> ' Old as I am, for ladies' love unfit,
> The power of Nina I remember yet.'

So, although I have nothing to say, and if I had cannot say it, ' I take up my pen,' as young ladies at boarding-schools say, to tell you that I hope you are getting better—much better—quite well. You have, I know, been attended lately by that great musician, Mr. F. L. ; and I trust that he has left you *determined* to be prudent and to get well enough to return to England. People may talk of Biarritz and Paris and other places of *fiction ;* but be assured that no place is like Old England—except Scotland.

"My wife has monopolised all the news, I know; from the latest discovery in astronomy to the delicate appetite of our dog Prinny (Prince) all is before you. I know nothing except about myself. I have been writing a book,* which has attracted the kind words of several of my friends on the side of the Malvern Hills. The flowers are all gone —even our three great national prodigies have disappeared. These were three enormous *thistles,* glorious emblems of our N.B., Scotland, seven or eight feet high, and, I imagine, descendants from William Wallace or Robert Bruce.

"You have found the road to my wife's heart— dress. She fancies herself already in her cloak Pyrennean. *I* have taken to scarlet—with blue trousers—and a sweet green waistcoat. I rather think that when I return to London some of the ladies will salute me—I mean with their hands— or curtsey, &c. When my friends return from foreign travel I cannot divine what *they* will do. Something extraordinary. Nothing so startling has come across human observation since the discovery of the Nyanza—what is the name? I mean the source or basin of the Nile.

"We have lately had—here amongst the residents in this Hotel—a Doctor Thompson, the Chief Sage or King of Cambridge, the Master of Trinity. Lest his elevation to this pinnacle should have daunted

* "Charles Lamb: A Memoir, 1866."

all his contemporaries, he has married a widow and come to pass the honeymoon amongst us unlearned Thebans.

"Kiss your children for me, and believe me, very truly yours,

"B. W. PROCTER."

[BARRY CORNWALL *to* MRS. F. LEHMANN.]

"WINTER AT PAU.

"32, WEYMOUTH STREET, PORTLAND PLACE, W.,
"*Nov.* 7, 1866.

"Will you have me in verse?   Will you have me
  in prose?
My dear Mrs. Lehmann—Ah! nobody knows
How hard (nay, impossible) it has become
To show all my heart in a letter from home,
Unless the receiver is able to turn
My phrases from ink into fire—and learn
The meaning of each—the *true* meaning I mean,
And then interpose some soft nothings between.
Now *you*—will you do this?   Come, Fred is away
And will not hear a syllable—What do you say?
He's in love with his fiddle, but *I* am—ah! you
May now give yourself up unto you know whom
  (who,
If correct, would the better have suited the rhyme).
He—he's thinking of nothing but ' tune' and the
  ' time.'
How bloom you, my Nina?   What's Nina? explain.
Caterina? Christina? Nerina?   In vain

I beat my dull brains.   The true versions depart,
They leave my head empty and sink to my heart,
And there 'tis all ' Ina ' and ' Nina ' instead :
These freshen the heart though they injure the head,
My heart therefore—' cœur ' or ' ma tendresse,'
    what is it ?
Most lovingly wanders to Pau on a visit.
And you, dear, how pass you the day and the
    night
Since Fred (the deceiver) resolved to take flight ?
He came t'other day here—oh, not to see me,
But my wife, whom he meets with detestable
    glee :
He's going to dine with *her*.   Will you believe
She smiled as she asked him, not asking my leave ?
But I'm forced to be calm though I know I'm
    de trop.
Well, patience, I'll pay him off nobly—at Pau ;
At Pau, where the sweetest of welcomes (divine
As the beauty of love is) will surely be mine.

.   .   .   .   .

Thus far—I can travel no farther, my pen
Becomes feeble and inkless.   What praises from
    men,
My dear Nina can vie with the shout and the jest
That spring from the children you still love the
    best,
Who cluster around you and tempt you to dream
Of the dear old North country, of mountain and
    stream.

In dream ?   Ah! perhaps you may dream of your
  Fred,
If so, I give up—there's no more to be said.

"B. C. aged 77 years.*   × his mark.

" Postscript.

" November 7.

"A letter—you tell me of roses and peas,
And of cream and of strawberries quite at your
  ease,
As if we in honest old England don't know
Such words are but boasts—fashioned merely for
  show,
Not realities.   No ! the true seasons are here,
Fawkes, frost and roast mutton, at this time of
  year."

The next letter was also written to Pau ; and
with it, as a gift, or soon after it, went " The
Mysteries of Udolpho," Mrs. Ann Radcliffe's blood-
curdling romance.   The book arrived safely, and is
referred to in a letter from my mother to my father
(12th March, 1867): " Ernie (aged seven) has just
been in a solemn manner to fetch himself a book to
read.   He has chosen ' The Mysteries of Udolpho,'
which Rudie has persuaded him to read aloud.
Rudie and Freddie during the performance sit
exploding at Ernie's mistakes—actually rolling on

---

* As a matter of fact Barry Cornwall was only a fortnight
short of completing his 79th year.

the floor in convulsions at passages. I just hear at this moment that somebody has been mixing in the 'gay and buzzy skanes'—in consequence of which Rudie and Freddie are both kicking on the ground, whilst E. calmly continues his reading without deigning to notice these unseemly proceedings."

" 27*th January*, 1867,
    " 32, WEYMOUTH STREET,
        " PORTLAND PLACE

" MY DEAR MRS. LEHMANN,—I like to return good for evil—soft words in return for neglect. It is the Weymouthian philosophy, which is peculiar to this district, and does not extend to Pau.

" My wife received (through Mr. Lehmann, whom his familiars call ' Fred ') a message from you ; but there was none for me. *N'importe.* Madame von Ousterhein, whom I am now rapidly attaching myself to, transmits many messages—jars of honey, to speak figuratively—invisible, untranslatable, and which I alone understand and feel. What is the French for kisses ? I suppose they, the Robespierrians and Dantonistes and Marats, have no word for it in their vocabulary.

.   .   -   .   .

" I am ashamed to say, after the foregoing natural emotion (indignation is the word), I was glad to hear that you and the children were well. By ' well ' I mean that you were mounting the steep hill on

which the Temple of the Goddess of Health is built
so firmly.

"In order that you may not relapse on account
of want of medicine, I have sent you some in the
shape of a book.   You recollect probably, from
your historical researches, the name of a celebrated
English physician, Dr. Ratcliffe?*   He bequeathed
a great library to the University of Oxford, which
indeed is there still.   Well, one book escaped and
came into *my* possession.   It bears a very unassuming name, and does not profess to expound (what,
however, it really does) all the abstruse mysteries
of the Stoics.   It is called, in modern phrase, ' The
Mysteries of Udolpho,' and is in the shape of a mere
story.

"This piece of old crabbed philosophy (in two
vols.), printed in the type of Walker or Dove or
Suby—for I forget which—*I* have sent to you.
With, I confess, some misgivings as to its security,
I have entrusted it to ' Fred,' who *says* that he will
forward it.   I hope you will read the book and
make a quick march up the Hill of Health and
reach the top.

"(I can scarcely write—and I cannot walk or
talk.)

"My wife will no doubt send you what news
she has.   I confine myself to Ratcliffian philosophy.
The domesticities are hers.

"You will be glad to hear that Mr. F. Lehmann

* His name, however, was Radcliffe.

has become an accomplished singer of the old song,
' The girl I leave behind me.'

" With all good wishes, I am, your sincere and injured

"B. W. P."

" 32, WEYMOUTH STREET,
"PORTLAND PLACE,
"22nd Nov., 1868.

" Many thanks, my dear Mrs. Lehmann, first for
your pretty verses, and secondly for your pretty
flowers. I wish I could send you any verses in
return ; but I cannot. I am overwhelmed by the
melancholy thoughts of old age. In former days—
i.e., before you and Mr. Lehmann were born—I
used to show my want of wit in divers ' nonsense
verses '; but to-day I enter upon my 80th* year,
and if I could properly offer you anything it would
be a sort of paternal (grand-paternal) blessing, that
you might enjoy all fruits and flowers (flowers as
pretty and sweet as those you sent me) for many
happy years to come.

" Dear Mrs. Lehmann,
" Your obliged and sincere,
"B. W. PROCTER."

The following stanzas are *printed* on a separate
sheet of paper. At the top is written the date,
1872, and then in my mother's handwriting

* It was his 82nd year.

follow the words, "Sent to me last New Year but one":

VERSES IN MY OLD AGE.
By BARRY CORNWALL.

"Come from the ends of the world,
  Wind of the air or sky,
Wherever the Thunder is hurled,
  Wherever the Lightnings fly!
Come, with the bird on your bosom
  (Linnet or lark that soars),
Come with the sweet Spring blossom,
  And the Sun from Southern shores.

"I hate the snake Winter that creepeth,
  And poisons the buds of May;
I shout to the Sun who sleepeth,
  And pray him awake to-day.
For the world is in want of his power
  To vanquish the rebel storm;
All wait for his golden hour,
  Man, and beast, and worm.

"Not only the seasons, failing,
  Forsake their natural tone,
But Age droops onward, sailing,
  And is lost in the seas unknown.
No wisdom redeemeth *his* sorrow,
  For thought and strength are fled;
No hope enlightens to-morrow,
  And the Past (so loved) is dead!
                    Dead! Dead!"

Barry Cornwall died on October 4th, 1874.

CHAPTER XI.

Mrs. Procter—Miss Jane Gape—Gossip from London—An
  Offer for a Harmonium—Life at Malvern—Lord Lytton—
  Mrs. Sartoris—Mrs. Procter's 82nd Birthday.

ENTER, now, Mrs. Procter, who thus writes to my
mother :

"ESSINGTON'S HOTEL, MALVERN WELLS,
  "*August 15th*, 1866.

"'Upon what pleasant slope or sunny field,
sweet, unforgotten Girl, are you delaying?' So
wrote Barry Cornwall forty years ago, not to your
humble correspondent, but to a lady, Miss Jane
——,* with whom he was desperately in love, and
now so writes his wife to Nina Lehmann.

"I have news of you from Mrs. Benzon, who
writes to me from the neighbourhood of Dunkeld—
where I once was. I well remember the Inn where,
upon my asking the Waiter what caused the dis-
agreeable smell in the sitting-room, he quietly
replied, 'Dead mice'! I sat up the whole night to
watch by my Adelaide, who was so nervous about
mice that unless I had done so she would have had
no sleep. We afterwards went to Glenfeschie, and
remained at Kinrara for weeks.

* The missing name is Gape, as will be seen from a subsequent
letter.

" And are you quite well, my dear, and happy away from home ? We left London in a great hurry. Dr. Quain said Edith must go, so we threw medicine to the dogs and came here. We were joined in a fortnight by my husband, and have now been here since the 23rd June. We have had some pleasant people in the Hotel, and have gossiped away the hours in a lovely garden under some cherry trees. Of course we had a nice young man, an Hussar officer, who certainly would have died of ennui had he not made our acquaintance. We sit in the garden all the morning, dine at half-past two, read and write a very little, and at five Edith on a donkey and I on foot ascend the Hills. I am good for six or seven miles, * and we come home at eight, very glad of our tea. One day is so like another that I begin to understand how prison life passes so quickly. I have a charming note from Mr. Chorley. He has been across the water to Boulogne, and is now at Gad's Hill. I have also a letter from Mr. Dickens, who really seems to like my husband's book, which was to have been dedicated to Mr. Forster, but Payne the bookseller has supprest it ; he having had a dispute with Mr. Forster. Bryan has remonstrated with him, and he replies, ' I have a right to do what I like with my own ' ! Of course my husband and Mr. Forster are equally angry. At present Mr. Forster is staying with Lord Lytton of Knebworth. I have a note from Mr. Sullivan, who has set Adelaide's

* Mrs. Proctor was very nearly sixty-six years old.

words ' Hush ! ' to music for Madame Dolby. We are expecting Mr. Kinglake here for a few days, and Mr. Collins promises, but I have no faith in his ever coming. It is a pleasant dream. We hope to go to Fryston this autumn, and to visit the Goldsmids; as usual they have taken a place for a year belonging to Lord Digby, I think, called Newnham Paddox, near Rugby. Of course, Rencome is not done. Will it ever be? And now enough of ourselves.

"My dear, I do not want you to write to me—I only wanted to tell you I had not forgotten you nor your husband, nor how good you both have always been to me.

"And the Highgate home: is it finished? We have *no* books—the second volume of 'My Novel' is at present my intellectual food, and very good food it is; only I should like the first.

"I read the marriage of your sister in the *Pall Mall*. . . . Browning is in Normandy . . . with his sister, who is going to live with him.

"I wish I could write you a letter—a mixture of Horace Walpole—as far as scandal goes, and . . . as far as love; you must fill up that blank as you like.

"My love to your husband.—Your affectionate friend,

"ANNE B. PROCTER.

" 32, Weymouth Street will always find me.

" Edith and my husband send their love."

The Chorley referred to in this and the next letter was Henry Fothergill Chorley, the musical critic of the *Athenæum*. Fryston was Lord Houghton's place in Yorkshire.

"32, WEYMOUTH STREET, PORTLAND PLACE,
" *Feb. 24th,* 1867.

" MY DEAR NINA,—You no doubt picture to yourself your friends looking all handsome, well dressed, and engaged in a continual round of delight, poets at our feet, painters longing to paint us. Nothing of the sort. Half the people have colds and some influenza; and altho' the prospect of Lent has given us some parties, they have not been worth much. I went on Valentine's Day to Mr. Chorley's. Only Peeresses dined, with a few men to do the agreeable. I found only the women and Chorley. Lady Molesworth in a *red velvet* jacket. Each of the ladies, six in number, found a Valentine upon her plate—a poem written by Chorley. He never treated me in that way. Sullivan played, and there was a whist-table. I shall always go, but people will not go to see others play at whist. About six people came in the evening. People are not easy to get; for instance, eighty folks came to me last Wednesday. They had only the free use of their tongues, and they were content. On Wednesday, 27th, I am again at home. Mrs. Benzon was poorly, and Mr. Frederick Lehmann writes me a note about a white tie! If he had come he would have made the acquaintance of Matthew Arnold. Dante

Rossetti came early, and we had a nice long talk together. My husband was as bright as possible, and chirped about amongst the young ladies. Charles Collins is no better. He still keeps his bed. Wilkie, of course, did not come. He had dined out, and had smoked; so, altho' some men who had dined at the same house came, he did not. Saturday, 23rd, he was off to Paris. I tried to frighten him about Charles Collins, but in vain. . . . Your admirer, Mr. Forster, is away at present. Macready and his wife have been at Queen's Gate House for a week, and a great bore they have been. He is grown old, fat, and stupid. Have you read Swinburne's poems? They are charming; a very few, perhaps six, not readable. One, a Ballad of Burdens, is perhaps the finest, and a Hymn to Proserpine beyond my powers of praise.

"Yesterday was like summer; we wanted parasols, and sat without fires. To-day it rains, and is cold and dull. . . . I am sorry you do not send your two boys to some boarding-school. You make such a great sacrifice in leaving England that it is a pity to let anything interfere with your recovery. I am so nervous myself that I cannot bear the noise and restlessness of children beyond a certain time. We have had all our dresses sloped away and look like extinguishers; but I have had a short dress made. Petticoat and sleeves and upper part of body blue corded silk, then over it a short black satin skirt, the whole trimmed with black lace and bugle trimming. I assure you it looks very well indeed.

I have copied out for you a list of the people who were here at my first party, and will also send you a list of the second. For small people should not attempt anything after Easter. I had the front drawing-room door taken off and a piece of net nailed across. It looked pretty and made it cool. The C.-J.* had dined at Chorley's. Millais tells me he has several pictures that will be ready for the R.A. Wilkie tells me his play ' Armadale' will be in *five* acts—last a whole evening. If it is a success in Paris it will be played here in England, and how badly ! How rich you and Mr. Lehmann will be—you, who have always your house full, and where the wine flows like a river, must be saving a fortune.

" I shall stop now ; perhaps Browning will tell me some news. None. He talked only of what the maids call *his-self*. . . . What an affair Cole, C.B., has made of the French Exhibition ! You will have heard what Bismarck said, speaking of the various advantages countries had had—Russia one thing, Prussia another. He gave France the Exhibition. Mrs. Cole and the Miss Coles have lodging and food provided for them by us, in fact.

" Your sister looked so pretty at our house !

" I am ashamed of my stupid letter, but I have done my best.—Yours aff.,

" ANNE B. PROCTER.

" B. C. sends his love."

* Sir Alexander Cockburn.

"MY DEAR NINA,—My mind is wonderfully relieved by hearing so good a report of the great Darling. I am now thinking of her hair.

" Yesterday I saw Hullah ; he has been at the Festival, Worcester, and says that it is impossible to speak too highly of A. Sullivan's ' Prodigal Son.' It is so fresh and so full of the deepest feeling. Sims Reeves sang to perfection. It is an excellent subject. It is sure to be given in London, so let us go and hear it.

" I am reading ' The Vicar of Bulhampton.' It is excellent, but one has read it all before. Edith and B. C. have both got very bad colds. B. C. has had a Seidlitz Powder at nine ; tea, egg, and buttered toast at ten ! . . .

" We have had such droll letters about the harmonium. Here is one. It was offered for three pounds ten shillings :

" ' The Rev. Wm. Allport Leighton will be obliged by being informed whether the harmonium is in good condition, and how long has it been used ? What is the *very* lowest price ? Would a large musical box playing four tunes (in mahogany)—viz. " Here's a health," " Mad Jem," " Pray Goody," and " Rondo Italien," be taken in exchange ? And who is to pay the carriage ? '

" I have copied his letter exactly. No wonder my three darlings joined the Catholic Church. This

is the first time anything he ever wrote was copied.
It ought to play ' Foolish William.'

"Yesterday we had a young friend of my girls
to spend the day. She is French, and when they
were children came for two shillings an hour to
speak French with them. They have always
looked after her a little. She is now married to
an actor — has two children. He is hired at
Drury Lane. They have a lodging in Alfred
Place, two pair of stairs. You know what that
means in London. Without meaning to complain, she gives one such dismal insights into
life. The husband's health is very delicate. She
said, 'He is not strong. When he carries my
eldest girl, two years old, the large drops pour
down his face! We have such poor Cooking!
He's very good, only cares for potatoes, and
they never boil them enough.' If it were you,
you would boil them, and if it was me I would
try; but what I call the half-gentlewoman is such
a failure. . . .

"My love to your Frederick, and never forget
that I love you. Our house looks so fresh and
clean; only, tradespeople will call and lean their
backs against the clean paint.—Your affectionate
old admirer,

"A. B. PROCTER.

"I only put A.; perhaps it is Adolphus who
writes, or Arthur. Nourish the fond delusion that
it is a coat without the petti."

Here follows a letter to my father:

"ESSINGTON'S HOTEL, MALVERN WELLS,
"*August 2nd*, 1870.

"MY DEAR MR. LEHMANN,—I have a way of thinking of you and your dear Wife, and now in this beautiful quiet place you are more than usually in my thoughts. I know that you must be anxious about this war in which many of those you love must be engaged. I think of little else. I suppose that being so far away from the business of life fighting seems like murder. Tell me what you think about this quarrel. You perhaps do not know that my forefathers were German—I trace my descent from Scheffer the Painter, and bear his Crest, *a greyhound*. At the time when foreigners were persecuted in England we altered our name to Skepper. I proved my relation to the great man to the satisfaction of Watts of the British Museum. After this piece of family history you will see that I must be for Germany. How far my love for the family Lehmann completes this we will not inquire. And Nina—where is she ? I pass a very quiet life here, being almost entirely out of doors. Edith is carried up on a Donkey, and the old lady is still good for six or eight miles. We have a pretty garden half-way up one of these hills, where we sit and work or read under some Cherry-trees. We rise at seven and go to bed at ten. Edith is wonderfully well, and we are counting the days that are left with great care. The

Hills are beautiful and the gorse is in full bloom. The Hotel is a quiet little place; we can only receive four sets of people.   We are mainly clergymen and Doctors — not your fashionable London Doctor who makes love to his patients, but the old one, who only took your money—not your heart.

"And Wilkie?   No, I will not speak to you of him, because you will then revenge yourself by writing about some wretched woman.

"On the 12th we go home.   My husband is very dull; altho' he likes quiet, still he misses the small excitement my presence gives his home.

"The people here are very simple.   Some complaint was made at Grt. Malvern about the small quantity of water furnished to each house, one man saying that the water cost as much as beer would.   A member of the Council said what he advised was—not to dig for wells or bring some water into the town, but *put your trust in Providence!*

"The Princess Christian is here, and went to a Flower Show.   They wished to fire some cannon or guns, but having neither, borrowed the blacksmith's anvil and beat a welcome on it.

"I shall be so much pleased if you will write me a few lines, telling me about yourself, your wife, and your children.   I have been thinking of Mamie [Dickens] so much; she wrote me word they would leave Gad's Hill on the 1st.*   That making a new

* Charles Dickens died on June 9th of this year.

home is dismal work. I don't think I ever can make you believe how much I like my shawl. I have made many friends (enemies) unhappy and jealous.—Your grateful and affec. old friend,

"ANNE B. PROCTER."

In the summer of 1872 the Procters rented the Vicarage at Highgate. Our own house in South-wood Lane, from which we were, however, tem-porarily absent, was little more than a mile away. Barry Cornwall was now eighty-five.

"*August*, 14*th*, 1872.
"THE VICARAGE, HIGHGATE, N.W.

"MY DEAREST NINA,—I want to have a little talk with you, and altho' I have wanted that for a long while I must write to-day, because yesterday I walked to Woodlands and sat for nearly two hours in that lovely garden. As in all charming homes, 'My Lady is in Scotland, Ma'am; she required a change. And my Lord is taking some German baths.' It seemed to me as I sat there that life could offer nothing better than to live there. Fluff [the cat] in Edith's lap was so happy. She occa-sionally opened her eyes, took a look, and went off to sleep again. Edith had a large flat hat on, and it seemed as if Fluff thought it was you. Your garden is a blaze of colour. I felt sad as I sat there. It seems to me always melancholy being in a place without the friends who made it warm and bright.

Martin was most polite, and showed me round the Kitchen Garden. We looked at the Bees and the Pigs. It is a great treat to us to sit in your garden, and we shall go there very often. We took *three white* roses, but no beast appeared. Perhaps no beauty either. Martin showed me the young gentlemen's sitting-room—Princes' room—and yet I am wrong, for our Queen has no taste.

"My poor husband enjoys himself greatly here. He is taken out every day in a chair drawn by a Donkey, and he also sits in the garden. I forget whether you know this house. It is very comfortable, but we have frightful green papers in each room, and felt carpets—all patched! The price is eight guineas a week! We go back to Weymouth St. on the 12th Septr., and then Edith and I are going for a holiday somewhere.

"I have already had a short one—at Knebworth; but the society was not very congenial—first six women—and three men.—There was a Miss ——, very common; all her discourse was about inferior people and things. It is curious how one vulgar person drags conversation down. Lord Lytton and Mr. Forster both tried in vain to raise us, but after a little light we dropped down into dull, stupid, degrading gossip. My only happy moment was when Miss —— told Lord Lytton that people thought he ought to put clothing on the statues in the grounds! Miss —— has given Ld. L. a lovely old white satin quilt. He had better pay for it, and not pay through his friends. I had some quiet talk with Ld. L.; but as he is deaf and wished to discuss the question of what truth there was in the report that Mr. X. was a lover of Miss Y., I was nervous and afraid of being overheard.

"I have since I was here had many letters to write—one to my husband's oldest friend, a Mr. Kelsall. He listened to and advised B. C. when he first published his 'Dramatic Scenes,' the best thing I think B. C. ever did. Kelsall is now blind, and his wife wrote to beg for something to cheer his darkness. Lately has died B. C.'s first love— *Jane Gape.* He has dedicated his 2nd book to her, ' A Sicilian Story.'* He had forgotten her, and would have denied the fact, only the dedication remains. I think *we* are more faithful. Mr. Hayward has been at Lord Lytton's, and was polite enough to write and express his regrets to me for not meeting me there. Lady Molesworth came to see me to have some talk about poor Courtenay's death, but I had left Weymouth St. for this rural retreat. This garden is very pretty—we have a strong atmosphere of divinity. Bishops face you and learned D.D.'s look at your back. There is an excellent Library—all the new poets, Jean Ingelow, Trench, &c.

"Write to me, my dear, and for once follow my example and tell me all about yourself. My best love to Frederick.—Your affect. old friend,

"ANNE B. PROCTER."

* Published 1821.

In 1874 Barry Cornwall died, in his eighty-seventh year:—

"*October 4th*, 1874.

"DEAREST NINA,—My dear husband died at a quarter past four, very quietly—in fact, he fell asleep.—Yours affectionately,

"ANNE B. PROCTER."

"QUEEN ANNE'S MANSIONS, S.W.,
"*February* 11*th*, 1880.

"MY DEAREST NINA,—I had no good of you yesterday, and my cold and cough are so much worse to-day that there is no hope of my getting to Berkeley Square. I wanted to talk to you about Lady Charlotte Elliot. My husband once had some correspondence with her. She sent him her writings, and he was charmed with them. There was a notice of her in the *Athenæum*, and by that I learnt she was 'Stella.' I had forgotten this, but soon rubbed up my memory.

"And the dear old friends . . . one never replaces them. There is nothing like 'Do you remember . . . ?' As we grow older the doors close over old memories, and one has no one to talk to of those we loved.

"Did I tell you I had seen Mr. Sartoris twice? We sit and talk of Byron, Shelley, and Trelawney, and we are both thinking of *Her*.* One feels with

* Adelaide Kemble, the younger daughter of Charles Kemble, married Edward John Sartoris in 1843. Before her

M.   N

a man more restraint than with a woman. I have not courage enough to bring up the subject of his wife.

"It was such a relief when Lady Goldsmid said to me, after some feeble efforts about the weather, 'Now let us talk of Frank.' . . .

"It is a curious way we live. There are people whom I hardly care for, and we meet three or four times a week, and you whom I love so dearly I so seldom see !—Yours affectionately,

"ANNE B. PROCTER."

In 1882 we had taken Dunnichen, near Forfar, for the shooting season. My father was temporarily abroad, and Mrs. Procter, who, with her daughter Edith, was on a visit to us, thus writes to him :

"DUNNICHEN,
"September 7th, 1882.

"MY DEAR MR. LEHMANN,—It was a great disappointment to me to find that you are not coming here. I had some idea of commencing an action for 'breach of promise'; but having taken Counsel's opinion, R. Lehmann, Esq., I find I have no case such as a Court would recognise, although morally I have one.

"As I have not given any fee, perhaps the said opinion is not of any value.

marriage she had gained great fame as a singer. Her delightful book, "A Week in a French Country House," first appeared in the *Cornhill*, and was reprinted as a volume in 1867. She died in 1879.

"It is ungrateful in me to make any complaint, for we are so happy here, and every one is so kind to us. Still, 'Man never is but always to be blessed.'

"The weather is perfect. We sit in the garden or drive about in the Brake. I and the dear wife have long talks of 'Those days that are no more,' and your children look and listen to me as if I were some Antediluvian animal.

"I have many faults, but I am not ungrateful. I do not forget all you have done for me—kind welcomes, happy days, beautiful gifts—the most precious things I have I owe to you.—Your affectionate old friend,

"ANNE B. PROCTER.

"Since writing the above I have been out. Truth compels me to add the Wind is cold. It would have been nice had you come here on Monday the 11th. A. B. Procter, aged 82! I do not confess this generally."

Mrs. Procter was to live six years more, enjoying life and friendship and all her delightful memories to the last.

CHAPTER XII.

The Peculiarities of Martha Jones—A Cornish Man—A Fortnight with the Old Testament—Noah's Grandmother —A Drive to Irun—Maria—A Mute Inglorious Authoress —The Respectfulness of Martha Jones.

MANY of the letters which I have already published refer to my mother's stay in the South of France in 1866 and 1867. She had gone to Biarritz in the late summer of the former year, accompanied by my father. Later on he had established her in Pau, and had then returned home. The following letters from my mother to my father describe an excursion which she made in February, 1867, to Biarritz and St Jean de Luz. Her companion was her maid, Martha Jones, a gaunt, big-boned spinster with a shambling gait and a face severely marked with smallpox. The Chorley who is referred to was H. F. Chorley, the musical critic of the *Athenæum*, whose journalistic campaign against Madame Schumann and the music of her husband had created a certain amount of sensation. I shall have more to say about him in a later part of this series.

"BIARRITZ,
"*Wednesday Evening,* 13*th February.*

"Here I am safe and sound and miles and miles
better, if you know what that is. I came here on
Monday in time for dinner, of which I partook in
company with some depressed compatriots and one
gaunt elderly French couple. Not a word uttered.
I couldn't stand the depressed compatriots, so at
yesterday's dinner I took my place beside the
French couple, and boldly plunged into a conversation, to their great surprise, in their own tongue,
which was listened to with a melancholy respect by
the D. C.'s. Gaunt French couple were delighted
to find at last a sort of tame and acclimatised
animal in the great British travelling menagerie of
wild ones. Yesterday was a glorious day—blue,
crisp, sparkling, the sea thundering up in its own
particular grand Biarritz way on the lovely golden
sands. I was out sniffing, imbibing, revelling all
day nearly. The depressed ones do not go on the
shore. I see them wandering listlessly up and
down the deserted *magasin-fermé* street though with
Murrays and silk umbrellas. I had the shore all,
literally all to myself, and I felt my heart swell, as
I went along, with the sort of bounding elasticity
one feels on again returning to the great glorious,
life-giving, life-taking monster. I am a new being
already. I feel I have had no air in Pau. What
is the use of having one's lungs mended and fitted
for the proper reception and circulation of God's air
if there is none to circulate? Oh, how I breathe

in this healthy, strong, capital sea-breeze and bless
Heaven for it! I have got so enterprising, and am
driving into nooks and corners of Biarritz I never
penetrated before. It is a *glorious* place at this
season. I do it full justice now. Although we
stayed such a short time at the hotel here, the
servants welcomed me like an old friend, and shook
hands with the chastest of her sex (Martha). They
have given me a dear sweet little room on the *rez de
chaussée* as you enter at the front, with a window
looking over the sea towards, of course, the Villa
Eugénie. This and Martha's modest chamber cost
six francs a day. I have breakfast *dans ma chambre*
and dinner at the table-d'hôte, which is now in the
Maison Rouge, the Hôtel de France being shut up
in winter. I am able to eat once more, *and to sleep*,
which is a faculty that had singularly decayed in
Pau. As I have Martha for my sole companion
(not companion of my soul, though) here, I am at
present engaged in trying to elevate her mind by
instilling little historical and scientific facts (all as
nearly in one syllable as possible, not to alarm her
unnecessarily), but she is disappointing, very
disappointing. She has one answer and one alone
to everything I tell her. She brings it out alike
when I mildly try to prepare her for the beautiful
annular eclipse there will be next month, or when
I simply call upon her to observe that the nearer we
approach Spain or Italy the flatter become the roofs.
'Oh my, good gracious me, yes, 'm.' To-day I
hired a *petite voiture* for a drive to St. Jean de Luz,

and to give her a little pleasure I took her with
me. I instilled a little on the road at first, but the
idiotic ' Oh my's ' reduced me to silence at last.
I felt they were intended at once as an admission
of her own ignorance, and an implied compli-
mentary surprise at my astonishing amount of
information. One thing was delicious, and I take
great credit to myself for not exploding on the
spot. I saw her gazing reflectively at the side of
the road several times. At last she awoke me from
dreams of past and future to present by saying
timidly, ' If you please, 'm, is this the road to
Canton, and is it far, 'm ? '   ' Not the direct road,
Martha,' I said with a perfect and highly-bred
gravity upon which I congratulate myself, ' and
I'm afraid it's rather far.' ' I think, 'm, it can't be
so very far off, as I see the name on the mile-posts
all along the road, 'm.' Oh, Doochen, you see it,
don't you? I didn't even smile as I explained what
this deceptive and misleading post meant, and I am
proud of my manners. I enjoyed my drive and
little excursion to St. Jean de Luz immensely. I
fell in love again with the quiet, quaint, deserted
old place. I looked over great barracks, *maisons à
louer*, for the fun of the thing ; went through
Moorish-looking courts and halls, and up staircases
with old carved wood balustrades, up which Noah's
immediate relatives must have walked when the
Ark anchored at St Jean de Luz, as I am positively
prepared to assert it did. One lodging struck me
from the outside. Above a pottery shop, where an

old grey-headed, spotlessly-linened man was sitting with his cat beside him (both lineal descendants from the patriarch just mentioned, and the pair of cats he had on board at the time), I saw two open windows with snowy-white curtains waving in the breeze. 'Martha, I want to live there. Let's go in directly and see about it.' The polite old man took us up into the cleanest of rooms, with a large alcove with a bed in it. 'Martha, I see myself at that window with my worsted work on that table, don't you?' 'Oh my, good gracious me, yes, 'm.' At the other end of the clean little passage was the cleanest, the most old-fashioned kitchen in the world; a large old fashioned casement-window, deep in, with a seat looking on to a little garden; an alcove with a bed at one side. 'Martha, do you see yourself under that flowered coverlet?' 'Oh my, &c., me, 'm, I think I do.' I very nearly settled with the old man on the spot, but I didn't, and just took his name in writing. It was the most deliciously antique-looking place, just after my heart, with a squint of the sea if taken with the left eye, and not a soul to be seen in the street. Martha says she would cook for me and for herself, and she thinks 'it do look so like you, mum,' and she likes it immensely herself. And there's a market twice a week and fresh air at a moderate expense, and I'll make up my mind and let you know. In the meantime, good-night, dear love.

"Your own

"N. L."

"BIARRITZ,
"*Friday*, 15*th February.*

"I told you how I entered into conversation with the French couple at the table d'hôte here. Yesterday I thought I would try a terribly silent oppressed-looking compatriot who sat next to me—a pink man with a bald head and spectacles, and beard in the first stage of sprouting bristle. So I said in my sweetest voice, 'Isn't the sea magnificent at Biarritz, sir!'" I was startled by the surly abruptness of the answer, 'Nothing to Cornwall. Ever been in Cornwall?' 'No, never,' said I timidly. 'Thought not. You'd think nothing of this if you had. *I'm* a Cornish man.' 'Oh, of course,' I said, and not another word passed. *Of course* he didn't bow when I rose from table. Rude brutes these middle-class British are. On the other hand, I get on charmingly with my French friends. However, to-day is my last dinner in this bear-garden, and to-morrow hey for St. Jean and solitude. I hug the idea of my ark to my heart. I like the notion of living, moving, and having my being in the midst of Noah's relations. A fortnight with the Old Testament! What a novel thing! I'll write you at once from there, and describe it all to you."

"29, RUE NEUVE,
"ST. JEAN DE LUZ,
"*Saturday Evening.*

"Well, dearest, here we are, Martha and I. In *such* an ark. Oh, if you could see us! If you could see my old spotless landlord, who lives alone here with his servant.   His servant, did I say? She is no other than Noah's grandmother, whom he must have left behind when he sailed from this port.   She is much too old, much too withered, much too bony, much too brown, much much too tough *ever* to die.   Consequence is that, of course, she never has died, and is here still in the—well, no, I can't say in the flesh, for she has none, but in the bone.   It is impossible to convey to you any idea at all of this old old wifie, and the old old mannie, and the queer, queer kitchen, where just now I went inside the great chimney, and looking up it, saw *a star* quivering in the sky!   I take my meals in that chimney, Martha cooking them before my eyes.   I am revelling in bacon, sausages, eggs, and tea,—purchases I made myself, getting a dozen splendid eggs, a pound of 'lovely bacon as ever I saw, 'm,' half-a-dozen enormous oranges, and a great thick sausage, for two francs and a half.   I do all my writing and embroidery in the salon at one end of the passage, all my eating and my knitting in the kitchen at the other.   Out of the salon— no, in the salon, is a large alcove with my bed in it.   In the kitchen are two alcoves—one that of the chaste Martha, the other to be slept in by the revered ancestress of our first authenticated mariner.   To complete the queerness, this ancient person is a Castilian, and can't speak French, but understands a little Italian, and I positively have to stutter away to her in a mixture of Italian and

broken French, with a dash of Béarnais, which I
am in hopes she takes for Basque, a language she
is at home in.   It is all too funny, and I am in
a dream.   It's like Washington Irving's hero
reversed,—I have fallen asleep and awoke, not
years, but centuries *back!*   The shore is most
beautiful, most picturesque, enclosed as it is with
these dear blue-brown mountains, which look so
near me, I feel as if I could walk in a few steps
to their rugged sides.   Since the second day after I
came to Biarritz this horrid stifling south wind has
been blowing.   I have no appetite, of course, but
whenever this wind changes and the air gets its life
back to it, I shall revive.   There are six nice cats
in this house, a great comfort.   I think I must go
to bed now; I feel ' my legs is *that* wearit.'   We
drove from Biarritz this morning in a calèche, with
a sweet postilion all in scarlet and silver, with rings
on his fingers and bells on his toes. . . .

"*Monday Morning.*—You see I have missed a
day.   I wasn't in a writing mood yesterday, that's
the fact.   I took too long a walk for that, but it
did me good in other ways, and I slept like a top.
I have 'taken up' St. Jean de Luz, and mean to
swear by it for the future, and pity people who
haven't seen it, as Chorley did about Palermo.   The
situation is much more beautiful and picturesque
than Biarritz, being so near these mountains, which
seem to protect the poor old place.   The bay itself
is lovely, finished off at one point by a ruin on the
cliff, and at the other, which darts far out into

the sea, by the round fort of Socoa. Wherever you go, the grand peak of Haya goes—before you, beside you, behind you. You never lose sight of its triple-crowned head. Yesterday Martha and I walked to this fort along the shore—a goodish walk. In fact, I was out for four hours. It is impossible to converse with Martha, she is so soon surprised (always out of compliment to me, as it were), and she asks such idiotic questions. How can a woman exist on so little brain? I believe she is of the frog species, and would live quite as well without her head as with it. There's not an English soul in the place but ourselves, and we are the first of that great nation that the old man has ever had in his house. This perhaps accounts for the fact that, the first day I was here, he came softly up the stairs in his white canvas shoes every quarter of an hour or so to gaze at me—never speaking—and when I looked round inquiringly he only said, '*Bon zour, Madame; ce n'est rieng,*' and went down again. The old wife did the same to Martha in the kitchen, only she wasn't silent, but poured out a volley of mixed Basque and Castilian, which Martha declares she understood; but, of course, to the frog-brain one language is the same as another. Whenever I stopped yesterday on my way, to ask the peasants where I was, &c., they only shook their brown heads, and showed their white teeth (if they were young, otherwise they had none to show). Not a word of French can they speak. One girl, very well dressed though, and evidently the higher class of peasant, said, '*Ah,*

non comprend français,' for all the world just the
answer Martha would have given. Martha insists
upon it they all understand English. She says it
in a mysterious way, as if they had some diabolical
motive in concealing the fact."

"ST. JEAN DE LUZ,

"*Friday.*

"I went to Spain to-day. I hired a sarcophagus
and was driven there, namely, to Irun, in company
with Martha. I seized the opportunity of enlarg-
ing her mind 'by travel'; but to everything that
was grand, she said it was lovely; and what I found
majestic and stern she thought 'eavenly. I solaced
myself by saying at times, 'Idiotic,' of course not
aloud, and could still, to her, bear aloft a smiling
countenance.

"I liked Irun, the queer high-climbing, narrow
street, where I priced in my sweetest Italian-
Spanish a baby's cloak (so like me, eh?), and
sighed because I had no baby to put it on!

"Up the street we walked into the country, where
we diverged to have a more extensive view of the
dear mountains. The lane would have been yellow
with primroses, had it not been purple with violets
and scarlet with berries! I gathered what Miss
Jones called 'an 'eavenly bookie,' which I bore
home with me. We walked about for two hours.
To the left, Fuentarabia sat quaintly on a peak that
went sharp into the sea. I got an old man with a
big bunch of keys to let us into the old church,

and he drew all the curtains aside from the altars, and showed us the horrid distorted figures of the Madonna and Jesus, and doves, and hearts with things through them, for the modest sum of five-pence. Everybody stared at us. Every balcony had a face—two faces—many faces—staring kindly at the strangers—the mistress with her dress short, the maid with hers trailing in the dust. We left St. Jean de Luz at twelve, and were home about five. I had heard from a shop-woman that she had two English ladies lodging with her, and so, after I read my papers, I handed them in for these ladies, thinking they would be *très contentes* to see the *ournaux anglais*. So as I came back, there was Mrs. L'Estrange, the English lady, come to thank me, and we had a long chat. She is here for the winter. One other English family is here also. She loves the place as I do, and can't think why it has never been found out as a winter residence. That is my surprise too. She is oldish—blue eyes, with the colours run; a general air of wiggishness over her head,—attire neat but simple—dress in one syllable. Hoped, *oh*, how I saw she hoped I was a fixture here for months, and begged me to call on all the people, that being the *mode* for the stranger, till I dashed her to the ground by the fell assertion I was here for one week longer only ! . . . At Irun we saw all the women come from the sea with baskets of fresh anchovies on their heads, of which fact they were good enough to inform us in that fearfully shrill cry you know of as connected with ' *sardines fraiches* ' at Biarritz.   I bought a great lot of them, almost leaping with life, and brought them home, and M. and I have just had them for supper, done like whitebait, and excellent."

"ST. JEAN DE LUZ, *Monday.*

" It was very good of you and R. to find so much to be amused at in my letter to her, but I can't remember having said anything especially funny. The awful difficulty to me is to write different things to all my friends, and I don't always succeed. I have about a dozen to twenty letters to write, all in pretty much the same set.   It harrows my very soul to think of it sometimes.   I wish people would consider one letter from me an equivalent for three from them ; but you can't get people to do that.   I have written again to Tuck,* with the purpose of prevailing on her to bring the Chief to her feet by singing at his house the day after to-morrow.   She can't refuse, as I have asked her to do it *for my sake*.   And even if she is nervous, she must be encouraged into going on till she grows inspired.   Good Lord ! when I remember one day Mrs. —— shouting and howling at Miss Gabriel's like a whole family in the middle of a street, the father with one leg and the baby in his arms, the mother with the other three clinging to her petti-coats, and *all singing*,—when I remember this scene, and poor Mrs. —— growing crimson, scarlet, and magenta in the face with the exertion, and people

* Mrs. Rudolf Lehmann, my mother's sister.

thinking they thought it ' grand,' and when I compare our Tuck ! ! !

" My dear, you should see the touching passion
the poor old Spanish woman, the hard-worked servant sixty years of age, has taken for me. It is
funny, and quite affects me. She flies to do what
I want—is never happy but when she is doing
something for me—is so careful to have my fire
good when I come home after walking, and is so
grateful if I am pleased with what she does. I
don't understand above two words an hour of what
she pours out to me in her affection. *Buenos—
hermosa*—such words I catch as a drowning man
does a straw, and then I say ' *Si, si,*' and she is
quite satisfied. At the market I bought her two
dreadful coloured prints in frames for a franc each,
on the Virginian System as to subject, of course,
and I think if I had given her an entire outfit of
clothes or an annuity payable quarterly, she
wouldn't have been so grateful as for these wretched
daubs. To be sure, I bought them on purpose for
her, and carried them home myself (like Mama,
eh ?), and presented them. Yesterday being Sunday, and the news of these wonderful acquisitions
to poor old Maria's little picture-gallery having got
abroad, the house was crowded with her friends,
who had come to see them, and *me* if possible!
She never saw an English woman to her knowledge
before, certainly never spoke to one. She has been

twenty-two years with the old man. I gave her five francs this morning, for she has done so much for me and Martha, but she was almost indignant. However, I said she must buy something with it to wear for my sake, which soothed her. She has just knocked at my door and entered to show me a beautiful *mouchoir* for the head, and a pair of black cotton gloves that she has bought for the money. She went to the funeral of a Spanish friend of eighty-five the other day, and everything she had on was forty years old, the black dress, the black woollen mantilla she wore on her head—all, all had been worn by the poor soul before I was born, and were her *best yet*. How refreshing it is to find still such innocent unspoilt peasant natures. She told Martha she prayed for me night and day, and would do so all her life."

" Still St. Jean, *Wednesday Evening.*

" I'm disappointed at getting no letter from you for two days. Perhaps I shall not get any more from you directed here. Well, that will be made up to me when I return to my sheepfold, which I do *really* on Saturday. We thought it a pity not to stay the two weeks out, and the sea smelt so delicious, and looked so glorious after I had arranged to leave it, that I couldn't resist it and gave way. I never saw such waves as there are here. They come rolling in slowly and majestically, and when near the beach grow an immense height : then they curl over, and you seem to look into a great deep, clear, green cavern, when over they go, tumbling in a magnificent mass of white spray. Oh, how I long to have you here sometimes! how you would enjoy it—but most of all you would enjoy the downs, away at the end of the beach, high up on the rocks that suddenly pile themselves up. Oh, what a walk that is—miles and miles—all along the cliff—undulating beautiful downs covered with primroses and (scentless) violets, looking so simple and innocent, as if they were not a bit afraid of the monster that was roaring and dashing amongst the rocks below, and whose spray positively wets them at times, I daresay. When I go there I never see a soul but myself, and I go wandering along till I find some smooth secluded spot with a rock or two to shelter and seat me, and there I sit with a book for pretence, but my thoughts and dreams for reality —and they go far far away northwards, and I forget where I am. Sometimes I take my knitting with me (such a pretty sock for you), and ah, me! thoughts of the future wearer of that sock are knit into every stitch I do, with a stitch here and there for the children, and sometimes a whole row for Woodlands. There is a whole history of future love and hope, and all the sunshine of *home* knitted into these socks; so wear them advisedly! I had a letter to-day from Chorley. I enclose it for your strictly private inspection, then burn it. Poor fellow! you must only smile at his morbid vanity, and not be angry at it. I have answered it, and will quote bits to you that are answers to some of his statements. Of Madame Schumann, and of her admirers dropping him, I say I don't believe for a minute people that like Madame S. would give him up or like him less—why should they? There is myself—' to me there is something grand in that woman, something grand in her playing,' but that would not influence my opinion of him. Then I say I rather think Amelia is hurt with him for never calling since she came to town. She has never said so to me, but I imagine it. As to Mrs. ——, I say, 'Oh dear, how ill it would make me to have Mrs. —— singing to me through an open door; I wouldn't even like it through a shut one.'

. . . . .

"I am sorry poor Chorley demeans himself to so much unmanly spite sometimes; but such is my pity for him and my old-standing feeling of affection and tolerance, that I never for a moment bear him a grudge; and for my sake be good, be lenient, to the lonely, much-forsaken, affection-seeking (and so seldom-finding) old man. Think, he is going on for sixty now, and only by his dinners can he gain or hold for an instant the least regard. To me all his vanity is most pathetic. So, for my sake, I say it again, be good to him, and pay him some little attention which will make him think you care a bit for him. Will you?"

"St. Jean de Luz, 28*th* *February*.
"(Oh, I wonder is it leap year?)

"I should have been heart-broken if I had not heard from you to-day, because after to-day all my

letters go to Pau, I think—*Pave*, as my old Spanish
woman calls it, where 'Los Ninos' are. I
positively begin to understand a bit of Spanish, for
I found out very soon that *Castilianos* means the
Spanish language, not that the person comes from
Castile. Well, to-morrow is my last day in this
charming solitude. Dear me, if I were an old-
fashioned German lady, I should be writing such
wonderful sentiments spun out of my inner consciousness assisted by my outer surroundings. I
might then have become a classic, like Zimmer-
mann & Co. The fact is, I have had a try at an
article, as I think the place ought to be known as a
winter residence, but the letters I have to write
and do write take it all out of me. I wager
George Eliot and all those great writers don't
write letters to their fifty friends as I do. My
brain and my will and my patience get exhausted,
and I can no more. I am a mute inglorious
authoress. Amen!

.   .   .   .

"Can you imagine poor pedantic ——'s righteous
horror when Mamie said I played the Arabesque
better than Madame Schumann? But I do. She
doesn't touch it delicately enough. It is too fragile
a thing for her powerful hand, and I say this with
the greatest modesty and the greatest appreciation
of her magnificent playing. Some things which
require no power and no practice suit my slender
fingers better than her grand hammers. But it

would be centuries before a conventional person like —— would dream of such a thing.

.   .   .   .   .   .

" It has been pouring steadily since two o'clock. I shall pay my farewell visit to Mrs. L'Estrange to-morrow. She will miss me, as she does love to talk about mineralogy and geology in a tottery sort of way. She never ceases when she once begins, and is one of those old women who call a walk ' a ramble ' and a little boy ' an urchin.' I allowed Martha to sit in my room and read last night while I wrote, and I made the discovery that she is one of those people a century behind their time, who blow their leaves open instead of turning them over. She blew for half-an-hour at one page, and sat on the edge of her chair the whole time, and didn't like having the candle too near her—it looked too familiar. You know the species. I am getting morbid in noticing the small peculiarities of race and character. Adieu.

" Your own N.

" *P.S.*—She also held her book a good distance from her ; it looked more respectful."

CHAPTER XIII.

Of Thackeray I myself cannot even say "*vidi tantum.*" I find, however, the following reference to him in my father's " Reminiscences " :—

" I got my first glimpse of Thackeray in Edinburgh somewhere about the year 1850. He was then at the height of his celebrity, and while he gave a course of readings of 'The Four Georges' he was received with open arms and fêted to the top of his bent by all that remained of the once famous Edinburgh society. Lady Murray, the wife of the Scotch judge of that name, was very fond of music, and they used to invite to their weekly parties all those who were musically or otherwise distinguished in Edinburgh. Owing to the fact that I was a fairish amateur on the violin I was lucky enough to have the *entrée* there, and it was at Lady Murray's that I first met the great novelist. He came after his reading, and remained to supper, at which, I remember, Lord Murray offered him ' a little Hochheimer,' adding, ' What you in England cannot pronounce, and so you call it Hock.' When the party was over I was in the hall with Thackeray, supplying him with a cigar, and on the point of opening the door for our departure, when we were stopped by the following grotesque incident. All the other guests had left before us. We heard whisperings on the landing above. Lord Murray, on hospitable thoughts intent, was evidently consulting his *cara sposa* before inviting the great man to dinner. Heavily old Lord Murray descended the stairs; but before he had got half-way down, or even opened his lips, Thackeray stopped him by exclaiming, ' You are very good, my Lord, but I am unfortunately engaged every day of my stay here.' Then he opened the door, and we left a tableau of dear old Lord Murray speechless on the stairs, looking up at his wife.

"Many years afterwards I used to meet Thackeray in London at the Reform Club and at sundry dinners. He was fond of airing his German, and even went so far as to pun in quasi-German. ' This is really vortrüfflich,' I have heard him call out as he tasted a dish with truffles in it.

" We had many intimate friends in common, but it was never my good fortune to be on very intimate terms with Thackeray himself. He was to have dined with me on the day after he was taken ill, and his daughter, Mrs. Richmond Ritchie, has told me that when she left him on the evening before he died the last words she ever heard him speak were, ' Tell Lehmann.' She has been good enough to give me one of his original sketches to bind up with the *édition de luxe* of his works. It is a water-colour drawing of a very small girl holding in her arms a very large bundle, labelled ' Vanity Fair.' "

My own place at the *Punch* table (the "Mahogany Tree" which Thackeray celebrated in verse) is close by the spot on which he carved the monogram of his initials. The " Mahogany," I may add, is a poetic licence. Deal would be nearer to the truth; but no deal that I ever heard of has been more highly honoured. Impressed with these great initials it may vaunt itself above all the mere. mahoganies that ever were made into tables.

From Thackeray to Lord Houghton the transition is not difficult, for it was Lord Houghton who wrote the noble lines in which Thackeray's claim to a resting-place in Westminster Abbey was vindicated. I quote three stanzas:—

"O gentle Censor of our age!
    Prime master of our ampler tongue!
Whose word of wit and generous page
    Were never wroth except with wrong.

Fielding—without the manner's dross,
    Scott—with a spirit's larger room,
What prelate deems thy grave his loss?
    What Halifax erects thy tomb?

But, maybe, he who so could draw
    The hidden great, the humble wise,
Yielding with them to God's good law,
    Makes the Pantheon where he lies."

Poet, essayist, politician, and man of the world, the friend of all oppressed causes and of all persecuted men, Lord Houghton had warmed both hands before the fire of life. " I am going over to the majority," he said when he was very ill in the year before his death, " and you know I have always preferred the minority." I find in my father's " Reminiscences " the following account of the way in which Sir Alexander Cockburn, the Lord Chief Justice, attempted at a dinner party to browbeat Lord Houghton, who had spoken in defence of the notorious Plaintiff at that time prosecuting his claim to the Tichborne estates :—

" During the progress of the Tichborne trial (*i.e.* the ejectment action before Chief Justice Bovill) Sir Alexander Cockburn dined with me at my house, near Highgate, and Lord Houghton was one of the party. At that time public opinion had begun to go against the Claimant. For dear paradoxical Lord Houghton this was enough : he immediately ranged himself on the other side. On this particular day he came on to me straight from Holly Lodge, where Lady Burdett-Coutts had been giving a garden party. At dinner the conversation, of course, turned upon the Tichborne case, and I remember that Cockburn expressed his opinion very emphatically to the effect that the Claimant was an impostor. Houghton, however, argued upon the other side. Suddenly Cockburn cut him short by saying, 'I should have thought this impossible from anyone with the very meanest intellect.' Houghton paused, apparently overwhelmed, and then replied : 'But surely that was very rude'; upon which Cockburn, glaring fixedly at him, merely added, ' I meant it to be so.'

" We got out of the dining-room somehow, but the incident, as may easily be imagined, did not contribute to the harmony of the evening. Lord Houghton, the most placable and amiable of men, never forgot or forgave the affront, and years afterwards, as he and I were going home together from a pleasant meeting at the Century Club, New York, he spoke of this incident as a proof of Cockburn's ' terrible temper.' "

There is a reference to the Plaintiff in the following letter written by Lord Houghton to my mother :—

"FRYSTON HALL, FERRYBRIDGE,
March 7th, 1872.

"MY DEAR MRS. LEHMANN,—Lady Houghton has handed me your most kind note, and it reminded me of my neglect (just before I fell ill) of the charming one you sent me out of the pleasant-peopled hills of West Scotland. Ever since that time I have been more or less poorly—at one time quite laid up, and only now recovering. I tried London for a few days, but found I was not up either to its work or play. So we do not come up till after Easter. But in the meantime—that is in the Easter holidays—won't you and Mr. Lehmann and the fair Nina be persuaded to pay us a visit

here ?   We are not very far from Woodlands [near Highgate] when you once come down from your garden into the railway, from which I always think I see it as we enter London.   Would you object to meeting the injured and, alas ! unrecognised Plaintiff ?—I am yours and Mr. Lehmann's very truly,
                                        " HOUGHTON."

My own most vivid recollection of Lord Houghton springs from the time when he paid us a visit at Dunnichen in Forfarshire.   Mrs. Procter was with us on the same occasion, and where these conversational protagonists had polished their arms dullness could not exist.   During the day, while we were attempting to secure partridges, Lord Houghton used to drive about the country or saunter in the garden.   After dinner, when the ladies had departed to their beds, he arrayed himself in a voluminous smoking-gown and a red fez, and joined us in the smoking-room, where he kept us all alive with anecdotes and stories drawn from the great storehouse of his experience.   One evening, I well remember, he played an active and brilliant part in helping us to organise and carry through a series of " dumb crambo " performances.   After his visit he wrote to my father :

                    " TILLYFOURIE, ABERDEEN,
                          " Sept. 21, 1882.
    "MY DEAR LEHMANN, — I managed my little journey very well, and crept up here in the gloaming without catching cold.

" I find that some Americans I had been asked to meet had just gone off—the Hays, whom I had known in the States, and a Mr. Clarence King they talk much of. Who did you tell me wrote 'Vice Versâ'? They say here the writer only got £10 for it. Did not Mr. Payn* tell you another story? If you have Mr. Payn's note with its kind message to me in it will you let me have it as an autograph? —With kind regards to your pleasant social group, who were very good to me, I remain, yours very truly,   "HOUGHTON."

In the next letter Lord Houghton refers to his portrait painted by my father's brother:

" FRYSTON HALL, FERRYBRIDGE,
                    Aug. 15*th*, 1883.

"MY DEAR MRS. LEHMANN,—Will you give me a line saying how long you stay in Hampshire? I shall be going westward some time in this month or early in the next, and shall be very glad to spend a day or two with you *en route*. My picture by Mr. Lehmann is said to be a great success. At least he thinks so himself, and I myself as an Artist know when my poetry is at its best.—I am, yours and Lehmann's, very truly,   " HOUGHTON."

I cannot remember whether the suggested visit took place or not.

* James Payn, the novelist, at this time editor of the *Cornhill* and "reader" to Messrs. Smith, Elder & Co., the publishers of " Vice Versâ."

LORD LYTTON.

My father was made known to Bulwer Lytton by Charles Dickens, and was asked to pay a visit to Knebworth. I have before me as I write the formal note in which "Sir E. B. Lytton presents his compliments to Mr. Lehmann, and begs to express the sincere pleasure it will afford him if Mr. Lehmann will accompany Mrs. Benzon and Miss Griffith in the visit to Knebworth with which they have promised to honour him next Saturday. Sir E. hopes it may suit Mr. Lehmann's engagements to remain till Tuesday." The date attached to this is "Saturday evening," which must have been 4th May, 1861. There is in the third volume of Dickens's "Letters" a letter to Bulwer Lytton, dated Wednesday, 8th May, 1861, in which Dickens expresses himself as "anxious to let you know that Mr. Frederick Lehmann, who is coming down to Knebworth to see you (with his sister, Mrs. Benzon), is a particular friend of mine, for whom I have a very high and warm regard."

The visit duly took place, and my father thus describes his first impressions in a letter to my mother, written on the morning after his arrival at Knebworth :

"KNEBWORTH,
"Sunday, 12th May, 1861, 11 A.M.

"Just a line from this enchanted castle. The post leaves at 12, so there is not time for much. It is a wonderful place—a perfect Old Curiosity.

Shop. Everything that Wardour Street ever had in it for the last three centuries has found its way to Knebworth. Sir Edward received us at his own door. I always fancied I had seen him before, but I was wrong. His face in repose has hard, fierce lines all over it, but when he speaks and makes himself agreeable to you that impression vanishes. I repeat, the place is wonderful. There is enough of old leather, carved wood, tapestries, silk hangings, old armour, and stained glass to make an antiquarian mad with envy. The dining-room is a gorgeous banqueting-hall the whole height of the house, with a gallery at one end. There are banners, devices, a blaze of plate, and, I am sorry to add, an Arctic climate in spite of an enormous fire, to which Sir Edward drew his chair immediately after dinner and began to smoke. I did the same, and this liberty makes you feel at your ease at once. The drawing-room is a fine long gallery full of the most interesting portraits, about every one of which he has some story which he tells *con gusto*. The library I only had a peep at. If our bibliomaniac E—— had had that peep his peace of mind would have been gone for ever. The weather is terrible, and we have not been out of the house yet, but there is so much to see that no one can feel dull for an instant. My room is called the Hampden Chamber, and the paper consists of stripes of griffins alternating with the Lytton motto, '*Hoc Virtutis Opus.*' I wish I could draw it for you. It would drive one mad in an illness.

We breakfasted at 9.30.   Sir Edward has not yet appeared."

I continue the account of this visit from my father's "Reminiscences":

"Dickens gave me an introduction to Lord Lytton, then Sir Edward Bulwer, who asked me to stay with him at Knebworth in the summer of 1861.   The grounds of Knebworth are lovely, and the house itself is beautifully proportioned; but it is disfigured to my mind by heraldic monstrosities, and a strange jumble of Wardour Street furniture. Lytton himself used to go about all day in the most wonderful old clothes.   He stooped very much, and in his frayed untidy suit looked at least seventy years old.   At dinner time, however, a wonderful change took place in him.   It was as though he had taken a draught of some elixir.   He appeared in evening dress as spruce as possible, and seemed to have left about twenty years of his age in his bedroom with his ancient garments.   During dinner he was animated and most interesting.   His wine was claret, a bottle of which stood beside him, and as soon as experience had taught me that this bottle contained the only wine which was good to drink, I contrived to make him share it with me.   Immediately after dinner he smoked a large chibouk. We then used to adjourn to the library, a noble room containing fine family portraits.   Our host's conversation was most fascinating.   In a large party his deafness prevented him from joining freely in the general conversation, but in the midst of a few friends willing and eager to listen, no talk could have equalled his. He was essentially what I call a monologist, but Dickens—the only man who perhaps could have disputed the supremacy with him—used to call him the greatest conversationalist of the age. At about eleven o'clock the power of the elixir seemed to wane ; he became again a bent old man, his talk flagged, and he faded away from us to his bedroom, where it may be he sat down to work, for he was the most industrious of men, and was said often to write half the night through. I find in a letter I wrote at the time the following description of my experiences * :—

'. . . In fine weather this place would be a paradise. As it is, we are in a very fine old house full of curiosities, a splendid library, and Sir Edward B.-Lytton. Yesterday it rained mercilessly all day ; we read, talked, shivered, ate, and drank. After dinner Sir Edward was very entertaining. He passed all the principal orators of both Houses in review—Derby, the late Earl Grey, Bright, Disraeli, and Gladstone. He gave us his opinion of Louis Napoleon, anecdotes of Madame de Stael, Richard Owen, Fourierism, and an account of his experiences at Cannes with Lord Brougham, which would have made you die of laughing. Then suddenly he burst out into a splendid recitation of Scott's " Young

* This letter is written to my mother, and is dated May 13th, 1861.

Lochinvar." He thought the "Woman in White" great trash, and "Great Expectations" so far Dickens' best novel. He cannot read Tennyson. After a course of Emerson's "Conduct of Life," and some other philosophical writer whose name I forget, he happened to read Gœthe, and felt like a man escaping from a black hole into pure air. He said he was constantly impressed with the wonderful universality of the Germans, and in particular was amazed at Schiller's knowledge of history, philosophy, and all manner of studies which to Byron, for instance, were a sealed book. He lay on a sofa smoking a chibouk, and Elizabeth* sang very nicely. He expressed himself delighted, and thus delighted Elizabeth, although she knows he does not hear a note. Just now he has been in and said, "I cannot bear being idle ; if I only had a grotto to make, or any change in the garden to plan, I should be perfectly happy." You cannot imagine the desolation and melancholy of this place under the present leaden sky. Poor Bulwer is a lonely and unhappy man, and I was much touched by coming suddenly upon a little ivy-grown monument which stands in the garden, and bears the following mournful inscription :

> "Alas, Poor Beau !
> Died Feb. 28, 1852.
> It is but to a dog that this stone is inscribed,
> Yet what now is left within the Home of
> Thy Fathers, O Solitary Master,
> That will grieve for Thy departure
> Or rejoice at thy return ?—E. B. L."

* The late Mrs. Benzon, my father's sister.

'Round the banqueting-hall, high up, runs the following inscription:

"Read the Rede of this old Roof-tree. Here be Trust Fast, Opinion free,
Knightly Right Hand, Christian Knee,
Worth in all, Wit in some, Laughter open, Slander dumb.
Hearth where rooted Friendships grow, safe as Altar even to Foe.
And ye Sparks that upward go, when the Hearth flame dies below;
If thy sap in these may be, fear no winter, old Roof-tree."' "

Here the first quotation from the letter ends and the " Reminiscences " continue:—

" During this visit to Knebworth one of my fellow-guests was a Miss Mattie Griffith from Kentucky. Inheriting a number of negroes, she had set them all free, and had refused their urgent entreaty to be allowed to set aside part of their wages for her benefit. Her act made her not only penniless but drove her from home, her abolitionist views making it impossible for her to continue to live in Kentucky. She had gone to Boston in order to make a living by literary effort, and had come to Lytton warmly introduced by Boston friends. She was enthusiastic for the preservation of the Union, and felt deeply the terrors of war between the North and the South. When, therefore, Lytton spread out a map of the United States, and declared in his most didactic way that if any lesson was taught by history, ' such unwieldy empires must fall to pieces and split up into a number of states,' I was amused to see Miss Griffith dancing a wild Indian war dance behind his back, and shaking her little fist at him. On this subject I may quote from the same letter:—

'Miss Griffith is a poetess. I found in the library a little volume of pretty poems by Mattie Griffith, and in it an ode addressed to Sir Edward, and over-flowing with enthusiastic admiration which probably aroused his interest in her. She is one of the most modest and innately ladylike persons I ever met, but a perfect tigress if America is sneered at or in any way blamed. Her love for her country burst out into some fierce little quarrels with Sir Edward. He thought the Americans would be much the better for a queen and a few hereditary gentlemen. She scorned the notion, and said that if such a thing ever happened "it would just break my heart." '

" Lytton had a curious drawling manner of speech, his words being interspersed with frequent ' erras ' to help him out when he was waiting for the proper word. Then, again, he would emphasise a sentence or a single word by loudly raising his voice, a peculiarity which gave his talk a certain dramatic character. I remember once, when I was dining with him *en petit comité*, the conversation turned upon the universality of belief in a Divine Creator, and even now I fancy I hear him saying: ' When—erra—I had the honour—erra—of becoming Her Majesty's Secretary of State for the Colonies, I made it my first business—erra—to instruct my agents all over the habitable globe—erra—to report to me if they knew of any nation, tribe, or community—erra'; thus far he had spoken in a low melodious voice, when suddenly he changed his register, shot out the following words as from a catapult, '*who did not believe in a* GOD.' He added that he had only found one savage community with such a want of belief.

"In the garden at Knebworth he was fond of pointing out the tree under which 'young Robert' * wrote his poetry.

"He was always buying and selling houses in town or places in the country. Among the latter I remember Copped Hall, near Totteridge, in Hertfordshire, a tumbledown old house in which I found him settled one winter with H. W. Ernst, the famous violinist, and his French wife. I am told that in all these purchases and sales Lytton did well.

"I remember finding him and his brother, Lord Dalling, assembled among the guests for a dinner to inaugurate a new house of Sir Alexander Cockburn's, at 40, Hertford Street. As usual with Cockburn, the house contained merely the necessary furniture, but neither picture, engraving, nor, indeed, any work of art. I could not help expressing to Lytton my wonder at the extent of bare walls in the house of a man of taste like Cockburn. Lytton looked round and quietly replied, 'Just the kind of house —erra—for him to start from after breakfast—erra —*to hang a man.*'

* The late Earl of Lytton.

" Lytton prided himself upon his knowledge of agricultural matters, and was fond of being consulted about them. When my wife was going to keep cows, and in her total ignorance of the subject rather trembled at the prospect, I advised her to consult Sir Edward Bulwer, and I now possess his reply of nine pages bursting with professional knowledge.

" He was very fond of my little daughter, and once actually persuaded my wife to let her accompany us to Knebworth. The little lady was not over five or six, and accepted the most slavish devotion from Lytton as her due. It was touching to see our frail, bent old host in his usual toilet of ancient clothes wander hand-in-hand with his small friend through the gardens, wasting, I fear, much wisdom and good counsel varied by wonderful stories. I tried hard to impress her with the great honour done to her, but I am afraid quite in vain. She pined for her toys and companions at home, and did not care a jot for the glories of Knebworth.

" I well remember Lytton expatiating on Disraeli's unbounded ambition. 'But surely,' I remarked, ' he must be satisfied with being Chancellor of the Exchequer and leader of the House of Commons.' ' You mark my words,' replied Lytton, ' nothing will satisfy him until he is Prime Minister and an Earl.' This was said in 1867 or 1868. I may here relate a curious conversation which took place in my presence at Knebworth in 1866. Disraeli had brought the Tories into power for the second time, but the Cabinet was not yet formed.   All the

Knebworth guests were on the lawn near the house when some one asked Sir Edward, 'And, pray, Sir Edward, which portfolio do you expect to take?' to which he replied, 'One always likes to return to familiar places; and as I have had the Colonies [under Lord Derby in 1858-59], I presume I shall go back to the Colonies.' In the afternoon we all went up to town and discovered that Bulwer had been left out in the cold. Shortly afterwards the usual consolation of a peerage was applied and accepted. His increasing deafness, which made him useless in debate, was doubtless the reason for his exclusion, which, in view of Disraeli's staunch and loyal constancy to his friends, was probably as painful to him as it was to Lytton. The sudden appointment of Lytton's son to the Viceroyalty of India was brought about, perhaps, in some measure by Disraeli's consciousness that something was due from him to the memory of his old friend."

I have searched high and low for the nine-page letter on cow-keeping referred to above, but I have been unable to find this document. Two or three short notes in Lord Lytton's mystic handwriting are all that I possess. In one of these—which is signed " E. B. L.," and must presumably have been written before 1866, when he became a peer—he says, " I have one consolation for my loss of your invitation. I was seized by a tiger whom I never encountered before, and torn by him into pieces the whole day. I believe common people call the tiger a toothache, but his proper name is perhaps not known out of Purgatory." In another (also undated, but written, of course, after June 9th, 1870, the date of Dickens's death) he writes : " I dare not trust myself to write about the death of Charles Dickens. The shock is too recent."

My father was to meet Miss Mattie Griffith again when he went to America in the year following his visit to Knebworth. She played a very noble part in the fight for the abolition of slavery. Lydia Maria Child,* in a letter written in 1857 to Miss Lucy Osgood ("Letters of L. Maria Child," Boston, Houghton Mifflin & Co., 1883), thus refers to her :—" I have lately been much interested about the young Kentucky lady [Miss Mattie Griffith] who emancipated all her slaves in consequence of reading Charles Sumner's speeches. She and I correspond, as mother and daughter, and I should infer from her letters, even if I knew nothing else about her, that she was endowed with a noble, generous, sincere and enthusiastic nature. It is no slight sacrifice, at nineteen years old, to give up all one's property, and go forth into the world to earn her own living, penniless and friendless; 'but I shall earn my living with a light heart, because I shall have a

---

* Mrs. Child (1802—1880) devoted her life to literature and the anti-slavery agitation, in which she was one of the protagonists. Her " Letters " were published in 1883, with a biographical introduction by Whittier, and an appendix by Wendell Phillips. See also p. 323.

clean conscience.' I quote her own words which she wrote in an hour of sadness in consequence of being cut by friends, reproached by relations, and deluged with insulting letters from every part of the South. Her relatives resort to both coaxing and threatening to induce her publicly to deny that she wrote the 'Autobiography of a Female Slave.' The truthfulness of her nature fires up at this. In one of her letters to me she says, 'What a mean thing they would make of me! I'll die first.' She is true metal, and rings clear under their blows. Yet she has a loving womanly heart, made desolate and sad by separation from early friends. We abolitionists ought to rally round the noble young martyr. I wish you had a chance to get acquainted with her. She struck me as quite a remarkable young person. . . . I suppose you have heard what a glorious time Mattie had when she emancipated her slaves. They danced and sang and sobbed and would have kissed her feet had she permitted. Then they began to think of her, and insisted upon continuing to send their wages to her, because she was not strong enough to work. When she refused, they pleaded hard to send her half their earnings. She wrote to me about it, and added, 'I assure you, dear Mrs. Child, there are very few people who know the real beauty of the African character.' I believe it." Again, in 1859, in her famous reply to Mrs. Mason, who had attacked her virulently for having offered to nurse John Brown in prison, Mrs. Child thus speaks of Miss Griffith :—" Miss Mattie

Griffith, of Kentucky, whose entire property consisted in slaves, emancipated them all.   The noble-hearted girl wrote to me: 'I shall go forth into the world penniless; but I shall work with a light heart, and, best of all, I shall live with an easy conscience.'   Previous to this generous resolution she had never read any abolition document, and entertained the common Southern prejudice against them.   But her own observation so deeply impressed her with the enormities of slavery that she was impelled to publish a book called 'The Autobiography of a Female Slave.'   I read it with thrilling interest, but some of the scenes made my nerves quiver so painfully that I told her I hoped they were too highly coloured.   She shook her head sadly, and replied: 'I am sorry to say that every incident in the book has come within my own knowledge.' "

Some little time after the conclusion of the great war Miss Griffith married Mr. Albert G. Browne, Jnr., who was Governor Andrew's private secretary during the war.   She subsequently resided in Boston during Mr. Browne's career as clerk of the Supreme Judicial Court of Massachusetts, and then in New York, where he was connected with the editorial departments of the *New York Evening Post* and *New York World*.   Later they returned to Boston, and, after Mr. Browne's death, Mrs. Browne continued to live there until her own death in 1906.

Two letters from her to my father will be found in Chapter XXI. of this book.

CHARLES READE.

I wish I could have spoken at greater length than my recollection and my materials make possible of Charles Reade, that great-hearted, chivalrous, erratic genius. He was for many years the friend of my parents; but during that time I was for the most part away at school or college, and my own memory of him is but a dim one. Even to have known and to have shaken by the hand the man who wrote that glorious and tremendous description of the Indiaman's fight with the two pirate ships is in any case no small privilege. Where in fiction can that passage be matched? To find its peer you must go, I think, to Napier's deathless account of the battle of Albuera. The spirit and temper of the two pieces are the same. There must, indeed, have been in Charles Reade's mind an unconscious remembrance of Napier's words. Let me give a short extract from each:

(1) *Napier : The Battle of Albuera.*

" Such a gallant line, issuing from the midst of the smoke, and rapidly separating itself from the confused and broken multitude, startled the enemy's masses, which were increasing and pressing onwards as to an assured victory; they wavered, hesitated, and then, vomiting forth a storm of fire, hastily endeavoured to enlarge their front, while a fearful discharge from all their artillery whistled through the British ranks. Myers was killed; Cole and the three colonels, Ellis, Blakeney, and Hawkshawe, fell wounded; and the fusileer battalions, struck by the iron tempest, reeled and staggered like sinking ships; but, suddenly and sternly recovering, they closed on their terrible enemies, and then was seen with what a strength and majesty the British soldier fights. . . . Nothing could stop that astonishing infantry. No sudden burst of undisciplined valour, no nervous enthusiasm weakened the stability of their order; their flashing eyes were bent on the dark columns in their front, their measured tread shook the ground, their dreadful volleys swept away the head of every formation, their deafening shout overpowered the dissonant cries that broke from all parts of the tumultuous crowd, as slowly and with a horrid carnage it was pushed by the incessant vigour of the attack to the farthest edge of the hill."

(2) *Charles Reade: " Hard Cash."*

" The pirate crew had stopped the leak and cut away and unshipped the broken foremast, and were stepping a new one, when they saw the huge ship bearing down in full sail. Nothing easier than to slip out of her way could they get the foresail to draw; but the time was short, the deadly intention manifest, the coming destruction swift. After that solemn silence came a storm of cries and curses as their seamen went to work to fit the yard and raise the sail, while their fighting men seized their matchlocks and trained the guns. They were well commanded by an heroic, able villain. Astern, the consort thundered; but the *Agra's* response was a dead silence more awful than broadsides. For then was seen with what majesty the enduring Anglo-Saxon fights. One of that indomitable race on the gangway, one at the foremast, two at the wheel conned and steered the great ship down on a hundred matchlocks and a grinning broadside just as they would have conned and steered her into a British harbour. . . . Crash! the Indiaman's cut-water in thick smoke beat in the schooner's broadside; down went her masts to leeward like fishing rods whipping the water; there was a horrible shrieking yell; wild forms leaped off on the *Agra,* and were hacked to pieces almost ere they reached the deck; a surge, a chasm in the sea filled with an instant rush of engulfing waves, a long, awful, grating, grinding noise, never to be forgotten in this world, all along under the ship's keel, and the fearful, majestic monster passed on over the blank she had made," etc.

I possess but half a dozen of the novelist's letters. In one, presumably written in 1866, he asks my father if he could " send a hundred respectable workmen to the pit and amphitheatre of the Queen's Theatre early next week. It would, I think," he continues, " gratify the sons of toil, and also answer my purpose by giving publicity to my play in the City." How my father, then head of a large mercantile firm in the City, was to procure the workmen, or how the workmen, if procured, were to advertise the play "in the City," was not stated.

In a later letter he fulminates to my mother against servants: "The servants," he writes, "make all this mischief by pretending they will say who called and not doing it. If they would only say honestly, 'No, sir, I will not tell missus you called. Why don't you bring a card like other people?' how much misery might be spared." Only a genius (who, by the way, had also been Vice-President of an Oxford College) could ever have imagined that a servant would remember a casual caller.

JAMES PAYN.

And now I come to James Payn, a name to be held in grateful remembrance by many readers. He was my father's close friend and companion through many years, and to me, too, from boyhood up, he was, in spite of the difference in our ages, a friend beloved beyond most others. I never knew a man more genuinely affectionate and sincere, or more free from every trace of affectation. In his society one could think of mean things only to despise them and of pompous people only to laugh at them. And as to laughter, those who once heard Payn's could never forget it. The whole cheerful soul of the man went to make it up. It was the most joyous, overwhelming volume of sound I ever listened to, sent up in a great full stream from the very fountain of mirth. His friends were permitted to chaff him about it; but once, when the late Bernal Osborne ventured to comment upon it, he did not escape scot-free. "That man," said Osborne, "laughs like a cannibal." Like a flash came the retort, "At any rate, Mr. Osborne, I've never been able to swallow *you*."

In 1869 my father took my younger brother and myself to the Lake District, and Payn accompanied us. He had on hand the writing of a descriptive book, afterwards published, under the title of "The Lakes in Sunshine," by Simpkin, Marshall & Co. One incident of this tour remains vivid in my memory. Payn had been vaunting the merits of Professor Stokes's system of mnemonics, which, so he said, had enabled one of his daughters to accomplish the otherwise impossible task of reciting Southey's "Falls of Lodore" by heart. My father thereupon backed me (I was then not quite fourteen years old) to learn the poem and to recite it at the same hour on the following day without any adventitious aid. Half a sovereign was the amount of the bet, and I was promised the possession of it if I succeeded. No single omission or misplacement of a word was to be allowed. The task is one that I would not undertake for ten times the amount nowadays, for there is no necessary connection of any kind between one line and another throughout the poem. In those days, however, I was enterprising, and my memory was a quick worker. I duly performed the task and received the reward. Payn tells the story in his own more or less decorative way in " The Lakes in Sunshine." Being in danger, he says, of being used as a hare by us in a game of hare and hounds, he bought himself off by offering us five shillings apiece—on condition that we learnt the poem by heart. " Their countenances, which had gleamed with rapacity, fell almost to the depth of the cataract in question when I annexed the condition; but they both said very good-humouredly that they would try their best." On a later page he reports that " Gatty (*enfant gâté*), having much time on his hands and nothing to do with it, absolutely learnt that poem and recited it without flaw." The last few words are accurate.

Payn was certainly the very best company in the world, for, though he never monopolised the talk, his brilliant humour and the unceasing flow of his animal spirits always secured for him a leading part and helped him to bring out all that was vivacious in his companions. His wit and his laughter radiated so generously on those who sat with him that he gave each of them the feeling of having been lifted into a clearer, brighter atmosphere where everybody enjoyed the privilege of being witty without being malicious. Suffused with the delightful glow of his personality and sped along by the swift succession of his stories, the evening passed all too quickly till the time for parting came, and nothing was left but to make plans for a prompt reunion.   I wish I could summon all those evenings back and live them over again !

I have only a few letters written by Payn in the amazing hieroglyphics (more puzzling even than those of Lord Houghton and Lord Lytton) which distracted his friends and his printers.   When my father died in 1891, I handed back a large packet of letters he had received from Payn.   One I kept, and I shall print it here.   My first, however, is a letter from Payn to me, giving me advice as to the choice of a college.   I was destined for Trinity, Cambridge; but had shown an inclination to try for a scholarship at some smaller college there or at Oxford.   Payn was the most loyal of Cambridge men; but Cambridge to him was summed up in Trinity, and he scouted the idea that anyone could want to go to another college.   "I don't say," he wrote, "as the Trinity man said when defending the small college men, ' Let us remember that they, too, are God's creatures'; but such a supercilious remark could never have been made unless there had been *some* reason for it.   I speak of what I know in this case, whereas in my preference for Cambridge over Oxford I may be swayed by a natural prejudice without knowledge. . . . This, however, is certain, that it would be better for you to be a simple undergraduate at T.C.C. than a scholar at a small college; but with application you ought to be a scholar at Trinity.   Then I'll come down and dine with you."   I failed to secure the scholarship, but he came all the same.

The next letter shows him in his character of amiable and encouraging critic. I had been writing verse, and had sent him some specimens. There is no date to the letter, but it must have been written towards the end of 1876 :

"15, WATERLOO PLACE, S.W.

" MY DEAR BOY,—The poem is very nice—I mean really nice—but not so good as ' The Dolomites.' The last line is a metaphor drawn from the subject, which is contrary to the canons. Still, it is good. Why do you want to attempt the *Cornhill?* I happen to know that *Chambers's Journal* is in want of good verse. If you do not want to send a few specimens to your Uncle Robert I will send them for you. There! Love to Fred. —Yours ever,

" JAMES PAYN."

This is the one letter to my father that remains to me. It was written to him when he was within a fortnight of his death :

"'THE CORNHILL MAGAZINE,'
" *Aug. 8th*, 1891.

" MY DEAR OLD FRIEND,—Martin has just been here. What he has told me of your poor self wrings my heart, as it will wring my wife's heart. She often talks of you, and always with the deepest sympathy.

" If anything can help one in your sad condition it should be the knowledge that there are two persons in the world (outside your own people) whose memory holds nothing concerning you save your many acts of kindness to them.

"God bless you, dear old friend! When I think of the days we once had together my eyes are wet. —Yours *ever* affectionately,

"JAMES PAYN."

My last letter from Payn is dated April 29th, 1895, when he was very ill and confined to his house. It is written in pencil:

"MY DEAR BOY,—Your kind letter touched me very much. How well I remember, alas! the scenes of which you speak. We have heard the chimes not only at midnight, but at all hours. You have sent me enough asparagus to set up a shop with. It is very good of you to have remembered my little weakness—the only one in an otherwise blameless life.—Yours affectionately,

"JAMES PAYN.

"Do not come on Tuesdays or Fridays."

The prohibition in the last sentence may be explained by a quotation from the charming little memoir prefixed by Leslie Stephen to "The Backwater of Life," a posthumous volume of Payn's essays: "When physical infirmities made it impossible for him to frequent his old haunts, the whist club to which he belonged made an arrangement which it is pleasant to remember. Four members

went by rotation to his house in Warrington Crescent, Maida Vale, twice every week to give him
the pleasure of a rubber.   Few men, I fancy, have
received such a proof of the kindly regard of their
friends.   I am as incapable of playing whist as of
writing a novel; but to me, as to many others, it
was an act of self-indulgence to spend one of the
other afternoons at Payn's house."   I am thankful
to remember that I was able to be one of the
" many others."

CHAPTER XIV.

Musical Memories.

An Evening at Hallé's—Henry Fothergill Chorley—His Campaign against Schumann—Meyerbeer's Age—M. Carvalho and the *Times*—A Guy Fawkes Invitation—Sir George Grove—Arthur Sullivan—"The Tempest"—Frederic Clay.

Memories of music and of those who made music cluster thickly about the old letters which are before me as I write. Both my father and my mother were born musicians and had been well trained, the one to the violin, the other to the piano; and for many years their house was the gathering-place of those who were musically minded. In his uncompleted "Reminiscences" my father had meant, as I gather from a list of names on a loose page in his note-book, to speak of Mendelssohn, F. David, Ernst, Chopin, Moscheles, Hiller, Meyerbeer, Liszt, Thalberg, Molique, and many others too numerous to mention here. In regard to these I cannot supply his place, but I can say a few words about some others whom I myself remember and whose letters still remain to me.

Let me begin with a letter from my father to my mother, dated 24th July, 1860:

"It was a quarter past 9 before I got any dinner at the club, and at 11 I made my appearance at the Hallés. Had Hallé not happened to be on the landing and shaken hands with me as I came up I should never have been able to come near him or he near me the whole evening, so great was the crowd. Prince Galitzin was going as I came. His wife's English maid had that day died at her feet in a fit of apoplexy. They were terribly upset, and he is to take his wife away a little to get over the shock.

" As I entered the sacred temple the well-known priests and priestesses were there, officiating or performing their devotions. At the altar were Hallé, Santley, Balletti, and Mlle. Artot. The latter sang a pretty lullaby by Gounod, but may on the whole for my part vanish at once into infinite space, as Carlyle has it. Hallé played Chopin and Bach, one *suite*, &c., which I had never heard before and which was quite enchanting. . . . Our friend ——'s nose glowed more powerfully than ever and paled the ineffectual lights of lamps and candles. I noticed that a young lady's dress (close to him) appeared pink, while (away from him) it was white.

" Among the devotees was Chorley, transparent, with rosy skin and yellow hair. He had drunk the elixir of life just in the right quantity last night and was wonderfully youthful and frisky. Near him were the young and lovely Virginia [Gabriel] and the still younger and lovelier Volumnia [Miss Boyle]. Leighton whispered soft nothings into Virginia's innocent ears, the Prinseps with the Murillo daughter were attended by their henchmen Holman Hunt and Dick Doyle. Manuel Garcia told me the same story about Ernst playing a sonata of Bach's many years ago which I have patiently listened to twice before, and I fear strong defensive measures will have to be taken on the occasion of the next attack. Round this camp of gipsies a thin line of respectable heavy outsiders sat frigid, trying to overawe the turbulent mass, not without a certain effect. Lady Molesworth bestowed some of her amiable self on each of the two parties and still had plenty to spare. Mrs. —— gave me her hand to kiss, but I regret to say it was covered by a washed glove which smelt strongly of turpentine. Everybody inquired after you. Chorley and I walked home together as far as the corner of Park Lane. He had recently made Holman Hunt's acquaintance at Gad's Hill, and was very much struck by the notion that he paints Christ from his own face. In ' The Light of the World ' there is certainly some similarity. He quite hugged this discovery, as you know he does everything which he thinks he has found out."

Of Henry Fothergill Chorley I have a very distinct recollection, though he died thirty-six years ago. He was tall and thin. His eyes blinked and twinkled as he spoke ; and his quaint pecking gestures and high staccato voice made an impression which caused one of his friends to describe him as the missing link between the chimpanzee and the cockatoo. He was a literary critic, a playwright, a writer of novels, all long since forgotten, and of operatic *libretti;* but he was best known as the musical critic of the *Athenæum*, the staff of which he had joined in 1833. In this capacity he for many years waged war against Schumann's music, and against Madame Schumann, who was endeavouring to make it known and appreciated in England. The genius of the dead composer and the noble efforts of his living wife eventually prevailed against Chorley; but for some years, at any rate, Chorley's campaign was conducted with some success.

I take the following account of him from my father's " Reminiscences " :

" Chorley, the musical critic of the *Athenæum*, was in appearance and manners one of the strangest of mortals. His face was all out of drawing, and his high voice and curious angular movements made him a very conspicuous figure wherever he went. Some thirty years ago" [my father was writing in 1884] "music in London really meant Italian opera or Handel's oratorios; for anything else there was an extremely limited public. Good chamber music could only be heard during the season at Ella's Union, and was there heard only by a few hundred people. Arthur Chappell *a changé tout cela.* No single critic could now make or mar a musical reputation, but in the antediluvian days of which I speak Chorley, as the mouthpiece of the *Athenæum*, was master of the situation and ruled supreme. I am bound to add that he was thoroughly honest, and, though he had his favourites, he wrote without fear. But he had neither the natural gifts nor the education necessary for so responsible a position. He took the most violent likes and dislikes; an important matter, seeing that he, so to speak, made public opinion. He cordially disliked Madame Schumann (whom, by the way, he always called ' the shoe-woman '). There can be no doubt that by his ignorant but constantly expressed detestation of Schumann's music he for many years prevented that great composer from becoming properly known and appreciated in this country. On the other hand, Chorley adored Mendelssohn, and went so far as to consider any admiration of Schumann a slight upon his idol. All this has now become a matter of history, and in spite of Chorley's well-nigh forgotten efforts Schumann has taken his legitimate place in England as elsewhere. In those days Chorley was a writer of opera books, and he seemed to look upon the composer's part of the business as entirely secondary to his own. For instance, he always spoke of the ' Amber Witch,' for which he had written the libretto, as ' my opera.'

" At his little house, 13, Eaton Place, West, he saw very good company and gave many pleasant dinners, to which he invited artists and literary men of eminence. At the same time he had a curious way of alluding to those whose rank and means made it unnecessary for them to live by their brains as 'real people.'   I remember once meeting Meyerbeer and John Forster at his table.   Little Meyerbeer looked at least a hundred years old.   We happened to be talking about age, and I remember that Forster, in tones made most dulcet for the occasion, said to Meyerbeer, 'And might I ask, M. Meyerbeer, how old you are?'   But Meyerbeer was equal to the occasion, and merely replied, 'I think you might, Mr. Forster, but I am not sure whether I would tell you.'

" I remember a curious instance of the apparent impossibility of French people understanding how differently newspapers are managed in this country. M. and Madame (Miolan) Carvalho were dining at Chorley's with Tom Taylor, who was at that time the art critic of the *Times*, a fact of which Madame was aware but Monsieur was not.   Something in the musical criticisms of the *Times* had apparently displeased M. Carvalho, and he broke out into a fierce invective against the paper.   In vain his wife made signs to him and tried to stop him, until at last she electrified him by saying, '*Mais, mon ami, M. Taylor est du Times.*'   I never saw such a transformation scene.   Tom Taylor did his best to explain to M. Carvalho that he, as the art critic, had no more to do with the music criticisms in the *Times* than the man in the moon.   But poor Carvalho continued to make the most abject apologies, and entreated him to forget what he had said.

" Chorley was really a most hospitable man, but his hospitality sometimes took strange forms.   Once,

I remember, he asked me whether I was engaged upon a certain date, and upon my replying 'No,' he somewhat astonished me by saying that he would come and dine with me on that day. 'I shall have a blue-coat boy staying with me,' he continued, 'and I will bring him with me; it will do the lad good.' Chorley was as good as his word. On the appointed day he and his *protégé* dined with me at my house in Westbourne Terrace. The proximity of Westbourne Terrace to Paddington Station, from which the blue-coat boy was to start that evening for his home, was, I fancy, the chief reason for this singular invitation. Chorley, however, was, I am bound to say, profuse in his invitations to dinner at his own house, but occasionally his stream of dinners would cease, though he never consented to abdicate altogether the position of Amphitryon. For instance, he would meet you in June and say to you, 'I have quite made up my mind to have a little dinner on Guy Fawkes day; will you come?' And through all these intervening months Chorley would never meet you without reminding you that you were engaged to him for the 5th of November. This became a standing joke amongst his intimates, and any proposal to fix a festivity a long way ahead was at once checked by 'No Guy Fawkes invitation.'

"In his later days poor Chorley became very feeble, and used often to forget where he was, and to imagine when dining out that he was dining at his own house.

"On one occasion, when Charles Reade, Wilkie

Collins, and others were dining at our house near Highgate, a curious incident happened. When Chorley arrived before dinner he showed that he was not quite at his ease by saying to my wife, 'Dear friend, where am I?' To which she replied reassuringly, 'Oh, Mr. Chorley, you must consider yourself at home.' I take the following amusing account from a letter written at the time by my wife:

"'At last Chorley didn't in the very least know where he was, and again asked me confidentially if I could tell him. I said he was at Woodlands. He said, "Where's that?" During dinner he appeared to have settled it in his own mind that he was at home; consequently he kept on ringing the bell, giving Martin all sorts of orders, and calling him Drury (his own man's name). He was quite vexed with me for ringing once and giving an order myself. At the end of dinner he tottered up, held on for a moment as if the chair was a mast and he was crossing the Channel, asked me to be good enough to take care of his guests for him, and particularly to see that Mr. Collins got what wine he liked, feebly said "Drury," whereat Martin took his arm—and so vanished to bed. He was all right the next day, and is right now and most delightful, like his fine, bright old conceited self again. To-night we have a dinner-party in his honour, Charles Reade, Tuckie, Wilkie Collins, Mrs. Procter, Mr. Bockett, and one or two others.'

"Next day. 'I told you in my last letter about

the dinner we had arranged for Chorley. When we sat down, his delusion of being at his own table came on again. We were all known to him except Mr. Bockett. I saw him now and then puzzling over Bockett, unable to account for Bockett, but in his old-fashioned, chivalrous way with the greatest stranger, sending all the dishes round to Bockett, pressing things upon him. " Take the champagne to Mr. Bockett, please," &c., &c. After dinner, when Wilkie was proceeding to light his cigar, Chorley at once interfered, declaring that he never allowed smoking in his dining-room. There was, I believe, a little scene, but matters were amicably arranged afterwards. Afterwards, in the music-room, Chorley asked me how his dinner had gone off, was it good ? Then he said, " I shall certainly ask Mr. Bockett again, he's ver–r–y nice." " But," said Kitty, "have you ever seen him before ? " " Well," said Chorley, meditating, " no—but then " (with an important little snigger) " this little dinner of mine has been a complete ——— " perhaps he meant a complete surprise to himself, but he waved off the end of the sentence. Every now and then he quite recovered himself, and told us how confused he had been. During one of these intervals he went up to Wilkie and most touchingly apologised to him, but in 'a short time again he would ring the bell and think himself at home.' "

I must add to this, for my own part, that in his private relations Chorley was friendly, affectionate, and sincere, with a strain of whimsical oddity which was the delight of his friends. One testimony, at any rate, to his true goodness of heart I can give in a letter written by him to my father when my mother was lying seriously ill :

"13, EATON PLACE, WEST,
"*Tuesday, Jany.* 26*th*, '65·

"MY DEAR LEHMANN,—I cannot tell you how sorry I am that you should have any anxiety now ; but I *can* tell you that should you by any mischance (which may God avert !) want a relief, I am ready. I can sit up in any lower storey, without wanting to go to sleep, I can take directions, and I make no noise. I earnestly hope and believe that I shall not be wanted; *but* you would do me an unkindness if, supposing I could be of any good, you did not remember now how I am your obliged and faithful,

"H. F. CHORLEY.

"This note requires no answer save in the form of a summons."

SIR GEORGE GROVE.

I now come to our dear old friend Sir George Grove—"G.," as he was always known to his friends. The mere thought of him brings a burst of sunshine into the mind. There never was a man of more delightful humour or of a more abounding gaiety and amiability. Friendliness shone from his eyes and from every line of his face. Cheerfulness entered the room with him and stayed even after he had left, so infectious were his spirits. He was all his life a very hard worker, but his enthusiasms remained fresh and unimpaired to the end. I was with my mother when he stayed with her at Portobello in 1896. He was my senior by thirty-five years, but I felt in his society as though the essence of youth and goodfellowship had become happily embodied in him for my especial benefit. Here was a man who had begun life as an engineer and had helped to float the tubes of the Menai Bridge; who had been secretary of the Society of Arts for two years and of the Crystal Palace for twenty-one; who had contributed many articles to the " Bible Dictionary," and had for sixteen years edited *Macmillan's Magazine;* who had organised and edited a monumental " Dictionary of Music," and had been director of the Royal College of Music—here, as I say, was this learned and versatile man of seventy-six frisking and laughing and chaffing, and egging his companions on to laughter like a boy just released from school. It is a memory to be prized through life.

I think it was early in the sixties that my father and mother first came to know Grove, who was then, as he remained until 1873, secretary of the Crystal Palace and one of the presiding spirits of the famous Saturday Concerts. The relation between our two families soon became a very intimate and affectionate one. I have a letter of July 8th, 1867, from Grove to my mother, in which he says : " Thanks, dear friend, for your account of yourself. It is bad enough, but, thank God, not so bad as I had heard, last of all from old Chorley, who came trembling and crying to our gate yesterday morning quite a wreck of a wreck. Can't you keep yourself quiet, and recollect that you are a very weak, fragile creature, and also awfully valuable to all your friends, and put yourself into a big jewel-box and be looked at and aired only occasionally? Don't vote me a bore for preaching. Good-bye, my dear friend. Write to me again, and the sooner the better. I am going to dine with Arthur [Sullivan] to-night, and shall drink your health (to myself) with my first glass of claret."

The friendship thus established continued uninterrupted to the end of Grove's life. Here is another letter twenty-six years later:

"LOWER SYDENHAM, S.E.,
"Oct. 8th, '93·

"MY DEAR OLD FRIEND,—I have got an excuse to write to you which is very nice. The other day at Ragatz I met a lady and her husband who knew you and talked familiarly of many of our friends. . . .

"Why did I go to Ragatz? Well, my dear child, I went to cure my rheumatism, which bends me double, and makes me cross, and tires me, and is absurd. I have taken the baths all regular, and been massaged by a powerful Swede with an immense ball to his thumb. With that ball he not only rubbed and dug into the poor muscles of my back, but after each rubbing he slapped me with all his strength and his open hand till I was almost mad. *Souvenirs de jeunesse* he called it, but I never remember anything so cruel or hard to bear at school. When I began my muscles were all in lumps like potatoes. Now they are as tender and nice as a new-born babby's, and *yet* the rheumatic pains continue! What to do I don't know. I live a life of martyrdom. I have ' cut off ' my sugar, my wine, my beer—everything that makes life desirable, and yet I live in torture and am always on the point of breaking into two across my back.

" However, there are some consolations. I am doing a book on Beethoven's Symphonies, into which I am putting all that I know and feel. I mean it to be lively and readable; there'll be musical hints for those who like 'em, but what I want is to write a book which will ' carry people away.' I have done six of them, and have had the proofs read by one or two *test-objects*, and they give very good reports. It's splendid doing it. I get no time, but have to snatch half an hour now and an hour then, and so get on with it. . I suppose it will be out about Easter. It's hard work, and 7, 8, and 9 are big mouthfuls to digest—and bring up again.

" When I got to Ragatz I went to see the resident doctor, who spoke English fairly well. When he had finished his instructions, I said, ' I don't know your ways. What fee am I to give you ? ' ' Oh,' said he, ' what you usually give.' So I forked out a napoleon, and then I said, ' You remind me of a story told about Macaulay. He usually shaved himself; but having hurt his hand he sent for a barber, and at the end of the operation he said, as I did, "What am I to give?" And the barber replied, as you did, "What you generally give to the man who shaves you." "*Then*," said Macaulay, "I should give you three great cuts on each cheek." ' The doctor pondered a little while and then he said, 'Ah, Macküläy! He was a historian?' ' He was,' said I, and fled.

"Love to any of you who are there, and to you.

"G."

In the summer of 1894, when he was contemplating resignation of the directorship of the Royal College of Music, he wrote to my mother:

"You *are* a brick—nothing short of it—to think of writing to me like that—a regular little soap-bubble of a note, all floating about with prismatic colours of the sweetest and brightest! And it was very *à propos*—a great deal of aproposity about it (that's better); for I am sadly down on my luck— no, not on my *luck*, but overdone and tired and full of pain, and, oh my dear, *so* old! You can't realise it—you, somewhere in the fifties, can't feel with an old hulk, an old seventy-four, the *Téméraire*—that's it exactly.

"But, really and truly, my time's about come, and now that we've got into our new house [that is, the new buildings of the College] I must retire; only, there are two questions: Who's to succeed

me ? and, How am I to live ?   I can live on bread
and cheese.   Well, but even that will be hard to
pay for with nothing coming in, for I shall never
make anything with my pen. . . . I have not taken
the plunge yet, only talked to Arthur Sullivan and
Lord Charles Bruce.   The last two months has been
a bad time, and my factotum Watson (a splendid
fellow) has knocked up—all but paralysis—and left
everything to me.   H.R.H. has been very kind,
praised me no end, and spoke quite affectionately. . . . Do you know that, except Christmas
Day, I have not had one day's holiday since I came
back from Ragatz on October 2.   I had planned a
little run into Scotland—Kenmore, St. Andrews,
Portobello, &c., when Watson broke down and
stopped it."

The following letter also refers to his impending
retirement at a later stage :

"LOWER SYDENHAM, S.E.,
"*Nov.* 28 [1894].

"MY VERY DEAR FRIEND,—I wish I could come
to the wedding, but I can't manage it, and I would
have no talk to you.   I am rather down on my
luck.   Nothing exactly the matter—rheumatism, of
course—but horrible bad spirits and foreboding,
and an uncertain feeling which, I suppose, is inevitable under the circumstances.   I do dread the
next 3 months with their fogs and east wind and
frost.

"My people have behaved very well to me; have

given me a handsome pension (quite enough), have put me on the Council, and have passed the most comforting and appretiative* resolution. I hope to give up at Christmas, and then Parry will succeed at the New Year. I am much comforted about him, and see a new lease of life for the College. Good-bye. We will meet again soon, when I have got my breath again.   " G."

In 1896, as I have said, Grove paid my mother a visit at Portobello. On July 6th he writes to her from Lower Sydenham :

" MY DEAR OLD FRIEND,—Have you made up your mind when you go down to Portobello ? You were quite in earnest the other day ? If so, I should like very much to know somewhere about the time of my departure.

" I have just been talking to a nice Edinburgh girl (was Miss Kerr and is Mrs. Milton Green, wife of a doctor here—a great admirer of R ——'s).

" What a hot day !

" She is telling of her brother, who was a sugar planter in Jamaica ; but I don't think he can have it much hotter there than it has been here, only my recollection is of white jackets and trousers which were more comfortable than the thick things I am now encased in.

" Let me have a line please.

* Mr. Graves, in his " Life of Sir George Grove," points out that Grove always spelt this word and the words related to it with a " t," in accordance with their derivation.

"I went to hear *Tristan* on Saturday. Very impressive, very long, very loud; but my soul revolted. Remember the lovely variety of *Fidelio*—Rocco, Marcellina, the prisoners (bless them!), the soldiers—(and even of *Faust*), and then think of that savage, diabolical story (it only wanted a fight of gladiators to make it quite brutal) four and a half hours long—as monotonous as *could* be, all the themes and passages made out of the Vorspiel! Oh dear! oh dear! This is what we have come to after *Beethoven!* And all the house *raving*.

"Good-bye. Love to Rudie.—Your devoted,

"G."

Grove started for Scotland on July 27th, and stayed for a few days at St. Andrews, where he met my brother Ernest, my brother-in-law Sir Guy Campbell, and Mr. John Oswald of Dunnikier. On Friday, July 31st, he writes to my mother from Rusack's Hotel:

"DEAREST OLD FRIEND,—I must send you a line or two, though they will be illegible, partly owing to the original sin of this writer and partly owing to the vileness of this pen. Your Ernest has been awfully good to me. The way we have hunted one another backwards and forwards to our hotels is most amusing; but at last we met at E.'s hotel and had a very nice dinner—*à la mode ancienne*—splitting with jokes and stories all through (not without pathetic moments either)—Ernest, Guy, Oswald (a very nice fellow), and a certain G. of your acquaintance. It was really very nice. We go to-day to Mr. Oswald's house [Dunnikier] some ten or fifteen miles off till Monday morning (longer they cannot be absent from their irrepressible golf), and I think I shall enjoy it, though I confess I do feel dreadfully rusty now and then (but I don't *creak* as old —— used to do). Do you still want to see me on the 5th, or will this not be convenient ? Please let me know. . . . I have given up the Highlands. Weather too unpromising. . . . Joppa ! ! how comic ! Do you remember Forbes's poem in *Punch* (100 years ago) describing his tour in the East :

'Ease her, stop her,
Who's for Joppa ?'

But that was the real place.—Ever yours,

"G. GROVE."

The last letter I have from G. to my mother is dated from Lower Sydenham, Nov. 17th, 1896 :

"DEAREST OLD FRIEND,—A 1,000 thanks. I answer you at once lest you should be crowded out, though I fear I sha'n't interest or amuse you. I am anything but well : full of pain and of distress and fear. I lay awake from 4 this morning, fighting the devil—all about nothing, but just as bad as if I had disgrace and disaster before me. It's no use complaining, and as a rule I don't talk, but it is dreadful. I am just worn out with letters on mere routine that I have to write myself. . . . . .

I have seen A. S. [Arthur Sullivan] twice. He was thin, but I thought his face very much improved, and *very* nice to look at. We were quite on our old terms, but I had only two words with him. I am sorry about the small houses in Edinburgh, but on the other hand the *Mikado* is doing well here. The fact is that in music now (as there was in painting in pre-Raphaelite times) composers and hearers worship ugliness—that is, directness in any art. There has come a turn or *kink* in the brains and heart-strings of composers : they have no affection, no love for their music. That divine quality which made Mozart, Beethoven, Schubert couch their thoughts in the most beautiful forms they could find, and return to their lovely phrases and subjects over and over again, giving the melodies to one instrument after another, with small appropriate changes, and loving it better every time they came back to it—that is now all dismissed in favour of sound and fury. 'Slap into it, the more directly your thought is thrust upon your hearers the better; ugliness and smashing denote strength of feeling. So don't spare abruptness and roughness.'

" And so the old school, with our dear Arthur as its latest product, must go, and wait in the background till the *fad* has passed and reason comes back. The same thing happened in literature too, Carlyle setting the example. But there's a purer air and a bluer sky behind. These thoughts were forced on me by Schubert's 'unfinished' symphony

last Saturday.   But I've given you enough ! . . .
There's a nice article on me in the last *Saturday
Review.*   More anon.   " G."

SIR ARTHUR SULLIVAN.

Arthur Sullivan was another of our intimate
friends.   It was through Chorley, I think, that we
became acquainted with him shortly after he had
come to London after finishing his musical studies
in Leipzig.   He was then organist of St. Michael's,
Chester Square, a post he retained until 1867, when
he migrated to St. Peter's, Onslow Gardens.
Chorley and Grove were his devoted friends, and
did all they could to promote the success of the
brilliant young man.

The earliest letter I possess from Sullivan was
written to me.   This is headed with a drawing of
" Ponsonby Castle, sketched from life and from the
street by a distinguished Artist."   The " castle "
possesses no back or sides, but on the other hand
its front has eleven windows, in addition to a stack
of chimneys and a front door.   " The Artist " in a
large top-hat is shown contemplating it from the
left.   In real life " Ponsonby Castle " was 3,
Ponsonby Street, S.W.   There is no date, but
internal evidence goes to prove that it was written
on 2nd January, 1863, when I was about to complete my seventh year.

" My dear Rudie,—I write to wish you many
happy returns of the day—in other words, to tell

you how I hope you may live to be a fine old man, honest, upright, and good, always doing what is right, and especially being kind and affectionate to your parents, for think what they do for you.

"Now the Sermon is over, we will proceed to lighter matters. In the first place, I shall be delighted to avail myself of your kind invitation for to-morrow which you did me the honour to send. The prospect of Tea and Buns which you hold out is far too tempting to resist, particularly as Buns are the one great comfort of my life—in fact, the sole object, almost, for which I live. If you could throw in a few biscuits and a pickled onion in red currant jelly my happiness would, indeed, be more than I could well bear. No more of this, however, until we meet.

"Good-bye, my dear boy.—Ever your affectionate friend,

"ARTHUR S. SULLIVAN,
"his + mark.

"*P.S.*—[Here follows an assortment of complicated hieroglyphics.] This of course is between ourselves."

Next comes the description of a mid-Victorian phase of constabulary duty:

"3, PONSONBY STREET, S.W.,
"*Jan.* 9, 1863.

"My DEAR MRS. LEHMANN,—Your graphic account of the City picnic quite revived me when I returned home tired to death with teaching my gallant constables a tune in G *minor*.   No easy task, I can assure you.

"'Now, my men, what key is this in?'

"Dead silence.

"*Organist.*—'Don't all speak at once.   One at a time, if you please.'

"*Shy Tenor* (B 47).—'B, sir.'

"'Major or minor?'

"'Minor, sir.'

"The force looks approvingly at B 47 for having thus defended its honour.

"*Organist.*—'No, that won't do.'

"The force now looks suspiciously at Mr. Sullivan and B. 47 alternately.

"*Mr. S.*—'It's G minor.'

"Deep sigh from the force and sympathising looks at each other.

"This is the way things go on.

"Have you written to Mr. Chorley about the tickets for to-morrow? . . . Don't trouble to answer this, please, as I shall not get your letter before I see you.   I shall make my way to my new address (No. 139, Westbourne Terrace) with a black bag, pleasant demeanour, and hungry feelings.—I am, dear Mrs. Lehmann, ever yours,

"ARTHUR S. SULLIVAN."

Sullivan's music to "The Tempest" was played for the first time at the Crystal Palace on April 5th, 1862. It had a tremendous success, and was repeated at the same place a week later.   Here is a description of its production in Manchester in the following year :

"GREENHAYS, MANCHESTER,
"*Jan.* 23, 1863.

" MY DEAR MRS. LEHMANN,—I shall tell you all about last night's proceedings, but in few words, for I have not ten minutes. First, however, on Wednesday I was received by Miss Hallé most graciously, who entertained me until the return of her parents to dinner. We went to the ' Gentlemen's Concert ' in the evening : very classical and, *ergo*, very slow—Hallé, Molique, Piatti, Reeves, &c. Then I was taken to a ball and shown about like a stuffed gorilla! Mrs. Leisler is the name of the hostess. There I met a Mrs. Gleig or Greig, a sister of Rathbone's. She was very pleasant and likes you and Mr. Lehmann—wonderful exception to a general rule! I stood about the room in easy and graceful postures, conscious of being gazed upon; walked languidly through the lancers, and then talked a good deal to Mrs. Gaskell the authoress, and at half-past 2 was in bed. The next day we went down to the rehearsal, where I met with a most enthusiastic reception by the band on being introduced by Mr. Hallé. They played through the whole thing with good-will and took no end of pains about it. Then I went and got shaved (!), had an Eccles cake, a glass of sherry, and a cigar—looked at a few things of Hecht with him; home to dinner, and then to the concert.

" I sat with the Hallés in the two front rows (I on only one, of course). A splendid hall and well filled—nearly 3000, I am told:

"Overture, 'Egmont'	. . .	BEETHOVEN.
"Song	. . . . .	Miss BANKS.
"Music to 'The Tempest'	. .	A. S. S. !

" Well, I felt calm and collected, and smiled blandly at the few people that I knew. The 'Storm' begins, ends, and is warmly applauded. Things go on. The 3rd Act Prelude, also warmly applauded, at which your correspondent looks gratified, and wishes that a certain friend of his could hear the way in which certain points were taken up and certain passages got through without bungle.

" However, the audience warms up and applauds everything, especially the 4th Act Overture, which your correspondent thought as near perfection as anything he had ever heard. The band was superb —so bright ! Well, it is all over, and loud applause follows. The band applauds at me. Hallé leans over and applauds at me. The audience see that some-thing is up, and continue. At last Hallé beckons to me to come up. I wink, I nod, I interrogate with my eyebrows, and at last rush madly from my seat and up the platform. When I show myself my breath is literally taken away by the noise. It is gratifying, though. I bow six times, twice to the orchestra (who throughout have been so kind and friendly), and shake hands with Hallé; then down again, and all is over. I stay behind during the 15 minutes interval, and am overwhelmed with

— not reproaches — from critics, artists, rich merchants with hooked noses, &c. One gentleman sitting near Mrs. Hallé, seeing me rush away, said, ' What ! is *that* Sullivan, that boy ! ' (Oh that I had a dagger !) ' I thought he was a relation of yours.' Others thought I was a contemporary of Beethoven, or at least his immediate successor.

"Hallé won't let me go back to-day. He is teaching all the morning, and says he has much to say to me, and stay I must. Mrs. Hallé waits now in the carriage to take me to a sewing-school ! My love to the children.—I am, dear Mrs. Lehmann, ever yours,   " ARTHUR S. SULLIVAN."

In 1866, when Sullivan was only twenty-four, he suffered what he himself describes as the first great shock of his life in the death of his father. In the following letter to my mother he pays a beautiful tribute of sorrow and affection to his father's memory :

> " 47, CLAVERTON TERRACE, S.W.,
> " *Thursday night*, 18 *Oct.*, 1866.

" I was very glad to get both your letters. . . . In great pain of this kind one holds out one's hands in an agony to see if any one will clutch them and press them even for a moment only, and it would be sad to hold them out in vain. And what agony, what real physical pain, it is when the first great shock of one's life comes.

" I was at Sydenham on the Saturday night, asleep ; and in the middle of the night was awaked

by the servant to say my brother was there. I
thought my brother wouldn't come down at
4 o'clock in the morning without some reason, and
then he entered, himself looking so pale and odd.
He tried to tell me quietly, but broke down at
once. I got up and dressed, and then went out
into the pitch-dark night, and together we drove
home in a hansom which was waiting at the gate,
and gave out a little faint, glimmering light in
the midst of the terrible darkness.

"Oh, that was a dreadful night! My dear
father went to bed shortly before midnight, and at
twelve he was dead. He slept in the dressing-room
next to my mother's bedroom, and was already in
bed when she came up. He called her and complained of a pain in his side. . . . She ran for a
doctor, but it was too late. She was only away a
few minutes, and before she returned he was gone.
He never spoke a word, but gave a long sigh and
died.

"My dear, dear Father, whom I loved so
passionately and who returned my love a hundred-
fold if that were possible! Oh, it is so hard—it is
so terribly hard—to think that I shall never see his
dear face again, or hear his cheery voice saying,
'God bless you, my boy.' . . . I am able to be
strong all day for my poor mother's sake, who is
nearly broken-hearted (they have been married
thirty years, and known each other intimately
nearly fifty!); but at night, when I am alone, then
the wound bursts out, and I think of him and his

tender love and care for me, and his pride in all I
did—and now he is gone for ever.   Perhaps he can
look upon me and see all I do; and please God I
will try and never do anything that will make him
turn away his head and regret that he left me alone
here. . . .

"Keep me in affectionate remembrance.—Ever
yours,   " A. S. S."

I give the following letter from Sullivan because
it contains a reference to another bright and joyous
spirit too soon withdrawn from the affection of his
friends.   The " Freddie " mentioned by Sullivan
was Frederic Clay, the composer of much beautiful
music.   His opera " The Golden Ring " was produced at the Alhambra on December 3rd, 1883,
amidst warm demonstrations of popular approval.
As he was walking home from the theatre after
the performance he was struck down by paralysis;
and, though he afterwards rallied to a certain
extent, he never recovered his full powers.   He
died at Marlow in 1889.   I have a letter from him
to my mother, undated, but evidently written a
few days before the fatal 3rd December, in which
he says:

" Will I dine with you on the 13th?   *Won't* I,
indeed ?   Yes, with all the pleasure in life, and my
only regret is that the date is so far off! !   I am
ordering some new evening clothes, as I believe I
am getting too shabby.   I hope they will be ready
by the 13th,

" If I make a failure at the Alhambra I don't know what will happen. I shall never have heart to dine at all any more—so let us hope I shall pass muster on the opening night."

Here is Sullivan's letter to my mother :

" QUEEN'S MANSIONS,
    " VICTORIA STREET, S.W.,
        " 22 *Jan.* [1884].

" Bless you for your kind words and loving thought of me. I am all right again now, but a little bit pulled down, and am off next week some-where—whither I know not yet. I saw our precious old Freddy on Sunday for the first time. He is bright, cheery, full of appreciation and sympathy ; but, alas ! speechless still. How awful it is ! "

I began my budget of Sullivan letters with a letter about a birthday. I end it with another written to my mother about a birthday thirty-two years later :

" QUEEN'S MANSIONS.
    " VICTORIA STREET, S.W.,
        " 29 *May,* '94·

" Yes, I had a birthday about a fortnight ago (13th), but I sha'n't have any more. I am 52, and it is time celebrations should cease. Do you remember that I spent part of my 21st birthday with you, and —— I forget the others ; and with every gaiety of London open to us we chose the delirious dullness of Madame Tussaud's ! It seems a very short time ago. How many of our own relations and friends have gone off since then—even Edmund Yates has succumbed.

"I only see Nina about once a year, and when I do see her I always feel as if I never wanted to see anyone else—such is real love, isn't it? Am I never to see *you* again. Is Bourne End to claim you all the time, or shall you be in London, or will you come and stay with me at Walton—also on the Thames?

"Well, in any case let me know when you come south, and I will make (if necessary) herculean efforts to see you. What a lot we shall have to talk about!"

CHAPTER XV.

Landseer—His dispute with Sir Alexander Cockburn—Millais
—Letters in Verse.

MY father was the son of an artist and the brother
of two who followed the vocation of their father. Of
these two brothers, the eldest, Henry, began as a
pupil in the studio of Ingres and spent the greater
part of his life in Paris. He became a Membre de
l'Institut, and was employed to design and execute
the mural paintings in the Hôtel de Ville and the
Palais de Justice. These beautiful monuments of his
skill and labour were destroyed by the incendiaries
of the Commune.

The other brother, Rudolf, also older than my
father, married my mother's sister Amelia Chambers,
and eventually, after some years spent in Rome,
settled in London, where he became well known as
a portrait-painter. A selection from his drawings
of celebrated people was published as a book, and
the original collection was after his death bought
for the nation by the British Museum. Such being
the family antecedents in respect to the art of
painting, it is not, perhaps, surprising that we
were privileged to meet a considerable number of
painters on terms of familiar friendship. Many of
these I can myself remember; but it is only with

M.   S

regard to two of them, Landseer and Millais, that I have sufficient material for the purpose of these " Memories."

About Sir Edwin Landseer my father tells the following story in his " Reminiscences " :

" As great nations have often chosen to fight out their wars on the territory of inoffensive neighbours, so some remarkable men have thought fit to explode their animosity at my humble dinner-table or at that of members of my family. The late Lord Chief Justice, Sir Alexander Cockburn, was at one time a frequeut guest at my house. His innumerable gifts, his fine scholarship, and his animated conversation made his society delightful—when he was in a good humour. But his temper was imperious and vindictive, and his quarrels with intimate friends sudden and unaccountable. I remember Millais saying to me of him : ' You should never have that man on your premises without having the fire-engines ready to act,' and the point of the remark was forcibly brought home to me on two occasions.

" The first was in 1863 or 1864. At that time and for some years afterwards I was living some six miles out of London, near Muswell Hill, and both Sir Alexander Cockburn and Sir Edwin Landseer were· amongst my frequent visitors. They were old and very intimate friends. Sir Alexander promised to dine with me on a certain Sunday, and upon hearing that Landseer was also to be of the party, he offered to call for him in his carriage and drive him out, an offer which Sir Edwin cheerfully accepted. On the appointed day both arrived in an open phaeton, Cockburn himself driving. As usual, we sauntered in the garden before dinner, and I remember Landseer telling me that he always knew the quarter of the wind from the general aspect and colour of the landscape. Then came dinner. I forget who were the other guests, but I recollect that we were very cheerful and that there was abundance of good talk. When the ladies had left the table someone spoke of Shakespeare, and Landseer remarked that even Shakespeare had made mistakes, for in ' As you like it' he makes ' a poor sequestered stag ' shed ' big round tears.' ' Now,' said Landseer, ' I have made stags my especial study, and I know for a fact that it is quite impossible for them to shed tears.' Most of us were inclined to accept this statement as a curious and innocent Shakespearian commentary, but Cockburn suddenly startled us by turning upon Landseer and asking him in a loud voice, ' And don't you think you are committing a most unwarrantable impertinence in criticising Shakespeare?' A bomb exploding in our midst could not have created greater dismay than this violent and unexpected exclamation. Poor Landseer, the most sensitive of mortals, turned pale ; Cockburn continued to glare at him, and all I could do was to break up the party and bundle my quarrelsome guests into the garden. Cockburn joined the ladies, while Landseer remained with the rest of us almost beside himself with anger at this churlish and unprovoked attack. Now came a great difficulty. How was Landseer to be got home? We were, as I have said, some six miles from town, it was a Sunday evening, and no cabs were to be had for love or money. I therefore made every imaginable effort to bring about a reconciliation. With this view I entreated Landseer to forget and forgive. 'Remember, Sir Edwin,' I said, 'that long after he has joined all the other Lord Chief Justices and is forgotten, your name will remain as that of the greatest English painter of this or any other age.' 'That's true,' replied Sir Edwin, 'and I am willing to make it up and ride home with him, but,' he added, 'begad, sir, he had better know that if he begins again, I am the man to get down, take off my coat, and fight him in the lanes.' All attempts, however, to conciliate Sir Alexander were in vain. When I told him that Landseer was willing to shake hands and to go home with him, he shut me up by replying curtly, 'I will not take him.' He drove away alone, and we got one of the other guests to give Sir Edwin a lift home."

The following letter from Landseer to my mother evidently refers to this incident, and fixes its date a year later than my father had supposed:

" *Thursday*, 13 *July*, '65,
"St. John's Wood Road, N.W.

" Dear Mrs. Lehmann,—I have great pleasure in thanking you for your lovely roses. It is most amiable of you to scatter flowers in my path ! I think I know why just now you left your rosy tints at my gate. I much regret being out when you called, and sincerely hope *I* may never meet that ruffian again !—Truly yours,

"E. LANDSEER."

SIR JOHN MILLAIS.

The Millais family and our own were very old friends. " Do you ask me how long we have known one another," I once heard John Millais say to my mother. " Why, we use to rock one another's cradles ! " and one of his great jovial laughs followed to emphasise the declaration. I cannot remember any man who seemed to enjoy life and fame more whole-heartedly than Millais. His magnificent stalwart frame, with the noble head set splendidly on his broad shoulders, his resonant voice, and the rollicking, boisterous good humour of the man, would have made him remarkable in any gathering quite apart from the genius that has given him his place amongst the great painters of the world. He seemed to breast the waves of life like a strong swimmer rejoicing in his strength.

The letters that follow are all addressed to my father. I have to thank the Millais family, and especially Mrs. C. B. Stuart-Wortley (the " Carrie " of the letters) for permission to publish them here.

"ERIGMORE, BIRNAM, PERTHSHIRE,
"24th September, 1878.

"DEAR FREDERICK,—The Viper Hills is with us, and has sloped off to his bedroom to breathe some of his poisonous words into your ear, through the post; and as it is raining outside (no wonder, say you, in Scotland) I will also send you a line to say Heaven knows what, for the pen already falters and my brains are dry. The Commodore was here two days ago, and was reduced to a shadow with the exertions of Lawn Tennis, but is on the whole a healthy-looking Tar. He let go the painter, and is cruising south to incubate more Loans, and to increase that colossal fortune in which we all participate. Alas, all my pretty chickens are leaving us. George and Carrie go this afternoon, and only Mary and Tot will be left with us. Education, education, and when they are finished behold they know *nothing*. Talk about Foreign Loans being a swindle, how about family instruction? But my poor dear Fred, you have a regiment of Vulcan Sheffielders hammering out a fortune for you, whilst your poor dear, poorer friend can only turn out a fancy article occasionally, subject to the fickle approval of an insensible public. Why should you go to America? What is the use of telegramation but to keep friends at home. We must dine again together and have more whist. Give my love to your wife and Nina, and if you do go to the dismal swamp bring me a canvas-back duck.—Your affectionate friend."

Here is added a pen-and-ink sketch of a knicker-bockered artist painting the portrait of an all but inverted ballerina.

The next letter shows Millais clamouring (in verse) for the return of his daughter Carrie. She was staying with us at Dunnichen, Forfar:

"ERIGMORE, BIRNAM, PERTHSHIRE,
"24th September, 1881.

"My dear MacLehmann
Why this delay man?
Næthing can be plainer
You mauna marry
My sonsy Carrie
Wherefore then detain her?
I ken I oughter
With anither daughter
Rest and be satisfeed,
But somehow she
On the piano fortee
I'm wanting by my seed;　　Note—side.
I'm sure you dinna
Permit your Nina,
To gang awa for weeks
And kick her heels,
Wi' pawky Chiels
In kilts, and Southron breeks.
Look to it frind
And quickly sind
My daughter back to Birnam,
Or Mister Apilles,

Like the Machilles,
Will smite thee on the Sturrrnum.
The Mither's gane
And left me alane,
Nor fashed hersel' for the Lassie,
But if ought gaes wrang
She'll no be lang
Before she ca's me Assie.
So send me my bairnie
My bonnie ane Carrie
To gratifee my lugues   (lugs)
Wi' Rubinstein and Auld Lang Syne
And Bach's immortal fugues.
Wae's me, I'm auld
And feel the cauld
Nae wonder I'm dejected
When she bides wi' ye still
Sae silent and chill
What Father would feel but neglected;
For never a word
Has the familee heard
Of what the Creetur's aboot,
And it's just on the cairds,
She's aff wi' the lairds,
To find oot the mon whae will shoot.
A bawbee at maest
Would ha' sent through the Paest
A letter to keep us frae frettin',
But thoughtless and asy
The Cutty's too lazy
To write, or is aye noo forgettin',

" Remember me, Freddie,
    To your ane gude leddie,
    And forgie us this ebuleetion,
    I am no that daft
    But I ken my craft
    And can paddle it wi' discreetion.

" If it's no in your poower
    To read this, be sure
    To spier her for information ;
    You'll find her profeecient
    Wi' learnin' suffeecient
    To interpret the verse of her Nation.

" And let me just say
    They bodies wha hae
    Sic a chance as to cross the Tweed,
    Wha visit auld Reekie
    And eat cock a leekie
    Are fortunate persons indeed.

" Wi' sic beautiful weather
    And dry bloomin' heather
    We're a' of us boond to be happy,
    For the burns though on spate
    (Which seldom abate)
    Are never mair than a ' wee drappy.'
            " —Yours as before,
                        " Foo Erigmore."

Here follows a sketch of a waste of waters with
a mountain peak projecting from it in the background, an umbrella floating handle up in the fore-
ground, and a head, Millais's own, showing above

the waves on the right. Underneath is written,
" All that is left to tell the tale."

"DALPOWIE HOUSE, MURTLY, PERTHSHIRE, N.B.,
"29th September, 1882.

" DEAR FREDERICO,—Will you, will you, come
and see me (us) here? Welcome will you be.
Perhaps a game of whist if you can hit it off with
Sir Henry Thompson, who comes here early next
month, October. I tell you fairly I am all day on
the river fishing, casting, casting, sometimes *blasting*
that the fish won't rise. Yet have I been successful; a 21 lb. yesterday and many other 20 lb. and
one 24 lb. last week, so I can promise you salmon
at all times for your *tummy*.

" It would do your wife good to have a crack
with mine on the perfidy of man.

" Here comes Carrie!—With love to all, yours
ever,

"J. E. MILLAIS."

"2, PALACE GATE, KENSINGTON,
"1st December, 1882.

" DEAR FREDDY, will you come and eat,
 Next Sunday WEEK your dinner here,
At seven sharp, and you will meet
Some friends to both of us most dear?
One, a certain Robert Browning,
Too late, the latest Oxford Doctor,
The other always cap-and-gowning,
Ever dear, *young*, Mrs Procter.
And if your Missus is in Town,

And will come too, how glad I'll be,
To welcome here my very own
Ere she had cast an eye on thee;
Say ' Yes, dear Millais, certainly.'

" *P.S.*—
You owe this doggerel to fog,
Which fills my studio even now,
So as you call me lucky dog,
Don't spurn his little rhyme.   ' Bow-wow.' "

PART II.

AMERICAN MEMORIES.

CHAPTER XVI.

My father's business frequently called him to America. His first visit was made in December, 1852, when he went out with my mother—they had been married in the previous month. After transacting his business in New York, he took my mother on a trip to Philadelphia, Washington, and Richmond. I find an account of their experiences in a diary (mainly written in the form of letters), of which the first two pages are in my mother's handwriting and the rest in my father's:

"WASHINGTON,
"*Tuesday evening*, 1*st February*, 1853.

" Arrived at the seat of American government after decidedly the most pleasant railway journey I have yet experienced in this great country of equality. Equality is very noble, but not comfortable after all. All grades of society meet in travelling here in the one long, many-seated car, and I, not being republican, cannot help sighing as remembrances of the luxurious, exclusive, softly-cushioned, carpeted English railway carriage rise within me and excite a little impatience at the

contrast with the American car.   The crush, too,
owing to this universal scheme, is very annoying, and
one has to go before the time in order to secure a seat,
a proceeding which the traveller of every grade in
England would smile at, I think.   However, it is
absurd for one little woman stuffed with British
prejudices, as her husband declares her to be
(though she solemnly declares the calumny to be
perfectly unfounded and entirely false), to make
lamentations over a system which so evidently is an
admirable one for a community.   After all it is not
the liberty, equality, and brotherly love I complain
of, not at all, but oh! if the liberty, equality, and
brotherly love would only give up the habit of
spitting; far from that, Washington in particular
has little monuments to this filthy custom dotted
everywhere, in the shape, I need not add, of
spittoons.   This it is which makes the huge ugly
car to me an abomination.   Well, I don't think I
have told you where we came from to-day.   It was
Baltimore, and our resting-place for two days before
that was at Philadelphia.   Philadelphia made a very
favourable impression upon us, the more so as we
did not find that terrible pushing, rushing crowd
which flies along the streets of New York and
Boston."

[Here my mother's handwriting ends and my father's begins.]

"*Thursday, 3rd February.*

"Whether it was the splendid weather, a mild
sun of April, and one glorious expanse of blue sky,

on the last days of January, that made us look on everything in Philadelphia with brighter eyes, or whether it be the older and more dignified look of the town, we certainly took a fancy to it and had a run of being pleased with everything. Maybe our comfortable quarters at the Girard House, which certainly is the best establishment of the kind we have seen as yet in America, had a kindly influence, on our Anglo-Saxon hearts. The town is built as regular as a chess-board, but the streets are broad, the houses high, bright and comfortable-looking, and the few public buildings, the famous United States Bank that made the great crash I don't know when, the Xchange (as they write it often in America), the Post Office, &c., &c., are fine marble edifices in the Grecian style.

"On Saturday night we went to a theatre and saw Auber's 'Bayadère' performed most deliciously. The singing was so novel and wonderful that it kept us in a roar of laughter; the dancers were very republican, that is, they took great liberties with their legs.

"On Sunday we wrote letters in the morning and then went out to ——, where the —— have an old-fashioned cottage. They received us very kindly. He says little and she much in a very whining tone of Christian humility that makes me nervous. They were so very good to us that it was quite delightful to escape from this shade of perfection and high-toned morality where any funny story would infallibly have broken its neck.

M,   T

" Monday at two to Baltimore, a nice cosy, dirty town. Being in the capital of Maryland, where slavery is the law of the land, we were for the first time waited on by slaves. I am no sentimentalist, but I can never overcome a silent terror creeping over me when I see one of these wretched, list-less, vacant, shining black statues behind my chair.

" Saw some acts of ' Othello.' The audience enjoyed the sport and laughed heartily at every point of Othello's agony and Iago's falseness.

" Arrived here (Washington), leaving Baltimore at 4, about 6 p.m. on Tuesday evening.

" A most dreary, uncomfortable town this Washington. Such bragging great designs for a metropolis with such desolate results are quite distressing. Imagine the Capitol, a fine striking building on a commanding rising ground, at one end of the city, and the President's house, a large two-storeyed mansion of no great pretensions from an architectural point of view, at the other, with an interval of two miles of howling wilderness—that is, several huge barrack-looking townships of hovels and lots of poor little shops bordering a dirty broad road, at both sides of which poor thin trees try to make avenues but can't. Then there is the Patent Office and the Post Office *et plus rien.* I never saw anything more dreary and desolate. As I have more leisure here than I had in any other town through which I have passed, the hideousness of this hotel life becomes more apparent and depressing.

Here is, for instance, the National Hotel. Imagine a house with some 300 rooms, and accommodating as many families in rooms with white walls and as little furniture as can be, viz., bed, table, chairs, washstand, and looking-glass. No wardrobe, no pegs, in fact, going little beyond the furniture of which my Boston friend complained, viz., a small bed and a large Bible. The bells of all these rooms are centred in the office on the ground floor in a so-called electric annunciator—a huge frame containing all the numbers covered by a little ivory plate. When a bell is rung this cover slants side-ways and uncovers the number of the bell-ringing room. To marshal the waiters who answer these rings a large bell in the courtyard is kept in a perpetual agitation. The floor of the hotel is generally occupied by lounging smokers, for whose convenience easy chairs are ranged along the walls. Here the republican spitting habit keeps up a per-petual fire, or rather water. The floor is inundated with it, notwithstanding an army of spittoons. Round this parterre are bathrooms, the hairdresser's shop, the bar, the reading-rooms, and even the telegraph-office. A constant round of eating and drinking is kept up. Your board is charged so much, and for that each person may do his or her worst at breakfast, lunch, dinner, tea, and supper. And they do it too. You see delicate females have a beefsteak, eggs, buckwheat cakes, and hot corn-bread, with tea and coffee, for their breakfasts, and despatch it all in a bewilderingly short time. At breakfast, lunch, tea, and supper, parties drop in, feed, and slink off, and as one party succeeds the other the slow-coach who sits half an hour at these meals has at least something to divert his attention from the food.   And the dinner is of all meals the most unrefined, dreary, funereal, and dyspeptic affair in the world.   Two hundred people or more sit down at the same time in an immense room.   A printed bill of fare is put before you, counting up everything imaginable in the season.   You are very hungry, and pick out of this immense spread what you think will be a very nice dinner; but woe betide you.   As nothing is put on the table except the *entrées* (*anglice*, 'No, thank you's') you have to take the rest on chance, and then begin your disappointments.   Everything is done wholesale and badly, and you get almost every dish cold.   You try beef, mutton, ducks, and geese in succession, and give it up in despair.   Turkeys and cranberries are most to be relied upon, and I have taken to make my dinner of these items.   So much for the dinner, but the company—ugh!   There they sit, solemn, grave, and devouring, and the moment they find their stomach refuses to admit any further bolt into it off they rush.   The only amusing feature at dinner is the army of waiters putting down the dessert.   They are regularly drilled, and march at a given signal in military order two abreast to their different stations.   Arrived at his post, each waiter stands motionless with dish in hand until the commander-in-chief, *alias*, head-waiter, gives them the signal, when down go some fifty or sixty dishes with a noise like a peal of distant thunder.

" Pardon this digression and let us return to Washington. Our first walk was to the Capitol. It is, as I have said, a very handsome building, and overlooks the would-be city. Going up a broad flight of steps and entering, you find yourself in a high (I think 96 feet) circular hall lighted from the top. Round the walls are some seven or eight large, bad paintings commemorative of Columbus's landing, the baptism of Pocahontas, and several scenes from the war and the Declaration of Independence. These pictures are void of all interest except from the historical association, which is heightened by the fact that some of them were painted by a Col. Trumbull, who was himself of Washington's staff.

" To the right and left of this hall are the House of Representatives and the Chamber of the Senate. In both I admired the comfortable and business-like arrangements. Each room occupies a semicircle. Against the wall is the President's chair raised up a few steps and canopied by the wings of the American Eagle. Before him, a little lower down, sit the Clerks of the House, and before them again the Reporters. In the semicircle each member has his easy chair and a desk either before or attached to it. The arrangements in the Senate are the same, only the room looks quieter ; there is not the same number of members, not the same bustle, not the same talking, and last (though in America never least) there is less spitting. Both Houses are open to everybody, and the arrangement of a large gallery for strangers running round the whole room recognises in a very striking manner the acknowledged right of the public to be present at these sittings. No gruff porter has to be bribed, nor are you cooped up in a miserable little hole as in the House of Commons. On our entering, the porter immediately made two gentlemen rise from a front bench to make room for *a lady*, which great politeness and civility always comes upon you like a ray of sunshine from the general slovenly and taciturn manners of the Americans. It is but right to say that they are far before all other civilised nations on this point, and it would be well if the ladies were contented with their position and not anxious to stretch the thing to an impossible point, as they have latterly tried to do in the States.

"There was nothing of great interest going on in either House just at the time we were there, although the reading by the Clerk of a Bill conferring powers on a company to conduct a railroad and telegraph from the Mississipi to the Pacific in not more than ten years gave rise to thoughts of wonder at the onward flight of this majestic age, and made the inward prophetic eye look with awe at the destinies of this nation.

"Below the Senate Chamber is the Supreme Court of the United States, the Judges, in simple black robes, the Counsel without any of the paraphernalia that seem in England indispensable for laying down the law and bamboozling witnesses.

I may here add another word to my American vocabulary, as the Counsel spoke of testi*mony* as if it were written testi*mohny.*

"The President's house has been often described, and has little in it of interest, except that it is the domicile of the Chief Magistrate of the United States, where he lives in republican frugality and simplicity, and may be seen by all, and every day.

"On Wednesday night we went to the theatre to see Mrs. Mowatt in 'The Stranger.' The house is large, but ill-lighted. The actors were as good as in one of the better provincial theatres in England. The best of it was, that to lighten the intolerable burden of howling, whining, remorse, and virtue, Peter introduced a few tricks of the clown in one place, and was bodily put over Solomon's knee and whipped in another, both of which scenes of wit and mirth (*alias* disgusting buffoonery) tickled the audience mightily and made the house shake with roars of laughter. A song was introduced which was so horrible that I daresay it moved several people beside the 'Stranger' to tears.

"After dinner on the same day a Mr. Fuller, standing at the door of our hotel, was shot through the heart by a Captain Schaumberg. The latter owed Fuller money and, as he would not pay, Fuller placarded him all over the town as a Coward, Liar, Swindler, &c., &c., adding sundry sweet epithets. This seems to have stung Schaumberg to madness, and, declaring that the first time he saw him he would shoot him like a dog, he waited in the street before the hotel for two days, and when he saw him he shot him down and then gave himself up to the authorities. This truly American episode created little enough excitement, and now nobody speaks about it any more. It seems just what everybody would have done under the circumstances. We are somewhat tired of Washington and shall be heartily glad to get out of it, which event will come off at 7 a.m. to-morrow, when we go South to Richmond in Virginia."

"*Saturday, 5th February,* 1853.
 "*On board the ' Mount Vernon,' on the River Potomac, from Washington to Aquia Creek, en route for Richmond.*

"Amongst the lions of Washington I forgot to mention the Patent Office, a building in which models of all American patented inventions or improvements are kept. Not having a very practical turn of mind, I was less interested by these professed contents of the building than by a sort of Museum upstairs in which one large glass case particularly rivetted my attention. It contains the original 'Declaration of Independence,' this talisman of the American Republic. I could not overcome an involuntary shudder as I read in it, set forth in the most glorious language, that all men are born equal, and that man has certain inalienable rights, amongst which first and foremost is the pursuit of liberty, health and happiness—and the avenging spirit of slavery rose before me. Ugh!

Going into the barber's shop on board just now, I enquired of the barber, himself a free coloured man, whether a female servant on board, who struck me by her transparent white colour and as woolly a head of hair as that of any negro woman, was slave or free, coloured or white.

" 'Certainly she is a Mulatto woman, but she is free.' He went on telling me in reply to my enquiries, that Mrs. Stowe's tale was by no means overcoloured; indeed the reverse, and rightly so, because if she told the whole truth nobody would believe her. 'I know it from experience, Sir, because I have passed my whole life in the South, and on this very river we daily see those scenes she describes. And yesterday we had a gang of slaves on board, and any man might see the degradation of women, the separation of families and the examination of people like so many cattle. If you go to Richmond you have but to go into the slave market and you will see it all. You can buy a woman there as you buy a cabbage in other markets. To-day a trial comes off against a woman for teaching slaves to write and read. That is a penitentiary crime and punished by ten years' imprisonment.'

" These things certainly strike you with a sort of ghastly unnatural terror as they come upon you thus in shape and form, and the impression on a rational mind must be stronger than 10,000 Uncle Tom novels. One remains struck with a silent bewilderment at the incongruity of a free and enlightened republic forbidding to men who are

born their equals by their own gospel, the light of
knowledge.

" To return, however, to the glass case in the
Patent Office. It contained, in addition, Washington's uniform and sword, and treaties between
America and the most powerful European nations.
There were the signatures of Frederick Wilhelm III.
of Prussia; Francis, Emperor of Austria; Ferdi-
nand VII. of Spain; and then in a row Louis
the Sixteenth, 1783; Bonaparte, 1802; Louis
the Eighteenth, 1820, and Louis Philippe. *Sic
transit gloria.*

" We are sailing like a phantom ship enveloped
in a cloud of fog. The banks of the river may be
guessed but not seen, and thus we passed Washington's seat, ' Mount Vernon,' unbeknown to Betsey
Prig. Occasionally we run aground with a bump,
but somehow always get off again. The saloon is
on deck, the sleeping berths below, and very comfortable and airy they look, so that things seem to
have improved since the time of Dickens' experience
of berths like bookshelves in the saloon, the two
sexes being divided by a pinned curtain.

" The engine overtops everything, being a
high-pressure one. Such a steamer is a sort of
two-storied house, the quarter-deck being the
second storey, the saloon, first floor, and the
sleeping berths, ground floor. There is a ticket-
office, a post-office, a barber's shop, and sundry
other indispensable conveniences."

CHAPTER XVII.

The Diary continued—Richmond, Va.—Talk about Slavery—
Service in the Negroes' Chapel—A Sailor-preacher and
his Discourse.

"RICHMOND, CAPITAL OF VIRGINIA,
"*Sunday, Feb. 6th*, 1853.

" WE had left Washington shortly after 6, and
at about 11 o'clock the steamer reached Aquia
Creek, where the cars stood waiting for us on the
water's brink. With the usual American dispatch
passengers and luggage were transported from
steamer to railway and away we went, through
the most dreary and uninteresting country I have
ever travelled in. Large woods and immense tracts
of waste uncultivated fields made up the scenery
which, during a distance of 76 miles, was scarcely
enlivened by a single habitation or one human
being, if I except the town of Fredericksburg, a
straggling miserable little place that boasts of
having been the scene of Washington's childhood
and youth. As we stopped, crowds of negroes of all
shades of colour and gradation of lips and noses
gathered on the station platform, and their mournful, timid, sometimes brutish and vacant, oftener
wistful and imploring aspect made my heart turn
sick.

" For the first time since I have been in America

I got into a somewhat lengthened conversation with a fellow traveller. He wore a white cravat, and a white beaver hat, and might have been a clergyman.

"'From the north, I guess.'

"'No, sir, from England.'

"'Ah, and not long since you arrived in our country.'

"'Only six weeks.'

"'Landed in New York, I presume.'

"'No, in Boston.'

"'And going south on a tour through our country?'

"I nodded assent, and having thus far satisfied his craving for guessing and reckoning, I got to talk with him on *the* subject—Slavery, and my different questions brought out the following answers.

"'Believe me, sir, there is not a man in his senses here that does not see the bane of slavery. It is acknowledged by everyone to be the curse of this country. The land we travel through just now is literally accursed by slavery, for it has been worked till it will produce nothing, and had to be given up and lie waste; it's a curse to business, a curse and bar to all improvements, and a curse to society in every fibre and relation.

"'But the question is not the right or wrong of the thing. Nobody disputes that. But how is the evil to be remedied?

"'No doubt the negroes could be improved and might be educated to be useful citizens, but 200 years of slavery have so debased and degraded

the race that it will take more than 200 years
to raise them up to civilisation again.   The Abolition cry in the North is only a party cry and those
same people that are writing so furiously against
Slavery would not give a black man 50 cents to
help him in his escape to Canada.   You must not
forget that it is a question of property.

"'There are planters here who have from 150
to 500 "people" as they are called here (for in
the South only the coloured population are called
"the people," whereas the Whites are Ladies and
Gentlemen).   Now fancy yourself to be brought up
amidst Slavery with all the ideas about property
with which slaves are looked upon here, and
succeeding to an estate of, say a plantation with
300 people.   Well, every slave is worth at any
of the markets from 1,000 to 5,000 dollars, and so
the 300 slaves represent a property of about
400,000 dollars.   Now it is a very great question
if you would give that property up, lose all you are
worth and say to those slaves, "You are free."
There is where the shoe pinches.   There was a pro-
position made in Congress by Henry Clay to make
a loan of two hundred million dollars and indemnify
every planter for the freedom of his slaves, but it
never got as far as being brought in as a Bill, as
the North would not have consented to pay the
South her share of this sum.   Mrs. Stowe's novel is
quite true, and for a work of fiction it keeps wonderfully to facts, but there is a growing opinion against
all cruelties and injustices to slaves, and a man that

would separate a family would be a marked man in society. Why only the other day 200 slaves were sold in that very town of Fredericksburg, and not a family was separated.

" ' Some slaves will not have their freedom because they know they will be taken care of till they die, and if they are sick will have their master's physicians. You may say this spirit only shows how thoroughly their hard fate has broken them down, but still there's the fact, make of it what you can. Slavery must inevitably perish, however long it may take. Almost all the States of the North were slave states and have one after another abolished Slavery, and so it will go on.'

"The man spoke well, and you may form your own conclusions on his testimony which, as given on the spot, as well as proving the absurdity of the idea that the subject of Slavery may not be frankly approached in the South, was very interesting to me.

" The cars soon stopped, and it was not long after I had selected from a herd of the most monstrous and subterranean looking crowd of black, howling paupers the most ugly one, belonging to the Exchange Hotel, that we and our luggage were comfortably housed in pleasant quarters. The hotel is a square building with an open courtyard, in the middle of which a fountain in the form of a swan is just now vainly endeavouring to make an impression against the waters that are coming down in a veritable deluge of rain.

" The interior is vast and comfortable. Maybe we are mildly disposed after that hideous phantom of Washington. However, the public rooms are large and well furnished, the bedrooms comfortable, the food palatable, and the servants attentive.

" Amongst them is a man as white as myself, and the only remarkable feature about him is a crop of long and somewhat woolly fair hair. He is a slave, and was bought by the proprietor of this hotel some months ago. One of his fellow-slaves told me his history. ' I know all about his family,' he said. ' His father was a very rich merchant up the river, his mother a very bright but coloured woman. The father hated them and sold him and his mother south.' It may appear an unpardonable weakness to a philosopher that wherever a slave is found almost like ourselves, we feel a keener sense of the injustice, a more savage horror and disgust at the institution, than at the sight of a very black man, but still I think the feeling is but human. I cannot look at that man with his blue eyes, fair hair and European features without feeling painfully bewildered and awestruck. When I think that his master can sell him to-morrow to pick cotton on a plantation, can beat him almost to death, can prostitute his wife, can sell his children without any man having the right to interfere, my hair stands on end. Why, little X—— with his curly woolly hair and Mulatto features would look black beside him, and I must really write and warn him never to enter this Land of Liberty. If anybody had a spite against him, he would no doubt make out a claim against him and he would be sold down south and would not bring much either, as he is but a little fellow. But some planter might make him his groom or have him to wait at table, and he would have to be thankful.

"Dinner was served by 5 or 6 slaves, of whom the head waiter Eli has taken us under his especial care and patronage. I asked a shiny, good humoured little black boy, who did not seem to understand me: 'Don't you speak English?' 'No, Mas'r.' 'What do you speak then?' 'I speak Virginia.' After dinner (which was the first meal we had enjoyed for a week, as we ate it, not in the company of 200, but alone, as the dishes were therefore hot not cold, and as we could take our own time) we took a drive to see the town. It stretches beautifully down a hill and overlooks a fertile valley through which the river James winds its course. As we arrived at the top of an eminence which overlooks the place, sunset gave its last many coloured rays to light up one of the finest panoramas I have seen in America. I can't help believing that the town from its situation on this James River, which here recalls the Thames, was called after her of the Star and Garter of blessed memory. I presume that some courtier of Queen Bess who gave the name to this state of Virginia, got a grant of the lands hereabout from the maiden queen for some special services done to her Majesty, and he having eaten a great many good dinners at the Star and Garter of the 16th century, exercised the Christian virtue of gratitude, and in grateful recollection of these delicious feasts, founded here a town, the mere name of which would bring the water into his mouth, the smell of roses and fresh hay into his mind's nose, and the glorious old Thames to his mind's eye.

"Being tired with the journey, we went to bed very early, and as a never failing consequence got up very late. I had just time to finish breakfast before following the advice of my black friend Eli to go to their church, which had the finest choir in the country. To this church then I went. It turned out to be a Baptist chapel, and I do not remember having ever been so much edified and amused at the same time at any place of worship. The chapel formed as it were an aisle with two wings. At the top of the aisle was the pulpit and behind it an elevation on which sat three white men, or brothers, as they called themselves. Before the pulpit stood a long and somewhat elevated table surrounded by a motley group of what appeared to me black elders. Before them seemed to be a small number of seats set apart for the white lords. The rest of the whitewashed and clean but some-what-out-of-repair-looking chapel was well filled by coloured people of a variety of shades more numerous than I had conceived possible. In Europe we see so few negroes that somehow they all look alike, and I could never tell Brown, the black waiter at Mr. D.'s, from Jones, the black waiter at Mr. R.'s.

I went up to near the middle of the church and sat down a few benches below the table of which I have spoken. I immediately noticed a suppressed titter among the women near whom I sat down. Then a grave elderly black or blackerly elder came up to me, and invited me by gestures to come to the place preserved for the Whitocracy. I made a sign that I wished to remain, on which he retired. Another titter and another black entreating me to come to the place of honour. I thought I would see what it all meant, and told him to leave me alone as I was very well there. He bowed off politely, but immediately the woman that had sat on the same bench with me got up and took her seat beside several other coloured women, leaving me thus alone in my white glory, which I suppose the neighbourhood of any coloured person is supposed to darken considerably.

"During this little by-play a black had offered up a very long extempore prayer, the minister stepped to the pulpit and then began to read the Ten Commandments, interrupting himself occasionally thus:

"'Thou shalt not take the name of the Lord thy God in vain, for the Lord will not hold him guiltless that taketh His name in vain.

"'Now you see, my brethren, nothing can be more irreverent than to call upon God for mere trifles. I know some of you will stop in the street, and the one will tell a piece of news, whereupon the other will exclaim, "Lor'." Now that is very bad. " Good God " is just as bad, and I might go on. You should never speak of God as of a single man. The Jews called God Jehovah, which is made up of three Hebrew words, meaning Was, Is, and Shall be. And they had such respect for their Jehovah that in prayer they passed the word over in silence as too awful to be pronounced.'

" Then he went on to ' Thou shalt keep the Sabbath holy,' &c.

" ' Now you know there has been a little modifi- cation made in this by our Saviour, and works of necessity and mercy are excepted. I guess you don't know why we keep the first day of the week instead of the last as the Jews. Well, I'll tell you. The Jews celebrated the creation of the world, whereas we solemnize the resurrection of Christ. That is a fact.'

" Thus he got to the end. Then he asked the choir, composed of coloured men and women, opposite to give them a hymn, which the choir did, and very prettily too. They sang a sort of Methodist hymn, and the melody, as it was sung in very good tune and with occasional *pianos* and *fortes*, had something very touching in its rough simplicity and beauty. After that the minister informed us that Brother Congreve of New York was present and would address them in favour of a society for building churches for missionary sailors, for which object he was at present travelling through the country. He said he need not remind them that sailors were the most good-natured and honest and deserving class, and altogether straightforward, go-ahead Christians.

"Whereupon Brother Congreve, a chaplain in the United States Navy, and a regular smart Yankee, came forward with a very good face and a blue coat with gilt buttons.

"I wish I had been a shorthand writer and taken his sermon down as he delivered it, and, more than that, I wish I could convey his delicious Yankee accent, putting stress always on the indefinite article *a*, as well as surprising you often by putting English words into American pronunciation. But he carried such a strong spirit of truth and conviction into his words, and his roaring voice had such a fresh smell of the sea, so very different from the nasal twang of cant and imbecility I had made up my mind to when I went, that I gladly forgave him the nonsense he spoke now and then, and may say that I never listened to a sermon with so much pleasure. So much so, that I will try to give you a sketch of it.

"His text was taken from the Acts xxvii. 31. 'Unless these abide in the ship ye cannot be saved.'

"'Yes, my brethren, unless these abide in the ship, ye cannot be saved. Who are these? These are sailors. Unless the sailors abide in the ship you cannot be saved. Who said so? Paul did. When? On the occasion of his shipwreck. An angel had appeared to Paul and told him to be of good cheer, for that all that sailed with him should be saved. Now Paul believed the angel, but did that make him be idle? No. He cheered the ship's crew on, and in the storm they drive towards the land, and they cast out soundings' (accompanying the words with ship-shape gestures) 'and find twenty feet water, and they cut off the masts, and a short time after they sounded again and find fifteen feet water. Then during the night they threw four anchors out, and towards morning, as the storm continued to rage, did they give it up? No, not at all: they saw a creek and tried to steer the ship into it, they hove the anchors on board, they made the creek, and drove the ship on to a rock, where she went all to pieces. Well, those that could swim swam towards land, and those that could not floated ashore on the pieces of timber, and so all were saved. Now what does this teach us? Just that although we were ever so sure to be saved, we should use the means of grace, and just work for our salvation as if without it we were doomed to perdition. That's the sense hidden in Paul's story. But now let me come to what brings me here. I am here to speak to you of one of the most useful, the most honest, the best-hearted classes of the community. I am a sailor myself, that is, I am a minister of the Gospel, and for thirteen years I have been in the service of the United States Government. I have been more than five on the wide ocean. I have seen the sailor at his daily occupation, I have seen him in trouble, I have stood by him in sickness, ay, I have closed his eyes and seen him lowered into his watery grave to lie there until the day when the sea shall give up her dead. (Groans amongst the congregation.) Therefore I know the sailor and can speak of him.'

" He then continued to eulogise Jack Tar as the most virtuous and best of men, and very delightfully came to a climax with the question, 'And should we not try to convert these sailors? Should we not try to make Christians of them? Certainly; and in that you are to help me. We have got a church of Christ now opened in a chapel of Bethel at New York. You see the sailor is nowhere at home, he is nowhere long enough to have an interest in building *a* church. He stops but *a* few days when he returns from a distant part of our country or from *a* country to another. So you see we other Christians, who are dependent on him for comforts that have become necessities to us, should provide comfort for the soul of the poor sailor. And now let me just remind you of what our blessed Saviour did. He goes and meditates in the mountains, and when He thinks He is ready to preach, why He comes right down to the town, and to what town? To Galilee, a poor sea-port; and whom did He choose for His apostles? Why, fishermen and sailors. And in that He showed the wisdom of God, for where could He have found people to stand by Him and His doctrine as staunchly as did those very fishermen and sailors? Look at Peter. Why, Peter signifies a rock, and a rock he was in his attachment to his beloved Lord, except just once, when I guess he did not behave as he ought to have done, and that was when he denied Him.'

"After thus showing that God had chosen sailors to become the instruments of diffusing Christianity and converting Jews and Pagans, he argued in a most cogent and convincing manner that it was but fair for the Baptists to *convert* the sailors, but say what he would he said it in such a frank and fresh voice, and was so little put out by any nonsense he might occasionally spout, that you could not help admiring this rude eloquence; and so he went on giving instances of the gallantry and merits of sailors.

"'Why, there was a vessel on the coast of Oregon but a few months ago, and in *a* fearful hurricane the ship got among the breakers. The coast was uninhabited; there was but one way of saving the whole ship's company. The captain looked about him and said, "I will give 500 dollars to any man who'll go and take a line on shore." The sea was at that time rushing against the rocks in *a* most furious manner. *A* man came forward and said, "Sir, I'll try. I can but lose my life in the attempt." He put the line round his body and threw himself into the raging waters, and in twenty minutes he was seen waving his hands high on the shore. A communication was established and all the passengers and crew were saved. The man comes back on board and the captain says, "Here, my man, is your money." But the noble fellow said, "Keep your money, captain; such services are not done for money."

" 'Then look at our Collins steamer the other day. They are themselves fighting against a hurricane when they see a Scotch vessel in distress. There are sixteen people on board that vessel making all possible signals of distress. The passengers were all in the greatest excitement. The captain said, "We cannot leave those people to drown. We must save them if there's a chance." Well, they waited more than twelve hours before they could think of getting off a boat. Then the wind lulled, and the captain said, " Now or never is our chance. Who will man the boat?" " I," " I," " I," and " I," they answer him from all sides. They put off, and many there were that thought they would never come back. Such was the fury of the waves, that for fear of being shivered to pieces against the Scotch vessel they made the people drop into their boat, and when they had all dropped in, they put back. What a sight, now on the top of the wave, now quite hidden from view. At last they got all safely back to the steamer, and just when all were saved, to show the wonderful escape they had had, the lifeboat struck against the steamer and broke into atoms.'

"All these stories elicited the most intense groans of anxiety and interest from the congregation. Then he told them of all the sailors they had already converted, amongst others of a Swede called Nielsen.

" ' " Why," says Nielsen, " I'm going right off to Sweden to convert my parents and friends." Most natural when a man has got converted he wants to take his friends by the hand and say to them, " Come *right away* to Christ." Well, he did so, and people came to hear him from near and far, and at last the Government got wind of his designs and they cited him before *a* court. But what of that. He was made of the right stuff. Pretty perpendicular, I guess; as straight as the main-mast. There were the judges of the land and the greatest preachers of their own Church, which is the Lutheran (!) and therefore comes nearest to the Roman Catholic religion. But could they confound him. Not at all. He had his Bible in his jacket pocket and the spirit of the Lord in him. " Well, Nielsen, convince you we can't," said they. " And you must leave the country," and so they banished him from his native land. What did he do ? Oh, just goes to another country—to Denmark. There he raises the banner and founds *a* Church. There they just want somebody to stir them up, and he does it.

" ' But,' continued he, ' these sailor missionaries can do more. They go to Havana now, for instance. There the religion is Roman Catholic, and they don't allow a Protestant of any sort to preach, neither the Presbyterian nor the Church of England, nay not even the Lutheran, which comes nearest their own. Well, the sailor just goes on shore with some tracts in his pockets. Nobody notices him. He can talk Spanish, and he talks to one and the other. At last he finds somebody thirsty for tracts and he gives him some.'

" Thus he went on rambling and narrating to prove that your real converted Baptist sailor was the very best missionary you could get.

" ' And,' continued he, ' we have been considerable often accused of being too fond of the penny, but never mind that. Cheapness is *a* consideration, and sailors do our work cheap. We don't give them a farthing, nay they contribute to the funds to do the work. We have sixteen languages represented in our society, all without having cost us a single penny.'

" This climax could not be topped, so he wisely left the matter there, and the pastor, brother somebody, got up and said that, as for himself, he should do violence to his feelings if he did not contribute to this work, and whoever thought with him, should do the same and put his offering on the table before him, ' for,' concluded he, ' the Day of Judgment will surely come, and *there* (pointing to the gallery where the black choir sat) God will sit on his white throne and ask every one of you, " What have you done for the sailor ? " ' "

CHAPTER XVIII.

The Diary continued — The Richmond Slave-market — A
Tobacco Factory — Richmond to Charleston, S.C. — A
Slave Auction.

" RICHMOND,

" *Tuesday, 8th Feb.* 1853.

" I HAVE just returned from a second visit to the
Slave-market here. I went first yesterday morning,
and the scene so utterly unhinged my mind that I
found it impossible to write to you just then.

" Eli, the black head waiter, showed me to the
place. He seems to have taken a special fancy for
N. and myself, and told me that he belongs to a
speculator here, who hires him out at so much a
month. He is allowed to keep some part of his
wages, and with these savings which amount sometimes to $100 a year, the man hopes to buy his
freedom in time. He is married and allowed to see
his wife every night, which is a great favour.
When he gets his own freedom he intends to make an
arrangement with his wife's owner not to sell her
till he can release her too. I hope he may succeed.
The man is very active, serviceable, and quite
cheerful. The Slave-market was but a few steps
below the hotel. It was a wooden sort of low-
roofed ware-room. On the door was a sign-board
with—'R. Dickinson and Brother, Auctioneer,' and

somewhat below hung the usual red flag to intimate that a sale was going on.

"On a platform, raised a few steps above the floor, stood a negro, and the auctioneer, surrounded by the motley group of buyers.

"The negro did not show the least sign of resistance, nor did he, or any one of the many others that I saw sold after, show the least sense of his situation. He answered every question put to him, and seemed anxious to bring as high a price as possible, as the greater their value, I suppose, the better their treatment.

"'Now, gentlemen,' called out the auctioneer, who looked quite a mild and gentlemanly man, 'who will give me a bid for this boy? He is warranted perfectly sound. No mark on him.' Here his attendant tucked up the slave's drawers above the knee and made him take off his shoes. 'A good foot and leg, you see, gentlemen, fit for anything.' Then several gentlemen came up to him, felt his feet and legs, felt his throat, and asked him if he was quite healthy. The slave said 'Yes.' 'Grin, my boy,' said another, upon which the negro showed a set of the most magnificent teeth. 'Here is ivory for you, gentleman,' shouted the auctioneer, and the buyers, having touched him all over, looked down his throat and asked him what work he had done, to which the slave replied, 'I have worked on a farm, but I can drive a waggon and do most anything.' The bidding then began, and soon got very spirited. You must know that the

American auctioneer never stops calling out the bid until the article is sold. He shouts out the bid until he gets another, and so on, and repeats it as continually to himself. So you heard (*loud*) 700, (*low and very quick*) 700, 700, 700, 700, 700, 700, (*loud*) 710, (*low*) seven and ten, &c., &c., &c., and so on. The man was sold for $1,150.

"Then came another. He was walked out like a horse. 'Stand by, gentlemen, and look how he walks.' They could not get a bid for him. At last somebody bid 450 which was indignantly rejected, and the man stepped down unsold. A few minutes after, I saw a white man take a gentleman to him and heard the following conversation.

"White man to the negro : 'Now Jimmie, I have sold you privately and you have got into the hands of a real gentleman, so just you behave yourself and don't you drink and fight again.' Jimmie said he would not. White gentleman, who was very mild and seemed rather ashamed of buying the man : 'Some ladies that are with me will go up the river in a few days, and you can go with them right up to my house. There you can rest a day or two and then you must help some seven or eight black men I have there working on a road to finish the last mile. As for your wife, you see it will be a distance of sixty miles and you can't expect to go and see her more than once a month, that is, if I can get you the permission from her owner. You see you are in a different position, but I will see what I can do. Now you may go down town and do what you like.' The seller repeated his admonitions to Jimmie to behave himself, and Jimmie went off with renewed protestations.

" I asked the seller why he had sold him, and he told me he was a good enough man, but when he got leave of absence he would go on the spree and not come back to the time, so his owner was determined to sell him 'and you see I have had to manage it privately. Do you buy, sir?' 'No,' I replied, with a shudder, and turned away.

" 'Here's a boy, gentlemen, who has a mark on his forehead, he says from a rock he got thrown at him, and moreover his left leg is bad from the kick of a horse. He is whipt some on the back and I don't warrant him sound.' They made him walk, they made him strip, and at last he was knocked down for $750 to a Mr. Thomas.

Then came a girl. 'Gentlemen, that girl has got a scar on her leg, please to take notice. Jim, show that girl.' (The poor girl was stripped to show the scar.) 'Now then, my pretty girl, look alive. Quite healthy, I guess?' 'Yes, sir.' 'Let's see your feet.' They touched her all over just as farmers do a cow; asked her if she had any children. She said 'No'. 'Are you with child now?' 'No, sir.' He felt her body doubtfully. Then some other men asked her questions too revolting to be repeated. It was whispered that she had run off several times, and this sign of nerve and smartness seemed to increase the wish to own her. She could wash, and, as the saying is here, do most any work. She was sold for $850.

"So it went on, lame and sound, the defects being generally pointed out in a tone conveying the wish to deal fair. I could not stay any longer and felt both times a sort of nausea coming over me, and had to compel myself to stay and and be a spectator that I might really see what I had only read about, and what conveyed only a sort of dreamy meaning to me before. There were little boys and girls from five to ten and upwards. Their teeth were looked at, their ribs felt. They were made to count, which but one could do up to ten, upon which he was declared to be a likely boy. When the men and women were asked their ages they generally replied, 'My master says I am twenty or thirty.' One said to a question whether he was twenty, 'Well, I don't think I am, for a few years ago I was very young.' Men built like giants, who could break any of their buyers to pieces, submit like lambs to inspections and questions. They seem utterly used to it, and only with some poor fellows I thought I remarked their restless eyes following the bids and trying to find out who was really bidding (this is generally done by a nod of the head) and who would be their owner.

"I would not live in a Slave State for anything in the world. Their dark, shining, plaintive, subdued faces were haunting me the whole of last night. I heard the ribald jests round me, I saw nasty burly, bloated men chewing tobacco and spitting, and more than all a set of sneaking, lynx-eyed, guilty looking Jews that had disgusted me very much in the morning, pursued me in my restless dreams with their cunning, hideous expression.

"I thought I saw poor little X. put up for sale. He cried and had to be put in chains, but it was all no use, and I saw him sold to a giant of a planter who said he should wait an hour, and if he did not behave, by G— he would shoot him.

"At one time the scene was changed and the blacks had got the better of the whites and were selling them; and the black auctioneer called out, 'Gentlemen, his teeth are very bad and I don't warrant him sound, but he can read and write,' whereupon a black planter bought him to be his clerk. I lay in a fearful perspiration at this hideous phantom and was glad to wake when the auctioneer knocked him down for $600.

There is a young and beautiful lady in this hotel. She is very imperious to the black waiters, and I have noticed that every time she speaks to them thus, she looks up at me with a half ashamed air and guilty eye. Her husband, a canal contractor and a wild, jolly sort of man, went with me this morning to secure seats at the theatre. On the way there he said, 'I don't like the Northerners. I am a Southern man to the backbone and I like the people here. The Northerners have interfered with our institutions and by G— we'll maintain them. I would fight for them any day.' I said to him that

I had been told they had only been made stubborn by the interference of the Abolitionists but that in the South they wanted themselves to get rid of slavery if they only knew how.

"'Well,' said he, 'I'll just tell you what it is. These black people are a doomed race, and will be so until it shall please the Almighty God to change their lot. You see, that's just the whole thing, and no more's to be said about it.'

"I'm almost sorry to say I did not hold my tongue, as the stupidity and enormity of the speech were so evident, but I could not help asking him, 'Well, suppose your forefathers had said we are just doomed to be a dependent colony of Britain and bear our lot till it shall please Almighty God to change it, where would you be now?' 'Oho,' said he, 'that's another thing altogether.' So I just changed the conversation.

"It is, however, clear to me that the Abolitionists are injuring the cause they have at heart by their agitation, and I am assured on all hands that Maryland, Virginia, and Kentucky would be free States now but for the interference of the North."

"CHARLESTON, S.C.
"*Sunday Feb.* 13*th*, 1853.

"My last letter was from Richmond, and to-day I address you from the sunny South. The change of climate is so palpable and overwhelming that it has come upon us as if by enchantment. Perhaps the more so as we spent yesterday on the Atlantic.

M,   x

However that may be, here we are in a large room
with open windows, and thankful that the sun cannot reach us. While I remembered that we are
only in the first half of February, and how my
friends in Edinburgh, with its stern and dangerous
beauty, are at this moment probably fighting their
way to church against a villainous and hardhearted
east wind, or most respectably and solemnly taking
their afternoon walk out by their Dean Bridge,
their very red noses telling a woeful tale, when I
conjured up the snow-covered Pentlands, and the
county police carrying out the true spirit of Christianity by keeping a watch at Duddingston Loch
to prevent naughty and immoral little boys from
skating—while my mind performs this winter's
tale my heart leaps with joy at the glorious expanse
of blue sky which the sun claims in undivided
empire, without the smallest cloud to pretend to a
share in the government of his dominions. The
water in the bay reflects the joy of the regions
above, and has clothed itself in the deepest blue
to do honour to the Sungod's sparkling golden
messengers. Only mother Earth seems as if taken
by surprise with the near approach of his celestial
majesty. She seems to have made no preparations
for him, and the trees look ridiculous in their shabby
winter dresses. Only here and there a few of these
dignitaries seem to have put out their buds to see
what is going on, and I caught one rosebush actually
dressing himself for the unexpected guest in the
loveliest flowers, while some other shrubs were

coquetting with blossoms.   In a fortnight at latest, spring, that heavenly child, will shower its gifts and rule supreme here.

"On Wednesday I walked out some distance from Richmond up to the brow of a hill that overlooks the town and the valley of the river. The air was like the first vague presentiments of spring, not sufficient yet to make you feel in every fibre of mind and body the pulsation of returning nature, but just enough to produce dreamy meditation and speculation. I struck off the highway into a rough country road. Soon habitations got few and far between; now and then a Virginian grandee would ride past me on a lineal descendant of Rosinante, but otherwise I was little disturbed. The birds sang merrily and the sun shone bright on the James River, flowing away from me to the town.

"As I turned, beautiful little Richmond was before me in all her glory, her capitol crowning the whole, with the American banner fluttering gallantly in the breeze. It was a splendid sight, but one old negro, passing me and taking off his hat to me in listless humility, was sufficient to mar the effect of the whole, for it conjured up the hideous phantom of slavery stalking like pestilence through this fair land, and I returned home dejected in spite of what ought to have been an exhilarating walk.

"In the afternoon we saw a large tobacco manufactory belonging to a Mr. Grant. He manufactures only chewing tobacco, and we followed the leaf through its various processes of immersion, drying,

cutting, pressing, &c., till it comes out at last
in the veritable round package from which the
almighty Yankee cuts his plugs and sucks his
inspirations.   All the men and children in the
factory, to the number of upwards of 200, are
coloured people, and, of course, slaves.   A certain
amount of work, or, as it is called, task, is required
of them in virtue of their slavery, and for whatever
more they do they get paid.   This explained the
astonishing celerity of their movements, and I was
glad to learn that most of them earn $1 per day, and
some more.   They are all well clothed and fed by
Mr. Grant, and look ten times as strong and healthy
as a Manchester or Glasgow factory hand.   So much
for the honour of truth.   Wherever slavery is not
abused it gets very much the aspect of the regular
relation between employer and employed, but the
curse of the idea that all these people are utterly
at the mercy of one man remains the same, and it
will never do as an argument that in a great many
cases, perhaps in most, slaves are treated kindly, and
are as well off as the working classes in England.
The possibility and the fact of the exceptions damn
the institution all the same.

    " While I watched the pressing and packing of
the tobacco I could not help thinking of the oceans
of spittle that these selfsame packages would let
loose over the Union, and thousands of careworn,
lankhaired, sallow, taciturn faces crowded into one
grim Medusa image, spitting one everlasting fountain from the Atlantic to the Pacific.   I, fortunately,

was not allowed to leave the place with these unsavoury thoughts, for on one of the floors of the factory the blacks struck up a Methodist hymn. They sang beautifully in tune, the different parts working together like a trained choral society. They sang of Jesus and heaven. Fancy a nigger in heaven! The idea is preposterous here. I wonder if the Southerners will ask St. Peter before they go in whether he admits any coloured people or Abolitionists. If Peter answers in the affirmative, fancy the horror of a gentleman from Virginia or South Carolina. Query, will he go in?

"In the evening we saw Mrs. Mowatt in a stage transformation of Sir Walter Scott's 'Bride of Lammermoor.' Caleb Balderston's Scotch would alone have repaid the visit. The actor murdered this fine language almost as badly as the Scotch murder the English. Amongst other proverbs, I remember his saying, 'He who will to Keepar maun to Keepar.' I was very near calling out, 'Cupar, you rascal,' to vindicate and prove the very existence of that very cold metropolis of the kingdom of Fife, but I feared I might be arrested as a maniac, and swallowed this indignity with many others. Edgar persisted in calling Lucy, Alice, in his most heartrending speeches, thereby keeping my wife in a state of dreadful nervousness, until Mrs. Mowatt, whispering audibly, 'Say Lucy,' relieved my wife, and reformed the refractory actor. Mrs. Mowatt was very hoarse, but as the Americans never speak

of her except as 'that great tragedian,' I had rather
not say anything about her.

"On Thursday morning, the 10th, we left Richmond before daybreak by the steamer *Curtis Peck*.
Poor Eli, our faithful black head-waiter, patronised
us to the last. I had to give him my card that he
might look me up if ever he came to Europe, and
after showing us every possible attention, he seemed
evidently quite distressed at our parting, and friend
K., who left Richmond a day after me, told me he
lamented the shortness of our stay in most vivid
expressions.

"A little lower down the river we saw the ruins
of Jamestown, the first settlement of the English,
called after James I. It is now utterly forsaken,
and the ruins reduced to a few crumbling walls, as
if the never-varying fatality of everything connected with the Stuarts had made it die a premature
death.

"Amongst the passengers was Brother Congreve,
whose sermon at Richmond I gave you at length.
He was a shrewd, pleasant man so long as you
didn't mention the Baptists.

"The sail was delightful, the sun shone out, and
the bright sky made the water look deep blue in
contrast with the green pinewood shores. Habitations you saw none along the banks, and it seemed
as if Nature was left as much to herself as in the
time of the Indians. Slavery has, I am told, made
people here so inert and indolent that shipbuilders
from the North actually come down here, fell the

timber in the woods, float it down the river, load it on vessels to the North, and build the ships there. Here, where Nature has offered every facility for shipbuilding, the people have too little enterprise to attempt it. The negroes make bad mechanics, and where there are slaves the whites won't work.

"The meals on board our little steamer were taken below deck in a saloon that received its dim light from above. At the sound of the gong everybody came down in dead silence, then fell to devouring what was on the table, and in less than fifteen minutes slunk off, apparently disgusted that man can't get on without this troublesome operation of feeding. Every remark that N. or I made to each other in a whisper was heard by the whole company in that universal silence, and altogether we were delighted when this funereal service was over.

"By sunset we were at Norfolk, a little town most beautifully situated at the mouth of the James River and Chesapeake Bay. It reminded me of some of the Baltic ports in its quiet doziness and little shipping. If there were enterprise they might trade with Europe, for the harbour is of the best, and the situation near the Atlantic magnificent. But everything seems to sleep in the South. We were politely received by a Mr. Reynolds, the landlord of the National Hotel. He is an Englishman by birth, and, for the honour of the old country, gave us the best room in the house.

"On Friday morning we left Norfolk, and

travelled all day by rail to Wilmington. Twelve weary hours did we rush through what appeared as one huge pine forest. No town, no villages on the whole long way. Here and there a few wooden huts, with black inhabitants, formed a station. At the only place where food was obtainable the train was too late, and there was no time to get out, and so we had to live on apples bought at the road stations, for bread was not to be got for love or money. The soil of this part of Virginia is poor and sandy, and turpentine is the only thing produced here. The pine trees are for that purpose stripped of their bark at the bottom. A hole is cut into them, in which the turpentine collects, and thence the negroes gather it.

" On we rushed, and our engine and cars, with the telegraphic wire running alongside of us, seemed like the spirit of civilisation looking with amazement on the wilderness around and panting to leave these silent deserts behind it.

" Between eleven and twelve at night we reached Wilmington, a little town within some twenty miles of the Atlantic. Even the doubtful beds of the little hotel there seemed a blessing to our wearied limbs. On Saturday morning at eight we left by steamer. The weather was glorious, the Atlantic like a mirror; and after a splendid passage of fourteen hours, we arrived here late last night.

" Among the passengers was a gentleman from Sweden, to whom a lady in Gothenburg, an intimate friend of my wife's, said (in joke) before he left for America, ' If you should see Mrs. Lehmann in America, give her my best compliments.' This gentleman was therefore quite delighted at the strange chance which made us fellow passengers and enabled him to deliver his message, and it was certainly curious to receive greetings entrusted and addressed so vaguely from the North of Europe to America.

" Making the passage much quicker than usual, we were not expected in Charleston. No cabs, no porters, no omnibus. Time, 1 o'clock a.m. I hurried to the hotel to secure rooms, but all my endeavours to impress a very sleepy porter with my wishes seemed to founder on the rock of perfect apathy and indifference with which he received me. He only congratulated me on the good passage and informed me that the superintendent was asleep. I told him that I had not the least objection to that arrangement, provided he would let me sleep also and show me the *sine qua non*. At this he turned to a gentleman in the bar and asked him if he thought he might give me eighty-two. The gentleman answered, ' Well, I'm sure I don't know. I rather think eighty-two is occupied.' Having delivered himself of this sentiment, he resumed his cigar in silence. This was rather too much for me, and I began to speak rather loud and furious. But the gentleman in the bar told me he was sorry I seemed annoyed, but he only stayed in the hotel, and could not help me. After that the porter concluded to call up the superintendent. Half an hour elapsed before he returned and told me I might have eighty-two. I went to see it, and found a miserable little hole. Seeing me still dissatisfied, he said the only other room held three beds, but perhaps I would not mind that, and so he showed me into a very large room, where one of the three beds was already occupied by a negro, whose black head loomed out from the white clothes. As I had told him that I was with my wife, the offer of this room with a black man already in possession seemed to me such a delicious idea that I was fairly convulsed with laughter, but my sleepy porter preserved his gravity, and merely remarked, ' You see, I told you eighty-two was the best room.' So I took possession of it, and the passengers and luggage having by this time got to the hotel, we were glad to creep in somewhere and get to bed about two.

" All this is, however, forgotten, as I am writing you from a delightful large room, which was given to us this morning."

" CHARLESTON,
      " *Feb.* 15*th*, 1853.

" The town is most beautifully situated, being on three sides surrounded by an arm of the sea forming a beautiful bay. Along the water runs a promenade called the Battery, which is the fashionable resort of Charleston. You cannot imagine anything more delicious than to inhale here the pure and gentle breeze from the sea. All the better houses have a large verandah to each storey, many are built entirely of wood, and all clearly convey the idea of being built rather against the rays of the sun than its absence.

"I am told that it is one of the most exclusive and aristocratic old towns of the Union. The South Carolinians pride themselves upon being the lineal descendants of the Cavaliers, just as the New England people boast of the Puritans as their ancestors. Everybody that can afford it has a private carriage; it seems to be the stamp of gentility, which must be had here at any cost, and no matter how it looks. I am told that on this account Charleston has, in proportion to the number of its inhabitants, more private carriages than any other American town. But you see the funniest turnouts that ever were got up. Immense rumbling family coaches of the last century, with the most miserable horses to match. All the streets are macadamized, and the dust consequently insufferable. The black population seems almost to outnumber the white. You see them everywhere. There is a fine long market-hall. All the women in the stalls are black, and they keep up an unceasing palaver, and the air rings with their merry laughter.

"'Buy cabbage, mas'r. Buy sweet potatoes,' &c., is their constant address to you.

"These market women generally belong to speculators, who get so much out of their earnings.

"The Post Office stands in the principal business street. At each side of it is a sort of open square, and the one to the left of the P.O. is employed for

slave auctions. Here, while the ordinary business
of life is pursued all around, while people read their
letters as they come from the P.O. with a large
thoroughfare before it, men, women and children
are sold like so many beasts of burden to the highest
bidder.

"I saw scenes of misery that made my hair stand
on end. Stout men, crying like children at being
parted from their wives, and children clinging in
vain to their mother; and more agonies than I have
a mind to recapitulate. They sold amongst others
an old coloured woman of above sixty. She was
palsied and had a continual shaking in all her limbs.
What anybody could have wanted with her I could
not imagine, for she repeatedly declared she could
do no manner of work. Still the bidding went on
slowly. A brute of a fellow shouted 'Sixty-five.
Now knock her down to me. I want her, old age
and all.' Then he went to her and said, 'How old
are you, my pretty girl?' knocked her in the ribs,
and pulled her about. Just as the auctioneer had
almost finished a man drove up with a cart right to
where the crowd had collected round the old negro
woman, and cried with a stentorian voice, 'Now,
gentlemen, I'll sell this horse and cart as it is here.
Who will give me a bid?' Thereupon ensued an
altercation between him and the auctioneer, but he
kept his post, and the two biddings went on simul-
taneously, the one for the horse and cart, the other
for the old woman.

"I could stand it no longer, and ran away very

sick. When you speak to benevolent Southerners about such a scene as this, they shrug their shoulders and say that that is the evil attending the institution ; at the same time they maintain that the Bible proves that the whole race is accursed on account of Ham ridiculing father Noah in his cups.

" One feels quite astounded at the wicked idea of imputing to the all-merciful Supreme Being an unquenchable thirst for revenge. Were it not better that the Bible had never been printed than that the code of love and brotherhood should be turned into the service of this vile and horrible institution ?

" I have seen enough of slavery. Not all the happiness of negroes in the plantations, not all the kindness and benevolence of their masters, will make me change my feelings with regard to the enormity of the laws that give man power to buy a fellow creature."

CHAPTER XIX.

IN 1855 my father was again in America; this time, however, without my mother. The two letters that follow were written to her. The first describes a sermon by the famous Unitarian divine, Theodore Parker, delivered at the Melodeon and Music Hall, Boston. Theodore Parker died at Florence, whither he had gone for the sake of his health, in 1860:

"77, BOYLSTON STREET, BOSTON,
"*February 26th*, 1855.

" I went to hear Theodore Parker yesterday, and had a real intellectual treat. He preached no sermon, but rather delivered a lecture. His appearance is not prepossessing, as he is a slender man with broad, plain, though intellectual features, and his delivery, although fluent, requires your strained attention owing to the often indistinct tone and accentuation; but he handled his subject with an ease and perspicacity, and had at his ready call such beautiful imageries that my heart warmed towards him. He treated (I suppose as one out of a series of subjects) of *manners* as an element of elevation, with reference to himself and others, not at all adequately considered and appreciated. He defined good manners as consisting of, and emanating from, good sense, good feeling, and good taste. I will not spoil his ideas by attempting to reproduce them in so abridged a form. Suffice it to say that I was highly elated and diverted at the identity of his ideas with those that had formed the subject of repeated conversations I had with your father when he was staying with us. Parker prefers real good manners based upon an equipoise of respect for yourself and respect for others, a charitable, benevolent, sympathetic way in the small change of life, to all the creeds in the world, if untempered by love of humanity. Amongst other good things, I remember his saying, ' I wonder often that good manners have never been constituted a test of Church membership.'

"He drew a beautiful line between elegant (*i.e.*, fashionable) and good manners, and without deprecating the former as a step on the great ladder, he elevated the latter almost to a next-of-kin to virtue.

"He preached in the Music Hall, which you know, to a large assembly, who followed his perfectly unshackled, unbigoted, ' uncanty,' beautiful, cosmopolitan lecture with evident appreciation and gusto. When it was over I went up to him and told him that I felt impelled to thank him for the great intellectual treat he had procured me, and I think I must have shown him that I was quite electrified by his humane, philosophic, and æsthetic treatment of morals, which had touched a chord within me that vibrated with assent. We shook

hands.   He asked my name, and, after some conversation, he asked me to spend that (yesterday) evening
with him.   I was so tired that I did not go, but I
mean to call on him before I leave Boston.''

The next letter describes a visit to Professor
Agassiz, the great naturalist, at his home in Cambridge.   Agassiz was born in Switzerland, in 1807.
After a brilliant European career, he had come to
America in 1846, and had established his reputation
as a popular lecturer on scientific subjects.   In 1848
he had been elected to the chair of Natural History
in the Lawrence Scientific School at Harvard
University, and for the rest of his life, with the
exception of sixteen months spent in a scientific
trip to Brazil, he remained in America.   He died
in 1873:

"77, BOYLSTON STREET, BOSTON,
    "*Sunday, March 4th*, 1855.

I have just been hearing Theodore Parker
again.   He delivered a sermon *of* (as he always
words it, not *on*) the ultimate triumph of truth and
right over all falsehood and wrong.

" It was a grand, impassioned lecture, and something wonderfully different from all that you could
hear from any of the thousands of pulpits in England or Scotland.   The local colouring through
which he adapts himself to his special audience,
blended with his gatherings from the science and
history of all nations, and all brought to bear on
the boldest and freest conclusions of moral philosophy, makes his sermons easy and nourishing.

" I have still to tell you of a most pleasant party at Professor Agassiz's in Cambridge on Friday last. I was agreeably surprised to find him a native of German Switzerland, where he has lived all his life and written all his books until about nine years ago, when he came to America. He is a man of portly, easy bearing, tall, and looking about forty-five to fifty. He has a fine large head, beautifully shaped, and his face, without being handsome, is most pleasing through an unmistakably benign and noble expression.

" His first wife left him three children, a young son and two girls, one about fifteen, the other eighteen. The present wife was a Miss Cary, of Boston. They have been married four or five years, and have no children.

" The small party consisted of three or four Cambridge professors, Mrs. Agassiz's two sisters and mother, Mrs. Howe, Mr. and Mrs. Ward, Mr. and Mrs. Benzon, Anna Loring, and myself and Mr. Dresel. One of the Miss Cary's is a pupil of Mr. Dresel's, has a very beautiful voice, and sings Franz's and Schumann's songs with German words (although she does not speak German) most admirably. She and Mrs. Benzon took joint possession of Dresel and the piano, and made a compromise how many songs each should sing. The piano was poor, but Mrs. Agassiz explained, pointing to a human skull (which her husband had that day received from France, and which had been found in a cavern along with a number of tools all

M,   Y

made of bone, and proving that they had been manufactured before iron had been in use), 'You see,' said Mrs. Agassiz, 'I can't afford a new piano as we import skulls from France.' They live together in most beautiful affection, I am told, but sometimes she cannot quite share all his idiosyncrasies. Awaking one morning, she was frightened by finding a little snake in her shoe. In terror she exclaimed, 'Agassiz, Agassiz, here is a snake!' But he, equally startled, said, 'Dear me, where are the other five?' remembering that he had brought six into the room the day before.

"He was in Edinburgh in '34, but only for a few days. He remembers papa, but only very slightly. He spoke much to me of poor Dean Buckland as his dearest friend, with whom, and at whose house, he had spent many happy hours. Of Mrs. Buckland he speaks with an affection almost amounting to veneration.

"As evidence of the intimate terms on which he was with the Bucklands, he told me, jokingly, that on a tour through Scotland they had to sleep all three (Prof. and Mrs. B. and he) in the same room. He would not believe that Frank Buckland was married and father of a family.

"He wanted much to know what he was doing, and I was sorry I could give him no special information further than that I believed he had already gained some celebrity through his scientific pursuits and writings. I told him much of our dear bright Mit,* but he only recollected her as quite a child.   He remembered dining at the B.'s with Arago, when Frank Buckland came in for dessert. Arago, making fun, wanted to prove to him by some trick that he had six fingers on each hand, when, after several repetitions, Frank Buckland looked at him seriously for a moment, and then, amidst general roars, told him, ' You must be a very stupid fellow.'

" Agassiz is entirely engaged in microscopic researches, and devotes his whole time to Embryology.   Talking of aquariums he said, ' Now I will show you my large and splendid one,' whereupon he brought a little flask, like one of your scent bottles, containing apparently nothing but a few small sea plants.

" By-and-bye he showed me some of the tiny creatures that were just visible to the naked eye like a grain of sand, and then made me look at his drawings of these tiny ones, as they appear under his powerful microscope, adding that his little aquarium had occupied his whole undivided study now for more than a year.

" He is not an American citizen, and talked beautifully about his feelings being all and unchangeably European.   He was nothing, and would be nothing, in politics.   As love of country, he acknowledged a peculiar attachment to the mountains and scenes of his youth, but his home was in science, and, consequently everywhere

* Frank Buckland's sister, Mrs. Bompas.

where they gave him his books and leisure. These he enjoys here to his heart's content. His chair as Professor of Natural History in Cambridge University obliges him only to lecture twice a week during about four months.

"I thought much of Philipson during his conversation on the peculiar nature of his pursuits, how he sometimes felt that he had created nothing, that he had not benefited mankind by any practical results, but how his branch of science was to him irresistible, and that he must admire and explore Nature in his own way. When I asked him if he did not sometimes feel the want of friction with other great men of science, he replied, ' No, I have always hated polemics ; I live here as I did in a remote village of Switzerland, much secluded ; I am not for society and society is not for me.'

"In spite of this, all concur in extolling his amiable social qualities. He was severe on Vogt,* the translator of the ' Vestiges.' ' I know him well,' he said. ' He lived four years in my house, but for many reasons I look upon him as a very dangerous man. Politically he acknowledges no principles except the claims of his party. In science he is one of the ablest of modern men, but socially he has made many enemies.'

"Agassiz was exceedingly civil, and devoted

* Carl Vogt, naturalist and politician, born at Giessen, 1817. Owing to his extreme political opinions he lost his professorship at Giessen, and transferred himself to Geneva. He was a strong supporter of Darwinism.

most of the evening to conversation with me. I
was much impressed with his urbane and manly
appearance. He reminded me much of the well-
known portrait of Jean Paul, and I left him with
the conviction that I had seen one of Nature's
noblest productions. He talks of coming to Europe
ere long, when he and his wife will be sure to
come and see us in Liverpool.

" On Wednesday, the 7th inst., I proceed through
Portland and Bath in Maine to Montreal and
Quebec, Hamilton, Toronto and Niagara Falls.
Thence letters will decide my further movements.
The journey will take me about sixteen to seventeen
days, and Mr. Lodge will accompany me. I have
had fine skating by glorious moonlight here, and
now that the first whiff of spring begins to agitate
the air I shall plunge back into deep winter. I
shall report faithfully. Your letters will follow me,
and your next will be sent to me at Montreal.

" I must conclude to-day, but will leave the
letter open in case I have something to add
to-morrow.

" I have forgotten to say that our dear friend
Mrs. Child,* the authoress, came to town last
Thursday on purpose to see the Benzons and
myself. She has removed from the pleasant little
village where you and I found her, and has gone to
attend her bedridden and very morose old father,
who finds the only alleviation to his sufferings in
her presence. She has resigned herself entirely to

* Lydia Maria Child ; see *ante*, p. 213.

this filial duty, and allows none of her friends to visit her. I understand she has been very busy all winter writing a book on all known religions,* the investigation of which subject leads her, I believe, to the conclusion that they are all alike a mixture of good and bad. She is as cheery as ever, and spoke of you with the affection of a mother or an old friend."

* "Progress of Religious Thought through Successive Ages." 3 vols., 8vo. New York, 1855.

CHAPTER XX.

IN the late summer of 1862 my father was again
called to America by pressing business affairs.
There he found himself in the very thick of the
commotion and agony produced by the Civil War.
He remained in the United States till late in the
year, returning again, after a brief stay in England,
in the spring of 1863. The following extracts
from his letters written to my mother give a vivid
account of his impressions of the state of the
country, together with references to the distinguished Americans with whom he was brought
into contact.

The battle of Bull Run mentioned in the first
letter is the second battle of that name, and was
fought on August 29th, 1862.

" WILLARD'S HOTEL,
" WASHINGTON,
" *Sept. 5th*, 1862.

" I wrote you a hurried note on Saturday last,
August 30th, from New York, to say that, as the
news from Washington was threatening, I would
defer my visit. On Sunday morning the papers

published a despatch from Pope, claiming a great victory over the rebels at Bull Run. The despatch was dated Friday night, and people thought the danger over. Early on Monday I left New York, and got here the same night. Ever since I have been in the midst of the intensest and most painful excitement. Instead of a victory for the Federals, they had been shamefully and fearfully beaten. Rumours flew thick and fast, and by Wednesday morning it oozed out that the whole army was back in, or coming back to, the old camps around Washington. The army is utterly disorganised, and wants rest, drill, and reinforcements. Washington is a camp. This hotel contains Sigel, Banks, and endless minor lights. Generals and colonels all over the place, orderlies flying, troops moving night and day, artillery rumbling, cavalry marching quickly, infantry slowly. In the midst of all this I have to attend to the most important interests of the firm, and think I have been very successful. Whenever I wanted to write to you, somebody called, a telegram came or had to be sent, I had to dance attendance at the War Office, or write pressing letters. I meant to go back to New York yesterday, but business kept me, and I shall not get off till this evening. . . .

" Washington is now considered safe, and if the rebels cross into Maryland, people think they can be checked. However, all is conjecture. They are probably too clever to risk themselves so far from home."

"BREVOORT HOUSE, NEW YORK,
"*Sept. 8th*, 1862, 10.30 P.M.

"Here I sit sweltering, with nothing on but a shirt and a pair of trousers. The heat has been maddening to-day, and it is 80 degrees now by the glass which hangs by the open door of the hotel; and in spite of all this terrific heat, which almost unfits one for anything but rest of mind and body in a darkened room, one has to be up and doing. The devil is loose. The Confederates are in Maryland, threatening Baltimore and Philadelphia, and scaring the North from its propriety. The poor bewildered Government at Washington, with its Ministers and Generals, is at a discount, and perhaps before many days are over will be among the things that were.

"I trust they may weather the storm yet, and retrieve their fortunes by a defeat of the bold Southerners, who are playing a dangerous game. *Nous verrons.* In the meantime, let us be joyful that I am safe back in New York and have not to throw myself upon the protection of the British Minister, or take ignominious flight on a Federal gunboat.

"The humiliation of this people is not a pleasant sight to behold. The wailing and impotent gnashing of teeth of a great nation is a deplorable spectacle. I have written over forty pages of letter-paper to-day, and, in spite of the heat, have to keep my head cool to steer our own old ship safely through the breakers. No fear of it, but I am thankful I am here; and only now and then, when the picture of you and those dear boys, and that lovely angel baby, and the fresh greensward at Woodlands will mix itself up with ever such incongruous and anomalous circumstances and surroundings, my head grows weary and my heart sickens for home, sweet home. . . .

"However, there is a good time coming, when I shall press you all once more to my breast. Amen. I do so long for your next letter to tell me you are all at Shanklin enjoying the dear old sea and the pebbles, the 'diamonds' and the little crabs, the roses and our old friend the hydrangea at the Lovers' Cottage, the breezy cliff and the waving cornfields, the shady woods and the rich green fields, the toothless Sampson and the absence of the X.'s."

Recruiting advertisement enclosed in the foregoing:

"HARRIS LIGHT CAVALRY.

"POPE'S ARMY.

"This regiment—well known for its brilliant service at Falmouth, and for three dashes within the lines of the enemy at Anderson's Beaver Dam and Frederick's Hill on the Central Road of Virginia, Jackson's main line,

NOW WITH GEN. POPE'S VICTORIOUS ARMY

in the healthy and cool region of the Rapidan, the most fertile and beautiful part of Virginia,

WILL RECEIVE

RECRUITS

at 600, Broadway, N.Y.

" The Cavalry Soldier, spared the more irksome
duties of the profession, mounted on his trained
charger, armed with Pistol, Carbine, and Sabre,
represents the Knights of Old, and like them can
gain Glory by individual prowess and daring. It,
therefore, requires the best men, and none will be
received but young men of good physique and
habits. Promotion depending on Merit. The new
recruit will have chances with the old.

" Come, share with us our experience, our past,
and future.

" All bounties, Land Warrants, &c., given to this
regiment.   " J. MANSFIELD DAVIES, *Col.*"

" PARKER HOUSE, BOSTON,
      " *Sunday, September* 21, 1862.

" I left New York at five p.m. yesterday, on
board the Fall River steamer *Metropolis*, one of
those wonderful floating hotel contrivances for which
the Americans have an especial genius. The voyage
was very pleasant, the sea smooth, the scenery, as
long as daylight lasted, lovely, the arrangements
for food and sleep marvellous, considering the host
of passengers, and altogether the mode of transit
highly preferable to the railway. At half-past four
this morning the boat poured us out (like coals
from a cart into a cellar) into a railway train, which
brought me here about seven. This is a new hotel
on the Brevoort Hotel plan, where you can take
your meals *à la carte* at whatever hour you please,
and preserve your individuality. Both in New

York and here I have had a sitting-room, a bed-room, with bathroom attached—a very complete and comfortable arrangement, which you could not have in London although you might be willing to pay for it. My daily breakfast consists of a glass of iced milk, a couple of eggs, gorgeous peaches (cost-ing only one penny to three-halfpence each), pears like the big French ones, and a melon. Bread-and-butter, of course. Never later than eight o'clock, and often earlier. This simple and cool diet in the morning suits the climate wonderfully. At lunch very little meat, and again fruit, and only one solid meal—dinner at half-past six to half-past seven. I was so tired when I arrived, as the night had been so much broken into, with rising at half-past three, that I went to bed and slept till ten o'clock. After breakfast Sebastian S. came, and we took a lovely ride and walk together to Jamaica Pond. The country is really charming about Boston, and I dare say E. saw it clothed in all its summer beauty in his mind's eye when he used to point out the shivery and icebound landscape as objects of ad-miration. It is a lasting pity you and I were not here together in September and October, instead of those dreary winter months. The great heats seem to be well-nigh over, and the weather is really enchanting. I wanted very much to take a few days of Lake George and Lake Champlain, to see the best of American scenery in its prime, but I cannot get the time. To-morrow I have only one month more of America, and I must make every day tell while I am about it.   The last thing I did in New York was to reconstruct the whole office. They had all *talked* about the irksome present arrangement, so at last I cut the Gordian knot, had an architect in, got my plan down on paper, had an estimate made, and decided the thing. . . .

"I said good-bye to Mr. Owen and Miss Griffith* on Friday evening. Poor thing, she is in sore tribulation about the course of events in this country. On Monday last we had a victory announced by McClellan.   Then nothing was allowed to transpire officially from him until Friday, when at last we heard: 'The Rebels are retiring to Virginia, and Maryland and Pennsylvania are safe.'   'As you were,' and all to begin again *ab ovo*. I half thought that now some compromise might be attempted. Both North and South have failed at invasion, and might now come to terms, 'sadder and wiser men'; but nobody seems to think that there is the remotest chance of peace.   It is awful!   Such carnage has never been known.   There seems to be no generalship, no manœuvring, but just a butchery that lasts a week.   Whoever gets most reinforcements and holds out longest kills most and keeps the field. The victor buries his own and the enemy's dead, and nothing further happens.   No victor has ever followed up one of these great holocausts to any great success.   This is now the third within three months.   The week's battles of the Chickahominy,   the   week's   battles   at   Manassas   and

* Miss Mattie Griffith. See *ante*, pp. 208, 213—215.

Centerville, and now again a whole week's carnage at Sharpsburg.

" On the boat last night, a Philadelphia clergyman, on his way to do duty for a brother-clergyman in Boston, opened his heart to me. 'The country is mad, and the Government is hurrying us on to ruin with ever-increasing speed. I have only one wish, and that is to go away for ever and live in England, where you have peace and liberty.'

" I sent to Dr. and Mrs. Howe to see whether they were at home, but both are in the country. So I went up to poor old Dresel. He lives in the fifth storey of a Hotel Garni at the corner of Boylston Street. When you are up there you can almost overlook the whole United States.

" I must tell you some Irish-waiter stories. When Seb. L., Dr. Mackay, and Livesey were dining with me, and we were in the heat of discussion, the waiter whispers into my ear, ' Shall I leave the vegetables on the table, sir, when I bring the partridge ? ' I said ' Yes,' in a half-angry tone at the stupid interruption, whereupon the waiter retires happy, saying, ' Thank you, sir; just my style,' which disarmed me.

" The next I may have told you before. I was dining with Livesey at the splendid new Fifth Avenue Hotel. There were different kinds of pastry, and Livesey, pointing to an open greengage tart, says, ' Let's try the broad gauge system.' The waiter at once corrected him, ' Greengage, not broad gauge '; but he saw his mistake by our laughter, and quietly observed to himself, 'Sold again.' Later on, nearly everybody had left, and Livesey said, 'I fear we shall be the last,' when the facetious waiter, anxious for his innings, remarked, 'Though last, not least.' Imagine all this in England. . . .

"Just another word before closing this letter. At last we have great news in the President's proclaiming all slaves of people in rebellion on the 1st January next free for ever. There is no going behind this, and slavery is now doomed in the United States, whatever that may be at the end of the war. As the South will certainly not submit before the end of the year, the proclamation amounts to virtual abolition wherever the North may succeed in planting its flag.

"I am delighted, but I see no peace. On the contrary, the war will probably only begin in earnest now, and get more inveterate and savage as it proceeds.

"I saw Mr. Fields yesterday. They expect to be back in town in a few days, and hope to see much of me then. The weather here is supremely beautiful. Just as pure, crisp, and exhilarating in its summer or autumn as in its winter guise. There is not the frightful rush and noise of New York; and instead of immense distances, everything is close at hand."

CHAPTER XXI.

In my father's "Reminiscences" I find the
following passage relating to Hawthorne and
Emerson :

" Hawthorne was sent as United States Consul
to Liverpool in 1854, he being one of the many
examples of the American Government's constant
practice of doing honour to their eminent literary
men by appointing them to distinguished public
positions.   I was invited by an American friend of
mine in Liverpool to meet Hawthorne soon after
his arrival.   His appearance was very striking, his
face handsome and intellectual, and the large
liquid eyes were full of latent fire and poetical
imagination.   He was not only reticent, but almost
taciturn, and, when he did speak, was apt to pause
and then jerk out the rest of the sentence.
Americans have, as a rule, a very remarkable
facility of expression.   Here was a curious exception.   I remember condoling with him for having
exchanged Boston, the hub of creation, for un-
congenial Liverpool, when he replied: 'Oh,

Liverpool is a very pleasant place' (then a pause sufficiently long for me to look surprised, and then suddenly the end of the sentence) 'to get away from.'

"After Hawthorne left Liverpool we did not meet again until my visit to America in the autumn of 1862, under the following circumstances. Robert Chambers had given me a letter for Emerson, which made him ask me to spend a day with him at Concord. He seemed to be the beau ideal of a contented and virtuous sage. Placidity and serenity were, to my mind, the chief characteristics of his face and manner. His conversation flowed without the slightest effort, copiously and harmoniously. He took me all over Concord, pointing out the lions of the war of independence. He seemed proud of the wealth of his New England orchard, the apple trees having done specially well that year. All his surroundings, not only his family, but his house and furniture, seemed to fit Emerson, and left upon me the very pleasant impression of my having come in contact with a master mind living in refined frugality. Among others, Emerson had asked Hawthorne to meet me. As usual, he hardly ever spoke, and I only remember his breaking his apparent vow of silence when appealed to by a Mr. Bradford.* This gentleman, after a fiery denunciation of the South, having come to the end of his peroration, passionately turned to his silent listener with the words, ' Don't you agree with me ? ' Then

* See p. 338.

M.   z

Hawthorne astonished him by uttering the monosyllable 'No,' after which he again relapsed into silence.

"Emerson told me that Hawthorne's increased taciturnity caused much anxiety to his family. My recollection of him is of one gloomy and much troubled, while I shall always think of Emerson as pellucid and at peace."

The visit to Emerson is described in the letter to my mother which follows. The Fields, of whom my father speaks in this letter, were Mr. and Mrs. James T. Fields. Mr. Fields was the well-known Boston publisher, the friend of Dickens and Wilkie Collins.

Russell Lowell, in his noble Memorial Ode on Robert G. Shaw, thus refers to his two nephews of whom my father speaks as having fallen in the last battle :

> "I write of one,
> While with dim eyes I think of three ;
> Who weeps not others fair and brave as he ?
> Ah, when the fight is won,
> Dear Land, whom triflers now make bold to scorn
> (Thee from whose forehead earth awaits her morn),
> How nobler shall the sun
> Flame in thy sky, how braver breathe thy air,
> That thou bred'st children who for thee could dare,
> And die as thine have done !"

Oliver Wendell Holmes's son, who is mentioned in my father's letter as having been shot in the neck, eventually recovered from his severe wound, and is now a Judge of the Supreme Court of the United States.

"PARKER HOUSE, BOSTON,
"*September 27th*, 1862.

"I have just returned from Concord, where I have paid a visit to Ralph Waldo Emerson. I sent him papa's [Dr. Robert Chambers's] letter of introduction, and received the enclosed kindly reply. I went out at eleven by rail, found Mr. Emerson waiting for me at the station in his buggy, and recognised him at once by portraits I knew of him. A charming old sage, with the kindest and most refined manner. He speaks well, and likes to speak about all manner of interesting men and things. From his writings I had expected a sort of oracular Carlyle, but a total absence of affectation or mannerism put me at once at my ease. The day was bright, pure, and serene beyond description. He drove me about through the dreamy, quiet village of Concord, pointing out its lions. A small gray obelisk records the spot where the first blood was shed between the Colonists and the English in the revolutionary war. The clergyman of the place asked all his congregation one Sunday to join him next day, each with a young tree to be planted near this monument. It was done, and now they have grown up to a pretty grove and avenue. Near it stands the manse, about which Hawthorne has written so charmingly. On we drove to a slight eminence, whence Emerson pointed out the different villages. One was said to be built on shoes, another upon peach-stones, and a third upon milk, according to their respective trades.

z 2

"We got to his place about two. Nothing could be simpler and more unpretending. He had asked Hawthorne, William Ellery Channing (a poet),* and a Mr. Bradford (a literary man),† to meet me at dinner, at which his wife and daughter completed the party. Hawthorne remembered me and you quite well before I gave him a note of introduction which Fields had volunteered. He is just the same shy, monosyllabic man, apparently with oceans of thoughts and talk if he could only turn on the stream.

"Emerson asked much after papa, and everybody seems always most anxious to make sure of his being the author of ' Vestiges of Creation.'

"The conversation was so pleasantly animated

* William Ellery Channing, born 1818, was a nephew of the Rev. Dr. Channing. He studied at Harvard, but did not get a degree. He married, young, a niece of Margaret Fuller, but they did not live together long. After a period of miscellaneous journalism in New York, he retired to Concord, where he spent the last thirty or forty years of his life. He was of the Emersonian school of transcendentalists. Emerson set some value on his poems, and every now and then there is to be found in them a poetic touch which indicates something more than an imperfect gift of versification. He died only a few years ago.

† Bradford was some ten or twelve years older than Channing. He, too, found the world too rough for him, and, after some years of preaching and school-mastering, he retired to Concord, where he lived a cheerful, simple life for many years. He died about twenty years ago. He and Channing may be associated with Thoreau as lovers and observers of Nature, as protestants against the materialism of the time, and advocates of plain living and high thinking. Their advocacy would have been more effective had their natures been of stronger fibre.

that the six hours and a half had slipped away before I was aware of it.   Hawthorne pressed me twice to come and see him.   All except him thought the South would soon give in.   Fight them with abolition of slavery, and they had no chance. It is quite inspiring to see men like Emerson quietly ignore what some others call the stern logic of facts, and continue to declare their unshaken faith in the triumph of the North and the restoration of the Union.

"I have breakfasted twice with the Fields, each morning at eight, at my request.   Their house is a perfect gem of brightness and cleanliness.   They have a charming view over the blue Charles River. Each room is full of books and engravings, everywhere portraits of English authors, everywhere autographs and letters from eminent men; an atmosphere of literature and refinement pervading the whole.   We had a long walk yesterday, and to-morrow he will take me a walk of twenty-five miles to the Blue Hills to show me the country about Boston.   We are drawn together by our common great affection for dear Dickens, whom he worships.   I was glad to be able to give him one of Dickens's good *cartes de visite*, and have promised more from England.   Fields took me to poor Longfellow, who received me very kindly, and was glad to hear my news of his literary friends in England. He lives in a little paradise.   Since the frightful loss of his wife, Longfellow is completely crushed, and just barely vegetates.   He had fame, money, and perfect domestic happiness, a loving wife and charming children. One little match, which she ignited by treading upon it, did all the mischief. Agassiz has just lost a brother-in-law, Dr. Cary, and is in deep distress. Russell Lowell lost two nephews, fine young fellows, in the last battle. Wendell Holmes, the life of Cambridge, had started off to the battlefield to find and tend his wounded son, shot in the neck. To-day I hear he has found him, and is bringing him home with every hope of his recovery, at which there is great rejoicing. Fields took me to Lowell; but he was not at home, and, considering the loss he has just had, I was scarcely sorry. You see the war is spreading death and desolation through all these bright homes, and still none of them talk of giving in. They scorn the idea. . . .

"I enclose two letters from poor Mat Griffith which may interest you. I had heard her lamentations so often that I could not help writing her a letter of congratulation when the President's proclamation came out. I find that everybody here knows and esteems her. The Fields and Emersons talked with great regard of her. . . .

"Do you know *Train*? The humbug has come back, and is addressing enthusiastic audiences of two thousand people *against* abolition. The fellow reviled Boston's best men—Tremont, Sumner, and Phillips—and the ruffians cheered him to the top of their bent. When you cite the fact to people as a curious phenomenon and an evidence of division, they merely shrug their shoulders and say it means

nothing. In fact, there are two stereotyped phrases :
(1) You do not understand the Americans, and (2)
I guess we shall come out all right in the end. . . .

"As for news about the army, you in England
know just as much of it as we do here."

Enclosure No. 1 in the foregoing :

"CONCORD, MASS.,
" *Sept.* 25*th*, 1862, *Thursday Morning.*

" FREDERICK LEHMANN, ESQ.

" DEAR SIR,—I am very happy to hear from Mr.
Chambers, and it will give me great pleasure to see
one so nearly allied to him as yourself. I am at
this moment confined at home by a sprained foot,
or I should go into the city to-day to fetch you.
Meantime, my house is but an hour's ride from
Boston by the Fitchburg Railroad, and if you will
take the eleven o'clock A.M. train on Saturday we
will show you our little village, give you a country
dinner, thank you heartily for all the good news you
shall bring us of Mr. Chambers ; and, if you cannot
face a Sunday in the country, there is an evening
train to the city at 6.30 P.M.

" Pray let me expect you.—Respectfully,

" R. W. EMERSON."

Enclosure No. 2 in the foregoing :

[Miss M. GRIFFITH *to* FREDERICK LEHMANN.]

" 143, 2ND AVENUE, NEW YORK,
" *September* 23*rd*, 1862.

" MY DEAR FRIEND,—I enclose you a letter to Mr.
Phillips,* which you can deliver or not as you think

* Wendell Phillips, the great abolitionist agitator and orator.

best or see fit. I daresay you have so many friends in Boston that an additional acquaintance will only prove an annoyance. If, however, curiosity prompts you to call on Mr. P., my only direction is for you to walk down that narrow, dirty Essex Street, and stop at the smallest, shabbiest house you find, ring, and ask for Mr. Phillips. I think that advice will safely land you in the august presence, and when you shall have seen the man you will not remember the house. I should like you to know him, for he is different from anybody you ever saw, *sui generis;* besides, I shall like to have your opinion of him. Perhaps the best way will be for you to drop the letter with your address in the post-office, as he is now passing some time in the country, and I daresay he will call upon you.

"You do not know how sorry I was not to hear your argument on Friday night, as I have since learned from Mr. Owen and Mr. Dryckinck that you managed it with wondrous ability and cleverness. Do you not see the account of McClellan's (doubtful) great victories? I hope he may follow them up. What you told me of the letter in the *Post* relative to the treatment of the negroes by the Union soldiers has been terribly confirmed by additional public statements. Is it not frightful? Poor negroes, they have not deserved to be the ' *les misérables,*' the pariahs which the insolent American men have doomed them to be. I confess to you my heart sinks when I reflect upon all this horrid state of affairs. I am neither cheerful, nor strong, nor brave enough to bear this fearful process of regeneration through which the country is now passing. I am afraid we are to be ground to powder for our sins, so long persisted in, before we can be reconstructed, for I cannot yet doubt that the glorious ideal of this nation will be fulfilled both as idea and fact. But much I fear that the great battle between the child of the free and the bondman has not only to be fought in the two great divisions of the land, but in every community, almost every heart, before the terrible Ishmael, slavery, shall be banished to the blank wilderness of ' nowhere and nevermore.'

" I need not, however, weary you by ' carrying coals to Newcastle.' Shall you not be glad to get beyond the dismal sound of this war, and land once more on the peaceful, green shores of Old England? I am sure you will.

"I hope you won't work too hard and fatigue yourself overmuch, so that your dear wife and children will blame this naughty America. When you write give my best love to Mrs. Lehmann, and say that I often and always think of her with pleasure. — Adieu. Sincerely and affectionately yours,

"MATTIE G."

Enclosure No. 3 in the foregoing :

[MISS M. GRIFFITH *to* FREDERICK LEHMANN.]

"143, 2ND AVENUE, NEW YORK,
"*Sept.* 24*th.*

"Very many thanks for your nice letter of congratulation just received. Yes, I do feel, my dear friend, a little better to-day ; fresh air seems to be circulating now in the ' White House ' ; the Government begins to stir from its deep sleep, and as it stirs it feels round for its weapon, and suddenly lights upon the sharp one. However thankful I am for this favour, yet I cannot help seeing the botched way in which the President has done it. Why did he not at once win for himself an imperishable name by doing an act of justice *in toto*, sweep the whole disease out of the body politic, and not reserve a strip of the virus in those border States ? . . .

" Ah, yes ! the war will be more bloody and fierce after this. The South will afford no quarter anywhere. Yet I am afraid Jeff Davis will be shrewd enough to propose gradual emancipation to France as the price of recognition and intervention. Then, our 1st of January Jubilee will be destroyed. How do you think France and England would treat such an overture ? Surely Anti-Slavery England will not cheat us of this glory. I cannot believe it possible. If she does, I hope you will do all you can to set Exeter Hall eloquence into a blaze. We had, last night, quite a fusillade on the occasion. The poor blacks in Broadway wore happier countenances and appeared to walk with a more cheerful, elate step.

" I am glad you like Boston. It is a little Anglican in its way—that is, bears a family resemblance to Liverpool and Manchester. I know you will admire Boston people : they are so earnest, so cultivated, and, when you come to know them well, genial and affectionate.   I thought the climate would suit you better than New York, that is, just at this season ; but in the winter it is harsh, with a rasping east wind that cuts equal to a rusty razor.

"I do hope you will stay long enough to catch a peep of our delicious Indian summer.   It is a season peculiar to our country, and it defies the pen and brush.   You have to see it to know it, and then, after our hot summers, it comes so gratefully.   I want you to get a few of the brightest of our autumnal leaves to take home to Mrs. Lehmann, that she may see how we 'get up' autumns on this side the water.

"I have missed you a good deal since you spirited off to Boston, and hope you will soon come back. We will try to have less scorching weather, but I cannot promise that New York will be less 'on the rampage.'   The late Theodore Parker used to say 'New York seemed to him as if she could not get to destruction fast enough.'   I have written this letter in patches.   Fanny Garrison has just called ; she says her father is in a high state of rejoicement over the proclamation.   You know, of course, who 'her father' is—the leader of the Anti-Slavery party, the man who first took slavery by the horns in this country, and has been wrestling with it ever since, to the peril of his own head.

"Adieu. Come, or write, as soon as you can to one who will ever hold you in cordial and affectionate remembrance.

"MATTIE GRIFFITH."

CHAPTER XXII.

HAVING rushed back to England late in 1862, my father returned to America in the spring of the following year. He writes thus to my mother from Washington:

"WORMLEY'S HOTEL, 307, 1ST STREET, WASHINGTON,
"*Sunday, 5th April*, 1863.

"I wrote you a long letter last Sunday, and a few lines on Wednesday, the 31st ult., and both epistles went by the same steamer. The improvement in the aspect of my operation has continued at a rapid rate, and it only requires a slight lift over what engineers call the 'dead point' to make it a great success. I tell you of it because when I am so much alone, as at present, when the idea of the dear ones I have left is ever present, when the flesh-pots of Egypt rise up in sad remembrance against the unsavoury meals which fate sets before me, and when howling winter blasts and deep snow conjure up the balmy air and greensward of dear Woodlands, I naturally feel that all I have sacrificed in leaving you ought to bear compensating fruit, and that nothing but success in my enterprise could make me amends, while failure or losses, if brought about by my journey across the Atlantic, would be doubly cruel. Anyhow, I shall have the great satisfaction of having done my duty and made my utmost endeavours according to the lights within me, and that alone is a great comfort.

" On Wednesday I dined at Mr. Hewitt's and his father-in-law's, Peter Cooper (the founder of the Cooper Institute, a kind of free library and South Kensington Museum in one, but of the mildest kind), with General McClellan. The general is a small, quiet, unassuming man, without the faintest outward attributes of a hero. A poor, dull face, with a small forehead and lack-lustre eyes. If he ever saves this republic, physiognomy and phrenology are not worth a red cent. On Thursday morning I left New York, and arrived here about ten o'clock at night. This hotel, or boarding-house, is principally patronised by U.S. Senators during Congress, and by respectable people who want to be quiet and hate the rush and gilt of Willard's. Consequently, Wormley's was hard to find, and when found at last had gone to bed. Thomas, an old negro factotum, received us half asleep ; and to my expression of hope that, although the house seemed empty, they would come up to the good reputation I had heard of them, merely answered, 'Never you fear, mas'r ; we'll treat you *nicely.*' And so they are doing, all things considered. I have a nice quiet sitting-room and ditto bedroom. The food is fair, the guests only two or three, and the attendance black and kindly. With me, as my secretary and assistant, is one of our New York clerks, Mr. Francis Garlichs, an American from Missouri, born of German parents, and speaking German. His handwriting is so beautiful that I think the Secretary of War will find it difficult to decline offers written out by him in something like copperprint.

"This is Easter Sunday, 5th April, and we have a foot of snow in the streets, fallen overnight. A furious gale is blowing, and Washington is a howling wilderness. On Friday I sent my letters to Lord Lyons,* M. Mercier, and their two secretaries, Mr. Clay and M. Treilhard. Lord Lyons at once sent me an invitation to dinner last night. He received me very kindly, and said, ' You have brought me a letter from my dear friend Browning. You must tell me all about him, for we spent such happy days together in Rome,' &c., &c. He is tall, looks forty-five to fifty, and is the very personification of good breeding. Undemonstrative, perhaps cold, but suave, polished, and easy. He told me that a good many of the Legation had gone to Baltimore for the Sunday. There was only one stranger, whose name I did not catch, and two attachés, or rather one, and the secretary, Mr. Clay. The dinner was very fair, the attendance admirable, and the whole thing was over in less than an hour. Scarcely any wine was taken after dinner; and, there being no ladies, Lord L. gave the signal to rise. Having been told that he says very little, I was agreeably surprised to find him pleasantly

* Lord Lyons was British Minister in Washington.

communicative. He seems to believe that in the course of three or four years, if the conscription is not resisted, the North will get a good army, immediately under the control of the Washington authorities and detached from local ties, that they will then get some good generals, and will finally overcome all organised resistance of the South. We had a long chat, and once he said, 'My position here is one of constant worry and irritation, and, upon my word, I believe I am the only impartial Englishman left, unless, begging your pardon, you should happen to be the other one.'

"Fearing that I might tire him, and outstay my welcome, I left early. This morning he kindly sent me a note :

"'MY DEAR SIR,—If you have nothing more attractive in prospect than a dinner at your hotel, will you give me the pleasure of your company at seven o'clock this evening ?—Yours faithfully,

"'LYONS.'

"This is very polite, but I had to decline it, as I am to dine to-day with M. Mercier, the French Minister, who called upon me yesterday afternoon, and sat for an hour talking politics by the yard and nonsense by the mile. He explained to me that during the entire late mediation scheme he had been on the best terms with Seward, and is so now; that Seward had first shown him the text of his message to Congress (which was thought in England to give Mercier the lie direct), and that he had given assent to every line of it. There was at the time an intrigue against Seward, to which he (Mercier) would not lend himself, &c., &c. This is only another instance of unruffled peace between the diplomatists while the newspapers cry fire and sword, and the gullible public get frightened into fits. Mercier is satisfied that this war can only be ended by European intervention, and that if England had joined France, and both had said, ' Unless you settle your differences by a given time, we recognise the Confederacy and open the ports,' the North would have given in at once, ' *mais l'Angleterre n'a pas voulu. Elle a peur d'une guerre avec le Nord, mais elle l'aura cette guerre, elle l'aura, qu'elle fasse tout ce qu'elle voudra. J'aime beaucoup l'alliance Anglaise qui est après tout pour la France le seul moyen de garder l'équilibre et la paix en Europe, mais j'avoue que les Anglais sont des amis très difficiles et bien des fois très désagréables. Ce sont eux qui de leur côté apportent les difficultés et les obstacles dans l'alliance,*' &c."

"*Monday, 6th April*, 1863.

" Here I was interrupted yesterday by a visit from Mr. Clay, who stayed over an hour and made himself very agreeable. We reviewed a great number of mutual acquaintances in London, and did a very fair amount of small talk. He told me that I occupied the room in which Mrs. Fanny Kemble-Butler and her daughter had lived some eight months ago, and that they had had ' great fun ' here. When I told him how agreeably I had been

surprised by Lord Lyons's pleasant and communicative ways on Saturday night, he said, ' I assure
you I was no less surprised than yourself. Indeed,
I told his lordship so after you had left, as I have
never seen him so open and talkative before. You
have undoubtedly touched the secret spring to draw
him out.'   (Hear, hear.)

"I dined with M. Mercier. There were only
Madame Mercier and an attaché. He talked for
four, and sometimes very well. I had put on a
white cravat, as at Lord Lyons's, where I found
them all dressed up to their eyes. Mercier was in
his shooting-jacket, and, on seeing me, said, ' *Comment, avec une cravate blanche? Mais nous n'aurons
qu'un dîner tout à fait sans cérémonie.*' I told him
that it seemed *de rigueur* at Lord Lyons's, although
there was no party. ' *Oh! les Anglais,*' he replied,
' *je crois que Lord Lyons dînerait en cravate blanche
tout seul vis-à-vis de lui même.*' In the evening I
asked Madame to play, and she did play a few of
Chopin's Nocturnes, not without a certain taste and
a good deal of execution. She is a little like Miss
Gabriel *en blonde*, if you can imagine that. There
was a Washington banker there, a Mr. Riggs, who
came after dinner and took me from Mercier over
to his house, which is a very gorgeous establishment. I thought he was a bachelor, and was going
to give me a drop of whisky and a cigar, when I
found myself suddenly in a drawing-room full of
his wife and about eight daughters. The surprise
was terrific."

M.   A A

. . . .

" Last Sunday, in Washington, we had a snow-
storm, and I was tramping about with my big
waterproof overalls. To-day we have *summer*—not
spring, but hot *summer*. The transition has upset
me, and I am sneezing to knock the walls down.
Yesterday we had a great mass meeting in Union
Square, called a Sumter Meeting, to celebrate the
rising of the North after the taking of Sumter by
the Confeds two years ago yesterday. There were
six stands, and from each some hoarse patriot was
stirring up the people and defying the universe.
Tremont, Sigel, and *hoc genus omne* blazed away,
but the acoustics of the open air were much against
them. While they were talking the Confederates
down in Union Square, gold went *up* in the city in
consequence of news of a repulse at Charleston.
Tell papa, and who else may care, that, in my opinion,
the talk of war between England and America will
remain *talk only ;* it is not the *interest* of the North
to have a war with England. What Europe has
taken for granted from the first—*i.e.*, the impossibility of conquering and subjugating the South—
has not yet even distantly dawned upon the
Northern mind. They are perfectly, and almost
unanimously, convinced of the possibility of success,
and it will take years and years before they will
give up trying. No party that advocates anything

but war until they shall have recovered every inch of the former Union has the remotest chance of influence, or even existence. The ambition to be a mighty nation, equal to or greater than any in Europe, is the idea which holds possession of the Northern mind, to the exclusion and disregard of every other. All reverses will be put down to the administration or bad generals, but nothing will make them give up but utter and hopeless exhaustion. In my opinion the war is only beginning, and will last more years than I dare to think of. This, however, is England's safety, for as a war with England would mean an alliance between the South and England against the North, the latter cannot afford to fight the South *and* England.

"On the other hand, England is so well convinced that the evil of war with the North would immeasurably outweigh any benefit we might derive from opening the Southern ports, that I am satisfied England will do all consistent with her honour and dignity to prevent war.

"Hence I believe in endless palaver and angry correspondence between the two countries, but in nothing more. Ernest Clay came on here before me, and left again for Washington yesterday. He was very affable, regretted exceedingly that he had not seen more of me, as they 'did not often get such a godsend in Washington,' and promised to look us up when he comes to London, &c., &c."

My father eventually returned home to England firmly convinced of the ultimate victory of the North. I have already recorded how he tried and failed to persuade Charles Dickens of the justice of his views on this point.

Here I must bring these "Memories" to a close. Of those who are mentioned in this book only a few survive—

> "Like clouds that rake the mountain-summits,
>   Or waves that own no curbing hand,
> How fast has brother followed brother
>   From sunshine to the sunless land!"

Yet the task of recapturing from the past some echoes of the voices of old friends has been a pleasant one. Once more I have grasped their hands and have held converse with them in some pale shadow, as it were, of bright and happy days. Desultory, no doubt, the book is; but I may plead that its fragments are held together by the two persons in whom the friendships here recorded were centred. To their beloved memory I bring this tardy tribute of reverence and affection.

INDEX.

BRADBURY, AGNEW, & CO. LD , PRINTERS LONDON AND TONBRIDGE

Lightning Source UK Ltd.
Milton Keynes UK
UKHW021303261118
332984UK00014B/855/P